Market Abuse Regulation in South Africa, the United States of America and the United Kingdom

Howard Chitimira

Vernon Series in Law

VERNON PRESS

www.vernonpress.com

In the Americas:
Vernon Press
1000 N West Street,
Suite 1200, Wilmington,
Delaware 19801
United States

In the rest of the world:
Vernon Press
C/Sancti Espiritu 17,
Malaga, 29006
Spain

Vernon Series in Law

Library of Congress Control Number: 2017960057

ISBN: 978-1-62273-260-9

Table of Contents

To My Wife, Children and My Mother

RACHAEL, ARIANA, NOLAN, NATHAN AND DIANA

You have been and still are my constant source of inspiration

Acknowledgements

Completion of this book was made possible through the guidance, support and help of many people. In this respect, I would like to express my sincere gratitude to the following persons:

- God Almighty, the source of all good things and blessings. Praise, glory and the entire honor be unto Him.
- "This work is based on the research supported in part by the National Research Foundation of South Africa (Grant Numbers: 106056)".
- Professor VA Lawack and Professor PA Duplessis. Thank you so much for your mentorship and guidance. May God richly bless you.
- Professor TH Mongalo, Professor E Snyman-Van Deventer, Doctor TV Warikandwa and Advocate JC Kanamugire, thank you for your encouragement and support.
- My mom and dad, thank you so much for bringing me up in love, and in the knowledge of God.
- My dear wife Rachael Chitimira, thank you for all the prayers, enduring love, encouragement and support.
- All my pastors, especially Evangelist C Tembo and Pastors Dan and Ria Zimuwandeyi, thank you for your encouragement, guidance and prayers.
- Mr Hudson Chitimira and Mrs Viola K Zhou-Chitimira, thank you for your love, prayers and valuable support.

Abstract

Market abuse (insider trading and market manipulation) practices have continued to cause various regulatory and enforcement challenges in several jurisdictions, including South Africa, the United Kingdom (UK) and the United States of America (USA). Accordingly, this book usefully unpacks the adequacy of the anti-market abuse laws and their enforcement in the aforesaid jurisdictions in order to isolate the flaws embedded in such laws and recommend possible remedial measures in respect thereof. This book offers a novel comparative analysis of the regulation and enforcement of anti-market abuse laws in two developed and renowned jurisdictions, namely, the UK and the USA as well as South Africa which has one of the biggest regulated financial markets in Africa. To my knowledge, there is no similar book that has been specifically written on the comparative regulation and enforcement of the anti-market abuse laws in these jurisdictions to date. To this end, the book provides the rationale for regulating and effectively combating market abuse practices in the USA, the UK and the South African financial markets. Notably, the book comprises of separate but related short papers that are provided in its nine chapters. For instance, Chapters Two to Five provide a comparative analysis of market abuse regulation in South Africa and the USA. Likewise, Chapters Six to Eight provide a similar analysis in relation to South Africa and the UK. Chapters Two to Eight were previously peer reviewed and published as journal articles and are now re-worked with permission from the initial publisher to update, expand and provide more recent information on the regulation and enforcement of anti-market abuse laws in South Africa, the USA and the UK. Such recent information includes, *inter alia*, the uncertainty surrounding the UK's anti-market abuse regime following its decision to withdraw from the European Union (EU) after the 2016 British EU (Brexit) referendum. Moreover, the recent South African and the USA international banks collusion and market manipulation involving the price-fixing, market allocation and rigging in the trading of foreign currency pairs of the South African rand since 2007 by lenders and banks is another reason for this book. A current surge of market abuse regulatory challenges caused by disruptive technology such as automated financial services, computerised trading, algorithms and artificial intelligence, especially, in the USA financial markets also influenced the writing of this book. Each Chapter has its own distinct title, introduction, relevant analysis, related conclusions and reference list. The book equips the students, academics and other market participants with a simplified but updated and rich understanding of the regulation and enforcement of anti-market abuse laws in South Africa, the UK and the USA.

Keywords: insider trading; market manipulation; market abuse; regulation; enforcement approaches.

Acronyms

BCBS	Basel Committee on Banking Supervision
CFTC	Commodity Futures Trading Commission
CFTF	Corporate Fraud Task Force
CPS	Crown Prosecution Services
DBERR	Department for Business Enterprise and Regulatory Reform
DMA	Directorate of Market Abuse
DPP	Director of Public Prosecutions
DOE	Division of Enforcement
DOJ	Department of Justice
DTI	Department of Trade and Industry
EBA	European Banking Authority
ECA	Economic Crime Agency
EC	Enforcement Committee
EDGAR system	Electronic Data Gathering Analysis and Retrieval system
EIOPA	European Insurance and Occupational Pensions Authority
EU	European Union
ESMA	European Securities and Markets Authority
ESRB	European Systemic Risk Board
ERIC	Executive Regulatory Issues Committee
EDC	Executive Diversity Committee
EOC	Executive Operations Committee
FATF	Financial Action Task Force

FCA	Financial Conduct Authority
Fin-Net	Financial Crime Information Network
FPC	Financial Policy Committee
FINRA	Financial Industry Regulatory Authority
FERC	Federal Energy Regulatory Commission
FOS	Financial Ombudsman Service
FTC	Federal Trade Commission
FSA	Financial Services Authority
FSB	Financial Services Board
FSCA	Financial Sector Conduct Authority
FSCS	Financial Services Compensation Scheme
FSMT	Financial Services and Markets Tribunal
IFSG	Intermarket Financial Surveillance Group
IOSCO	International Organisation of Securities Commissions
JSE	Johannesburg Stock Exchange Limited
LSE	London Stock Exchange
LIFFOEAM	London International Financial Futures and Options Exchange Administration and Management
MOUs	Memoranda of Understanding
MSRMB	Municipal Securities Rule Making Board
MTFs	Multilateral Trading Facilities
MLAT	Mutual Legal Assistance Treaty
NASD	National Association of Securities Dealers
NYSE	New York Stock Exchange
NCA	National Crime Agency
NFA	National Fraud Authority

LSE	London Stock Exchange
OTC	Over the counter
OTFs	Organised Trading Facilities
PA	Prudential Authority
PSC	Policy Steering Committee
PRA	Prudential Regulation Authority
UK	United Kingdom
USA	United States of America
RDC	Regulatory Decisions Committee
SFA	Securities and Futures Authority
SIB	Securities and Investments Board
SFO	Serious Fraud Office
SOCA	Serious Organised Crime Agency
SROs	Self-regulatory Organisations
SEBI	Securities and Exchange Board of India
STORs	Suspicious Transactions and Orders
STRs	Suspicious Transaction Reports
SEC	United States Securities and Exchange Commission
SEETS	Stock Exchange Electronic Trading Service
TPSE	Trade Point Stock Exchange
TRP	Takeover Regulation Panel
TEU	Treaty on European Union
TFEU	Treaty on the Functioning of the European Union

Chapter 1

Introduction and Background

1 1 Introduction

Illicit insider trading and market manipulation (market abuse) practices[1] have given rise to several regulatory and enforcement challenges in many jurisdictions to date. Accordingly, these challenges have been, and are still being experienced in many jurisdictions such as the United Kingdom (UK), the United States of America (USA), South Africa and several other countries.[2] This could be attributed to a number of factors including, *inter alia*, the enactment of flawed market abuse laws and the use of few and less deterrent anti-market abuse enforcement approaches by the relevant enforcement authorities in many countries. Consequently, several anti-market abuse regulatory and enforcement authorities have grappled to effectively and consistently curb market abuse practices in their respective financial markets to date. The UK, the USA and South Africa were chosen to investigate and compare their respective anti-market abuse enforcement experiences. This was mainly done to isolate and recommend possible anti-market abuse enforcement approaches that could be employed in South Africa from both the USA and the UK's market abuse statutory regulatory frameworks. Accordingly, a brief comparative analysis of the enforcement of the market abuse prohibition in the UK, the USA and South Africa is undertaken in this book. It is hoped that this book will recommend possible measures that could be employed by the relevant enforcement authorities to improve the combating of market abuse practices in all the aforesaid jurisdictions.

The book discusses the adequacy of the market abuse prohibition in South Africa, the UK and the USA. Notably, market abuse is expressly prohibited at a national level in South Africa under the Financial Markets Act.[3] Likewise, market abuse is universally prohibited in the UK. Market abuse is also

[1] Definitions and further discussions of these practices will ensue in Chapters Two to Eight of this book.

[2] Notably, this book is mainly focused on the comparative analysis of the regulation and enforcement of anti-market abuse laws in South Africa, the USA and the UK. It is hoped that this book will isolate and expose the gaps in the anti-market abuse regulatory frameworks in these jurisdictions in order to recommend were appropriate, possible measures that could be employed to remedy such gaps. See Chitimira *A Comparative Analysis of the Enforcement of Market Abuse Provisions* (Unpublished LLD thesis, Nelson Mandela Metropolitan University) 2012, 1-6.

[3] 19 of 2012 (Financial Markets Act). See ss 78; 80; 81 & 82.

outlawed both at a federal and state level in the USA.[4] Consequently, the offences, penalties and other anti-market abuse enforcement approaches that are provided in the relevant legislation of the stated countries are discussed in this book. The book also provides the rationale for regulating and effectively combating market abuse practices in the USA, the UK and the South African financial markets.

Notably, the book is comprised of separate but related short papers that are carefully spread over its nine chapters. Chapters Two to Five provide a comparative analysis of market abuse regulation in South Africa and the USA. Likewise, Chapters Six to Eight provides a similar analysis in relation to South Africa and the UK. Accordingly, Chapters Two to Eight were previously published as journal articles and are now re-worked with permission from the initial publisher to update, expand and provide more recent information on the regulation and enforcement of anti-market abuse laws in South Africa, the USA and the UK. For instance, such recent information includes, *inter alia*, the uncertainty surrounding the UK's anti-market abuse regime following its decision to withdraw from the European Union (EU) after the 2016 British EU (Brexit) referendum.[5] Moreover, the recent South African and the USA international banks collusion and market manipulation involving the price-fixing, market allocation and rigging in the trading of foreign currency pairs of the South African rand since 2007 by lenders and banks is another reason for this book.[6] The introduction of the Financial Sector Regulation Act[7] which introduces the Prudential Authority (PA) which supervises all financial institutions that provide financial products and securities services and the Financial Sector Conduct Authority (FSCA) which regulate the conduct of all financial institutions is another new information highlighted in the book.[8] A current surge of market abuse regulatory challenges caused by disruptive technology such as automated financial services, computerised trading, algorithms and artificial intelligence, especially, in the USA financial markets

---

[4] Steinberg "Insider Trading Regulation–A Comparative Perspective" 2003 *The International Lawyer* 153 169-171; Chitimira "A Comparative Overview of the State Prohibition on Market Abuse in the United States of America" 2014 *Mediterranean Journal of Social Sciences* 54 54-68.

[5] This referendum was held on 23 June 2016. The majority of British citizens in that referendum voted to leave the EU. See SIA Partners (Banking and Insurance) "Brexit and the Impact on the UK's Regulatory Framework" (2016) 1-4 <http://en.finance.sia-partners.com/brexit-and-impact-uks-regulatory-framework> (accessed 12-07-2017); also see related comments in Chapter Six of this book.

[6] See further related remarks in paragraph 1 3 below.

[7] 9 of 2017 (Financial Sector Regulation Act) which was assented to by the President on 21 August 2017. However, the Financial Sector Regulation Act is yet to come into force on the day determined by the Minister of Finance by notice in the Government Gazette in terms of s 305 of the same Act.

[8] See Chapters 3 and 4 of the the Financial Sector Regulation Act. Notably, the FSCA is set to replace the Financial Services Board (FSB).

also influenced the writing of this book.[9] Each Chapter has its own distinct title, introduction, relevant analysis, related conclusions and reference list. The author adopted this unique approach after receiving numerous requests from students, academics and other market participants who struggled to access all the initially published articles, hence the decision to re-publish them as a unitary book. The book equips the reader with a simplified but updated and rich understanding of the regulation and enforcement of anti-market abuse laws in South Africa, the UK and the USA.

1 2 Overview Background Aspects

Various effects of market abuse-related problems have been felt in the UK's financial markets from time to time. As a result, the UK has, from time to time, enacted some anti-market abuse laws in a bid to, *inter alia*, combat such problems and enhance the competitiveness of its financial markets. Accordingly, the UK employs a separate and specific statute that prohibits insider trading[10] and another statute that broadly prohibits market manipulation and other related market abuse activities.[11] Despite this, the anti-market abuse provisions of both the Criminal Justice Act and the Financial Services and Markets Act have relatively failed to effectively deter unscrupulous persons from continuing with their illicit market abuse practices in the UK's financial markets to date. This implies that both the Prudential Regulation Authority (PRA) and the Financial Conduct Authority (FCA)[12] which replaced the Financial Services Authority (FSA) have relatively failed to consistently enforce the anti-market abuse provisions to effectively combat market abuse activities in the UK's financial markets. Related market abuse problems have also affected the financial markets in the USA as early as the 1920s to date.[13] Similar problems were reportedly rampant in the South African financial markets between the early 1970s and the mid-1990s.[14] In a commendable attempt to curb the

[9] Brummer "Disruptive Technology and Securities Regulation" 2015 *Fordham Law Review* 977 997-1003.

[10] See the Criminal Justice Act 1993 (c 36) (Criminal Justice Act).

[11] See the Financial Services and Markets Act 2000 (c 8) (Financial Services and Markets Act). See further Avgouleas *The Mechanics and Regulation of Market Abuse: A Legal and Economic Analysis* (2005) 307 and related discussions that ensues in Chapters Six to Eight of this book.

[12] These regulatory bodies replaced the FSA in accordance with the Financial Services Act 2012 (c 21).

[13] Chitimira *Enforcement of Market Abuse Provisions* 1-6, for further discussion and related discussions in Chapters Two to Five of this book.

[14] The South African financial markets had a very poor reputation due to rampant market abuse practices that occurred between the early 1970s and the mid-1990s. See Myburgh & Davis "The Impact of South Africa's Insider Trading Regime: A Report for the Financial Services Board" (25-03-2004) 11 <http://www.genesis-analytics.com/ public/FSBReport.pdf> (accessed 09-02-2013); Chitimira "A Historical Overview of the Regulation of Market Abuse in South Africa" 2014 *PER* 937 937-939, for related comments.

negative effects of market abuse practices and related regulatory challenges, various anti-market abuse laws were introduced in South Africa from the early 1970s to date.[15] Nonetheless, despite these positive efforts, the South African anti-market abuse laws have been sometimes inconsistently enforced by the relevant authorities from the early 1970s to date.[16] For instance, previous anti-market abuse prohibitions that were contained in the Companies Act,[17] the Financial Markets Control Act,[18] and the Stock Exchanges Control Act[19] were both flawed and inadequately enforced by the regulatory authorities. Consequently, undeterred market participants and other relevant persons continued with their market abuse activities in both the regulated and unregulated South African financial markets.[20] The Insider Trading Act[21] was enacted to remedy the aforesaid flaws but its provisions were relatively inadequate and mainly limited to insider trading offences committed by individuals and not juristic persons. Moreover, its provisions did not expressly prohibit market manipulation.[22] The Securities Services Act[23] later repealed the Insider Trading Act and extended its market abuse prohibition to both insider trading and market manipulation and introduced administrative penalties which were enforced by the Enforcement Committee (EC) through the provisions that were inserted in the Financial Institutions (Protection of Funds) Act.[24] Nevertheless, its market abuse provisions were still relatively inadequate for deterrence purposes. The Securities Services Act was repealed by the Financial Markets Act which introduced relatively adequate defences, civil penalties for

---

[15] See the discussions in Chapters Two to Eight of this book; Chitimira 2014 *PER* 937-965; Van Deventer "Anti-Market Abuse Legislation in South Africa" (10-06-2008) 1-5 <http://www.fsb.co.za/public/marketabuse/FSBReport.pdf> (accessed 05-05-2013); Myburgh & Davis (25-03-2004) 8–33, available at <http://www.genesis-analytics.com/public/FSBReport.pdf> (accessed 09-02-2013), for related comments.

[16] Scholtz, Paige & Van Zyl "Financial Markets, Market Abuse, Money Laundering and the National Credit Act" (31-03-2008) <http://www.legal500.com/index.php? option=com_content&task> (accessed 30-04- 2016); Chitimira 2014 *PER* 937 937-965; Chitimira "Overview of the Market Abuse Regulation under the Financial Markets Act of 2012" 2014 *Obiter* 254 255-271.

[17] 61 of 1973 (Companies Act); see ss 162, 229-233.

[18] 55 of 1989 (Financial Markets Control Act); see ss 20-23.

[19] 1 of 1985 (Stock Exchanges Control Act); see s 40. Myburgh & Davis (25-03-2004) 8–33, available at <http://www.genesis-analytics.com/public/FSBReport.pdf> (accessed 09-02-2013), for related comments.

[20] Myburgh & Davis (25-03-2004) 11 available at <http://www.genesis-analytics.com/ public/FSBReport.pdf> (accessed 09-02-2013); Chitimira 2014 *PER* 937-965, for related comments.

[21] 135 of 1998 (Insider Trading Act); also see "The King Task Group into the Insider Trading Legislation" 1995 (King Task Group); Chitimira 2014 *PER* 937.

[22] Ss 2-16 of the Insider Trading Act; Luiz "Market Abuse II–Prohibited Trading Practices and Enforcement" 2002 *JBL's Quarterly Law Review for People in Business* 180-183.

[23] 36 of 2004 (Securities Services Act). See ss 73; 75; 76 & 77.

[24] 28 of 2001 as amended (Protection of Funds Act). See ss 6A-6I of the Protection of Funds Act.

insider trading and maintained the administrative penalties regime.[25] However, more needs to be done to enhance market integrity and investor confidence in the South African financial institutions and financial markets by effectively curbing market abuse activities in these institutions and markets as discussed below.

1 3 The Rationale for Effective Market Abuse Regulation

Although it is still debatable[26] whether market abuse practices should be regulated,[27] the author submits that such practices must be statutorily and adequately prohibited in all jurisdictions to enhance the efficient and effective functioning of the financial markets. The effective regulation of market abuse enhances market integrity and public investor confidence in all jurisdictions. Moreover, the effective regulation of market abuse promotes free and fair financial markets that competitively attract foreign investment in several countries. The effective regulation of market abuse also promotes the creation and maintenance of transparent and efficient securities and financial markets where the price of a security accurately reflects its true value. Accordingly, the effective and consistent enforcement of adequate anti-market abuse laws by the relevant authorities is crucially important to the transparency and efficiency of such financial markets.[28] Thus, effective market abuse regulation in any country enhances the natural forces of supply and demand to accurately determine the price of securities in the financial markets of that country.[29] Put differently, anti-market abuse laws must be effectively enforced to promote market integrity, protect investors and to keep the financial markets free from market abuse activities and other illicit practices such as fraud.

---

[25] Chitimira 2014 *PER* 937-939; Chitimira "Unpacking Selected Key Elements of the Insider Trading and Market Manipulation Offences in South Africa" 2016 *Journal of Corporate and Commercial Law and Practice* 24 24-41.

[26] For instance, some academics argue that the regulation of market abuse activities is economically undesirable, see Akerlof "The Market for 'Lemons': Quality Uncertainty and the Market Mechanism" 1970 *Quarterly Journal of Economics* 488 488-500; Ali "Market Abuse: It's Not just a Wall Street Thing" 2006 *The Company Lawyer* 222 224; Fischel & Ross "Should the Law Prohibit 'Market Manipulation' in Financial Markets" 1991 *Harvard Law Review* 503 512-513 & 553. On the contrary, other commentators argue that the effective anti-market abuse legislation is vitally important to accurate and internationally competitive financial markets in all jurisdictions. See Chitimira *Enforcement of Market Abuse Provisions* 6-13; Anonymous "The Regulation of Insider Trading in the United States of America" (09-03-2008) <http://www.sec.gov> (accessed 08-06-2016).

[27] Henning & Du Toit "The Regulation of False Trading, Market Manipulation and Insider Trading" 2000 *Journal for Juridical Science* 155 155-165; Chitimira *Enforcement of Market Abuse Provisions* 6-13; Gething "Insider Trading Enforcement: Where are We Now and Where do We Go from Here?" 1998 *Company and Securities Law Journal* 607 607-627.

[28] Henning & Du Toit 2000 *Journal for Juridical Science* 155-165; Chitimira *Enforcement of Market Abuse Provisions* 6-13.

[29] Chitimira *Enforcement of Market Abuse Provisions* 6-7.

Moreover, the effective enforcement of anti-market abuse laws enhances the combating of market abuse activities that are still occurring in many jurisdictions, including the USA, the UK and the South African financial markets and financial institutions.[30] For instance, the ineffective enforcement of the anti-market abuse prohibition has culminated in a relative surge of market abuse activities in the South African financial institutions and financial markets in the recent years. The recent South African, the USA and other international banks collusion and market manipulation involving the price-fixing, market allocation and rigging in the trading of foreign currency pairs of the South African rand since 2007 by lenders and banks such as the Bank of America Merrill Lynch International Limited, JP Morgan Chase and Co, JP Morgan Chase Bank N.A, Macquarie Bank, BNP Paribas, Credit Suisse Group, HSBC Holdings, Commerzbank, Australia, New Zealand Banking Group, Barclays Capital and Barclays, Standard New York Securities and Nomura Holdings International is a case in point.[31]

Consequently, it is less prudent to assume that the enactment of adequate market abuse laws alone will automatically combat market abuse activities and give rise to increased market integrity and investor confidence in the USA, the UK and South African financial markets.[32] On the contrary, such laws will only effectively curb market abuse activities if they are robustly and consistently enforced by the relevant enforcement authorities. In other words, adequate anti-market abuse legislation alone is not sufficient since such legislation must be supplemented by effective enforcement of its provisions to combat market abuse practices. In a nutshell, adequate anti-market abuse laws must be consistently enforced in all the jurisdictions to enhance the integrity and efficiency of the financial markets.

---

[30] *Pather and Another v Financial Services Board and Others (57617/10)* [2014] 3 All SA 208 (GP), for related discussion on the role of the EC; *Zietsman v Director of Market* Abuse 2016 1 SA 218 (GP), which dealt with the meaning of "inside information" for the purposes of the insider trading offence in South Africa; the Directorate of Market Abuse (DMA) "Past Investigations" *DMA Media Release* 23 June 2015, 1-11; the DMA "Report by the Directorate of Market Abuse" *FSB Press Release* 31 March 2017, 1 1-3.

[31] Anonymous "How Banks Allegedly Colluded on Currency Trades" (15-02-2017) <http://www.fin24.com/Companies/Financial-Services/why-the-competition-commission-wants-17-banks-prosecuted-20170215> (accessed 21-03-2017).

[32] For instance, see Anonymous "Steinhoff, Brait Share Movements Probed for Insider Trading" (25-06-2015) <http://www.fin24.com/Companies/Financial-Services/Steinhoff-Brait-share-movements-probed-for-insider-trading-20150625> (accessed 21-03-2017); Burkhardt "Insider Trading Rocks SA Coal Mine" (15-03-2017) <http://www.fin24.com/Companies/Mining/insider-trading-rocks-sa-coal-mine-20170315> (accessed 21-03-2017); Anonymous "JSE to Investigate MTN for Possible Insider trading" *Fin24* (30-10-2015) <http://www.timeslive.co.za/local/2015/10/30/JSE-to-investigate-MTN-for-possible-insider-trading1> (accessed 21-03-2017); the DMA "Report by the Directorate of Market Abuse" *Financial Services Board* (FSB) *Media Release* 30 March 2016, 1 1-3, for further examples of market abuse activities that have been recently reported in the South African financial markets.

1 4 Concluding Remarks

Illicit market abuse practices may, *inter alia*, give rise to poor integrity and efficiency of the financial markets in any country where such practices are rampant. These and other negative effects have either directly or indirectly affected the normal functions of the financial markets in the USA, the UK, South Africa and other countries to date.[33] Market abuse-related problems have continued to be exacerbated by either the enactment of inadequate anti-market abuse laws and/or the inconsistent enforcement of such laws in many countries, including South Africa, the UK and the USA.[34] Given this background, it is submitted that South Africa, the UK, the USA and other countries must adopt a robust approach to regulate and effectively combat market abuse practices in their respective financial markets.[35] Accordingly, this book exposes the need for the enactment of adequate anti-market abuse laws as well as the robust enforcement of such laws in many jurisdictions as discussed above. This approach enhances and promotes competitive and efficient financial markets across all the jurisdictions.

---

[33] See paragraph 1 2 above.
[34] See paragraph 1 2 above.
[35] See paragraph 1 3 above.

References

Books

Bergmans B *Inside Information and Securities Trading: A Legal and Economic Analysis of the Foundations of Liability in the US and the European Community* (Graham & Trotman London 1991)

Brazier G *Insider Dealing: Law and Regulation* (Cavendish Publishing Ltd London 1996)

Ferran E *Company Law and Corporate Finance* (Oxford University Press Oxford 1999)

Gitman L *Principles of Managerial Finance* 9th ed (Addison-Wesley Reading Massachusetts 2000)

Hopt KJ & Wymeersch E (eds) *European Insider Dealing – Law and Practice* (Butterworths London 1991)

Manne HG *Insider Trading and the Stock Market* (The Free Press New York 1966)

Mitchell PLR *Insider Dealing and Directors' Duties* 2nd ed (Butterworths London 1989)

Velasquez MG *Business Ethics: Concepts and Cases* 5th ed (NJ Prentice Hall International Upper Saddle River, United States of America 2002)

Journal articles

Akerlof GA "The Market for 'Lemons': Quality Uncertainty and the Market Mechanism" 1970 *Quarterly Journal of Economics* 488-500

Ali S "Market Abuse: It's Not just a Wall Street Thing" 2006 *The Company Lawyer* 222-224

Brummer C "Disruptive Technology and Securities Regulation" 2015 *Fordham Law Review* 977-1052

Cassim R "Some Aspects of Insider Trading–has the Securities Services Act 36 of 2004 Gone too Far?" 2007 *SA Merc LJ* 44-70

Chitimira H "Unpacking Selected Key Elements of the Insider Trading and Market Manipulation Offences in South Africa" 2016 *Journal of Corporate and Commercial Law and Practice* 24-41

Chitimira H "Overview of the Market Abuse Regulation under the Financial Markets Act 19 of 2012" 2014 *Obiter* 254-271

Chitimira H "A Historical Overview of the Regulation of Market Abuse in South Africa" 2014 *PER* 937-965

Dooley MP "Enforcement of Insider Trading Restrictions" 1980 *Virginia Law Review* 1-89

Dye R "Insider Trading and Incentives" 1984 *Journal of Business* 295-313

Easterbrook FH "Insider Trading, Secret Agents, Evidentiary Privileges, and The Production of Information" 1981 *Supreme Court Review* 309-365

Fischel DR & Ross DJ "Should the Law Prohibit 'Market Manipulation' in Financial Markets" 1991 *Harvard Law Review* 503-553

Georgakopoulos NL "Insider Trading as a Transaction Cost: A Market Microstructure Justification and Optimization of Insider Trading Regulation" 1993 *Connecticut Law Review* 1-51

Henning JJ & Du Toit S "The Regulation of False Trading, Market Manipulation and Insider Trading" 2000 *Journal for Juridical Science* 155-165

Henning JJ & Du Toit S "High-pressure Selling of Securities: From Rigging the Market to False Trading, Market Manipulation and Insider Dealing" 2000 *The Company Lawyer* 29-36

Hu J & Noe TH "The Insider Trading Debate" 1997 *Economic Review* 34-45

Gething M "Insider Trading Enforcement: Where are We Now and Where do We Go from Here?" 1998 *Company and Securities Law Journal* 607-627

Jensen MC & Meckling WH "Theory of the Firm: Managerial Behaviour, Agency Costs and Ownership Structure" 1976 *Journal of Financial Economics* 305-360

Luiz SM "Market Abuse II–Prohibited Trading Practices and Enforcement" 2002 *JBL's Quarterly Law Review for People in Business* 180-183

Ma Y & Sun HL "Where Should the Line be Drawn on Insider Trading Ethics?" 1998 *Journal of Business Ethics* 67-75

Macey JR "Securities Trading: A Contractual Perspective" 1999 *Case Western Reserve Law Review* 269-290

Manne HG "In Defence of Insider Trading" 1966 *Harvard Business Review* 113-122

Manove M "The Harm from Insider Trading and Informed Speculation" 1989 *The Quarterly Journal of Economics* 823-845

Martin DW & Peterson JH "Insider Trading Revisited" 1991 *Journal of Business Ethics* 57-61

McGee RW & Block WE "Information, Privilege, Opportunity and Insider Trading" 1989 *Northern Illinois University Law Review* 2-35

Moore J "What is Really Unethical about Insider Trading?" 1990 *Journal of Business Ethics* 171-182

Scotland RA "Unsafe at Any Price: A Reply to Manne" 1967 *Virginia Law Review* 1425-1478

Case law

In *re Cady, Roberts and Company* [1961-1964 Transfer Binder] CCH *Fede Sec L Rep* 76 803

Pather and Another v Financial Services Board and Others (57617/10) [2014] 3 All SA 208 (GP)

Zietsman v Director of Market Abuse 2016 1 SA 218 (GP)

Legislation

Companies Act 61 of 1973

Financial Markets Control Act 55 of 1989

Financial Sector Regulation Act 9 of 2017

Financial Institutions (Protection of Funds) Act 28 of 2001 as amended

Financial Markets Act 19 of 2012
Insider Trading Act 135 of 1998
Securities Services Act 36 of 2004
Stock Exchanges Control Act 1 of 1985

Commissions, Committees and Reports

Directorate of Market Abuse (DMA) "Past Investigations" *DMA Media Release* 23 June 2015

DMA "Report by the Directorate of Market Abuse" *Financial Services Board Media Release* 30 March 2016

King Task Group into the Insider Trading Legislation *Final Report* 21 October 1997

King Task Group into Insider Trading Legislation *Minority Report on Insider Trading* 1997

King Task Group into the Insider Trading Legislation *Report* 15 May 1997

Thesis and dissertations

Chitimira H *A Comparative Analysis of the Enforcement of Market Abuse Provisions* (LLD-thesis Nelson Mandela Metropolitan University 2012)

Newspaper articles

Chanetsa B "Insider Trading is Notoriously Hard to Prosecute" *Business Report* (2004-04-26)

Internet sources

Anonymous "Discussion of the Need for Good Corporate Governance" (31-07-2008) on <http://www.oecd.org> (accessed 02-03-2009)

Anonymous "The Regulation of Insider Trading in the United States of America" (09-03-2008) <http://www.sec.gov> (accessed 08-06-2016)

Anonymous "JSE to Investigate MTN for Possible Insider trading" Fin24 (30-10-2015) <http://www.timeslive.co.za/local/2015/10/30/JSE-to-investigate-MTN-for-possible-insider-trading1> (accessed 21-03-2017)

Anonymous "Steinhoff, Brait Share Movements Probed for Insider Trading" (25-06-2015) <http://www.fin24.com/Companies/Financial-Services/Steinhoff-Brait-share-movements-probed-for-insider-trading-20150625> (accessed 21-03-2017)

Anonymous "How Banks Allegedly Colluded on Currency Trades" (15-02-2017) <http://www.fin24.com/Companies/Financial-Services/why-the-competition-commission-wants-17-banks-prosecuted-20170215> (accessed 21-03-2017)

Beny LN "A Comparative Empirical Investigation of Agency and Market Theories of Insider Trading" (08-08-1999) 15 *Harvard Law School Discussion Paper* 264 <http://www.law.harvard.edu/Programs/onlin_center> (accessed 03-08-2008)

Berwin SJ "Criminalising Market Abuse: The Shifting Sands of Enforcement by FSA" (13-06-2008) <http://www.legal500.com/index.php?option=com_content &task=view&id=2955> (accessed 15-08-2008)

Burkhardt P "Insider Trading Rocks SA Coal Mine" (15-03-2017) <http://www.fin24.com/Companies/Mining/insider-trading-rocks-sa-coal-mine-20170315> (accessed 21-03-2017)

Forum of European Securities Commissions (FESCO) "Market abuse: FESCO's Response to the Call for Views from the Securities Regulators under the EU's Action Plan for Financial Services Com (1999) 232" (19-03-2008) <http://www.europefesco.org> (accessed 10-05-2008)

Loubser R "Insider Trading and Other Market Abuses (Including the Effective Management of Price–Sensitive Information)" in the Insider Trading Booklet final draft (2015) <http://www.jse.co.za/public/insider/JSEbooklet.pdf> (accessed 10-06-2016)

Marques CF "FSA in Debate on Market Abuse Tactics" (13-06-2008) <http://www.legal500.com/index.php?option=com_content&task=view&id =2955> (accessed 05-07-2008)

Myburgh A & Davis B "The Impact of South Africa's Insider Trading Regime: A Report for the Financial Services Board" (25-03-2004) <http://www.genesis-analytics.com/public/FSBReport.pdf> (accessed 09-02-2013)

Scholtz J, Paige N & Van Zyl E "Financial Markets, Market Abuse, Money Laundering and the National Credit Act" (31-03-2008) <http://www.legal500.com/index.php?option=com_content&task> (accessed 30-04- 2016)

Van Deventer G "Anti-Market Abuse Legislation in South Africa" (10-06-2008) <http://www.fsb.co.za/public/marketabuse/FSBReport.pdf> (accessed 05-05-2013)

Chapter 2

Aspects of the State Prohibition on Market Abuse in the United States of America and South Africa

2 1 Introduction

Market abuse (insider trading and market manipulation) practices are now statutorily prohibited in many countries. For instance, market abuse practices are statutorily prohibited both at a federal and state level in the United States of America (USA).[1] Accordingly, the state prohibition on market abuse has continued to play a relatively crucial role in the curbing of market abuse in the USA financial markets to date. Given this background, this chapter provides an analysis of the enforcement of the market abuse prohibition in California, Delaware and Washington states. These states are discussed because they have relatively and consistently employed several anti-market abuse enforcement approaches in their respective financial markets to date.[2] Thus, it is hoped that some possible enforcement lessons will be adopted by the aforesaid states and incorporated to improve the statutory anti-market abuse regulatory frameworks in other countries such as South Africa.[3] Moreover,

---

* This chapter is influenced in part, by an article that was initially published in the *Mediterranean Journal of Social Sciences*, see Chitimira "A Comparative Overview of the State Prohibition on Market Abuse in the United States of America" 2014(5)(7) *Mediterranean Journal of Social Sciences* 54-68. Accordingly, the author has written this chapter with legal permission from the editors of the *Mediterranean Journal of Social Sciences.*

[1] Steinberg "Insider Trading Regulation–A Comparative Perspective" 2003 *The International Lawyer* 153 169-171.

[2] Langevoort "Federalism in Corporate/Securities Law: Reflections on Delaware, California, and State Regulation of Insider Trading" 2006 *University of San Francisco Law Review* 879 880-892; Crandall "State Securities Regulation and the Internet" 2001 *Legislation & Public Policy* 23 24-31. See further Bhattacharya & Daouk "The World Price of Insider Trading" 2002 *Journal of Finance* 75 75-108; Lyon & Du Plessis *The Law of Insider Trading in Australia* (2005) 159-168, for related comparative analysis in other countries & Avgouleas *The Mechanics and Regulation of Market Abuse: A Legal and Economic Analysis* (2005) 75-502, a related comparative analysis.

[3] Botha "Control of Insider Trading in South Africa: A Comparative Analysis" 1991 *SA Merc LJ* 1 1-18; Botha "Increased Maximum Fine for Insider Trading: A Realistic and Effective Deterrent?" 1990 *SALJ* 504 504-508; Chitimira *The Regulation of Insider Trading in South Africa: A Roadmap for an Effective, Competitive and Adequate Regulatory Statutory Framework* (Unpublished LLM dissertation, University of Fort Hare) 2008, 41–72. See related comments by Van Deventer "Anti-Market Abuse Legislation in South Africa" (10-06-2008) 1-5 <http://www.fsb.co.za/public/marketabuse/

relevant provisions and cases from the selected USA states will be contrasted with similar provisions and cases in South Africa. This is done to recommend possible anti-market abuse enforcement approaches that could be incorporated in the South African anti-market abuse regulatory framework.

2 2 Overview of the State Prohibition on Market Abuse

2 2 1 Prohibition on Insider Trading in California

An issuer or any other person who is an officer, director or controlling person of such issuer or any person who knowingly has access directly or indirectly, to material non-public information that relates to any securities by virtue of his relationship with the issuer is prohibited from dealing in such securities in order to prevent insider trading.[4] Thus, although no express definition of insider trading is provided, it is statutorily prohibited under the California Corporations Code.[5] Moreover, there is a requirement of knowledge on the part of the accused person that the material non-public information he obtained will significantly affect the market price of the securities in question before incurring any insider trading liability.[6] Such liability can only be imposed upon the accused if he fails to prove that the affected person was aware of the non-public information in question; or that the affected person would have purchased or sold the securities in question at the same price even if the material non-public information was made public.[7]

California's insider trading prohibition is limited only to officers, directors, controlling shareholders of an issuer (primary insiders) and/or any other

---

FSBReport.pdf> (accessed 05-05-2013) & see further Myburgh & Davis "The Impact of South Africa's Insider Trading Regime: A Report for the Financial Services Board" (25-03-2004) 8-33 <http://www.genesis-analytics.com/public/FSBReport.pdf> (accessed 09-02-2013). See further Osode "The New South African Insider Trading Act: Sound Law Reform or Legislative Overkill?" 2000 *Journal of African Law* 239 240-263; Bhana "Take-Over Announcements and Insider Trading Activity on the Johannesburg Stock Exchange" 1987 *South African Journal of Business Management* 198 199-208; Jooste "A Critique of the Insider Trading Provisions of the 2004 Securities Services Act" 2006 *SALJ* 437 441–460; Van Deventer "New Watchdog for Insider Trading" 1999 *FSB Bulletin* 2 3; Chitimira *A Comparative Analysis of the Enforcement of Market Abuse Provisions* (Unpublished thesis, Nelson Mandela Metropolitan University) 2012, 188-210. Also read the repealed Securities Services Act 36 of 2004 (Securities Services Act), in conjunction with the Financial Markets Act 19 of 2012 (Financial Markets Act) to trace the anti-market abuse enforcement approaches that are employed in South Africa.

4 S 25402 of the Corporate Securities Law of 1968 (California Statutes 1968, Chapter 88) also known as the California Corporations Code (California Corporations Code).

5 Ss 25402 & 25502.5 read with s 25502 of the California Corporations Code.

6 S 25402 read with ss 25110; 25210 & 25230 (which prohibits investment advisors and broker-dealers from dealing in securities without licensure or exemption) of the California Corporations Code.

7 S 25402 read with ss 25502.5 & 25502 of the California Corporations Code. See Bingham McCutchen Securities Litigation Group "California's Unique Treble Damages Insider Trading Law Applied to Corporations Incorporated Outside of California" 2006 *Securities Litigation Alert* 1-3 <http://www.bingham.com.01.2006/03> (accessed 26-10-2013, for further comments.

person who obtains non-public material information by virtue of his relationship with primary insiders.[8] Therefore, any violations by other persons who fortuitously obtain non-public material information not on the basis of their relationship with any of the primary insiders are not expressly covered under California's insider trading prohibition.[9] However, California's insider trading prohibition has an extra-territorial application that covers any violations that are perpetrated in California by primary insiders of a corporation incorporated in another state or country (foreign corporations).[10] Wherefore, accessorial liability can also be imposed on individuals who tip, induce or assist others to contravene any California's insider trading provisions.[11]

2 2 2 Prohibition on Market Manipulation in California

The California Corporations Code prohibits disclosure-based market manipulation, trade-based market manipulation, Internet-based market manipulation and commodity-based market manipulation. Trade-based market manipulation practices include:

(a) the use of a device, scheme or artifice to defraud or manipulate the price of a security;[12]

(b) effecting a transaction in a security which involves no change in the beneficial ownership;

(c) entering orders for the sale or purchase of any security with the knowledge that similar orders have been entered at the same price and/or at the same time for that security by the same or different persons; and

(d) effecting alone, or with other persons, a series of transactions in any security to create actual or apparent active trading in such security in order to raise or depress the price of that security for the purposes of inducing its sale or purchase by others.[13]

---

[8] S 25402 of the California Corporations Code; see further Langevoort 2006 *University of San Francisco Law Review* 886.

[9] S 25402 of the California Corporations Code.

[10] *Friese v Superior Court* (2005) 36 Cal Rptr 3d 558 (Cal Ct App) 563-568, which held that although the internal affairs doctrine (as codified under s 2116) stipulates that only the state of incorporation may adjudicate on insider trading and/or any other violations, the defendants' breach of s 25502.5 of the California Corporations Code did not merely give rise to fiduciary duties violations but to insider trading and as such, it was not rigidly subject to the internal affairs doctrine.

[11] S 25403 of the California Corporations Code.

[12] S 25541 of the California Corporations Code.

[13] S 25400(a) & (b) of the California Corporations Code.

Notably, disclosure-based market manipulation practices include the dissemination of false or misleading material information pertaining to the sale or purchase of a security by a broker-dealer or any other person so that the price of such security will or is likely to rise or fall (raising or depressing its market price) for the purposes of inducing others to purchase or sell that security.[14] Disclosure-based market manipulation practices further include the oral or written communication of false or misleading statements that relate to the sale or purchase of securities by any offenders.[15] Accordingly, liability for both disclosure-based market manipulation and trade-based market manipulation requires proof on the part of the prosecution that the offenders wilfully participated, directly or indirectly in the effecting of a manipulative transaction or in the making or dissemination of a false and misleading statement of a material fact relating to any security; or that they omitted to state such material fact in order to make the statement, in light of the circumstances it was made, not misleading.[16]

Commodity-based market manipulation practices that are outlawed include:

(a) wilful engagement by any person, in the making of a false report;

(b) entering any false record or untrue statement of a material fact and/or omitting to make the material fact in order to make any statement relating to a commodity, commodity contract or option false and misleading.[17]

Additionally, engaging in any transaction, act, practice or course of business which operates or would operate as fraud or deceit upon commodities investors and the employing of any device, scheme or artifice to defraud or manipulate the sale or purchase of any commodity is prohibited.[18]

Internet-based market manipulation, franchise-related touting and other manipulative practices are statutorily prohibited in California.[19] For example, the intentional making of any untrue statement of a material fact relating to the sale or purchase of a franchise is a felony under the California Corpora-

[14] S 25400(d) read with ss 25400(c) & (e) & 25401 of the California Corporations Code.

[15] Ss 25400 & 25401 read with s 25404 of the California Corporations Code.

[16] Ss 25400; 25401; 25541 read with ss 25404; 25500 & 25501 of the California Corporations Code.

[17] S 29536(b) of the California Commodity Law of 1990 as amended which is also part of the California Corporations Code.

[18] S 29536(a); (c) & (d) of the California Corporations Code read with s 29520; 29535 & 29538 of the same Code, which prohibits any person from purchasing or selling commodities without licensure or exemption and/or from concealing evidence or making untrue statements to the California Department of Corporations.

[19] Ss 31200 to 31204 of the California Corporations Code.

tions Code.[20] The California Department of Corporations also established the Internet Compliance and Enforcement Team to oversee the prohibition of Internet-based market manipulation by *inter alia* requiring all persons to obtain a permit before issuing any securities.[21]

2 2 3 Available Market Abuse Penalties and Remedies in California

Various anti-market abuse penalties and remedies are employed to combat market abuse practices in California. For instance, an issuer or any person who wilfully engages in insider trading or market manipulation and fails to rely on the defences as earlier discussed[22] will be liable for a fine not more than $10 million upon conviction or be imprisoned in a state prison (or pursuant to the California Penal Code)[23] for a period between two and five years, or be liable for both the fine and imprisonment.[24]

The Public Company Accounting Reform and Investor Protection Act of 2002[25] stipulates that an issuer as defined in this Act who commits insider trading, market manipulation or who violates any rule or order that prohibits market abuse will be criminally liable for a fine not more than $25 million upon conviction, or imprisonment in a state prison, or in terms of the California Penal Code,[26] for a period between two and five years and/or be liable for both such fine and imprisonment.[27] The California Corporations Code specifically imposes a fine not exceeding $10 million, or imprisonment in a state prison for a period between two and five years, or both such fine and imprisonment upon any person who wilfully employs, directly or indirectly, a device, scheme or artifice to defraud or manipulate the offer, purchase or sale of securities.[28] Likewise, an issuer as defined in the Sarbanes-Oxley Act[29] who wilfully employs, directly or indirectly, a device, scheme or artifice to defraud or manipulate the offer, purchase or sale of a security will be liable for a fine

---

[20] Ss 31200 to 31204 read with ss 31210; 31211 & 31220 of the California Corporations Code.

[21] Ss 25111 to 25113; 25140(c) read with ss 25400 & 25401 of the California Corporations Code. See further California Department of Corporations "Internet Investments Ordered to Stop Selling" *Press Release 98-11* (10-06-1998) <http://www.corp.ca.gov/ pressrel/nr9811.htm> (accessed 27-10-2013); California Department of Corporations "Department of Corporations Files Internet Market Manipulation Actions" *Press Release 00-11* (20-06-2000) <http://www.corp.ca.gov/pressrel/nr0011.htm> (accessed 27-10-2013) & Crandall 2001 *Legislation & Public Policy* 23-31.

[22] See paragraph *2 2 1* above.

[23] S 1170(h) of the California Penal Code.

[24] S 25540(b) of the California Corporations Code.

[25] Public Law 107-204, 116 Stat 745 (as codified in scattered sections of 15; 28 USC) (Sarbanes-Oxley Act) and its relevant provisions will be referred to only where necessary. S 2 of the Sarbanes-Oxley Act; also see Palmiter *Securities Regulation: Examples and Explanations* (2005) 23.

[26] S 1170(h) of the California Penal Code.

[27] S 25540(c) read with s 25540(a) of the California Corporations Code.

[28] S 25541(a) of the California Corporations Code.

[29] S 2 of the Sarbanes-Oxley Act.

not exceeding $25 million, or imprisonment in a state prison for a period between two and five years, or both such fine and imprisonment.[30]

Persons who violate the insider trading provisions are directly liable to the person who sold or purchased the affected security for the damages equal to the difference between the price at which such security was sold or purchased and the market value which such security would have acquired at the time of the purchase or sale if the information known to the defendant had been publicly disseminated prior to that time.[31] This civil liability also includes interest at a legal rate accruing to the plaintiff (affected person) provided that a reasonable period of time has lapsed for the market to absorb the publicly disclosed material information, or that the defendant failed to rely on any available defences.[32] Furthermore, any person other than the issuer who commits insider trading will be liable to the issuer or anyone acting derivatively on behalf of the issuer for civil damages of up to three times the profit gained or loss avoided as a result of the insider trading in question.[33]

Any person (defendant) who commits market manipulation will be liable for compensatory damages to any other person (plaintiff) who purchased or sold securities at an affected or manipulated price as a result of such defendant's illicit act or transaction.[34] This civil liability seems not to be limited to the plaintiff who initially bought or sold the securities that were affected by the defendant's market manipulation.[35] Moreover, any person who wilfully disseminates false or misleading statements which relate to any securities will be liable to the affected person, for rescission or compensatory damages.[36] It is not required that the plaintiff should have actually relied on the false or misleading statements in question before the defendant is held liable for such recessionary or compensatory damages plus interest at a legal rate.[37]

---

[30] Ss 25541(b); 25542 of the California Corporations Code read with s 1170(h) of the California Penal Code.

[31] S 25502 of the California Corporations Code.

[32] S 25502 of the California Corporations Code. This provision gives private rights of action to the affected persons in order for them to recover their insider trading damages directly from offenders.

[33] S 25502.5 of the California Corporations Code. These treble insider trading damages are determined by calculating the difference between the price at which the security was purchased or sold and the market value that it would have gained at the time of the sale or purchase if the non-public information known to the defendant or the offender was publicly disseminated; *Friese v Superior Court* 563-568.

[34] Ss 25500; 28900 & 28901 of the California Corporations Code.

[35] On the other hand, market manipulation offenders are apparently exempted from any liability that could arise from routine statements such as press releases and quarterly reports that are not intended to induce others to sale or purchase any securities, see s 25500 read with s 25400 of the California Corporations Code.

[36] S 25501 read with s 25501.5 of the California Corporations Code.

[37] S 25501 read with s 25501.5 of the California Corporations Code.

Furthermore, there is secondary civil liability for controlling persons, aiders and abettors who participated in disclosure-based market manipulation.[38]

The California Corporations Code further imposes separate criminal penalties on any person who commits commodities-based market manipulation offences.[39] Such a person will be liable for a fine not more than $250 000 or imprisonment in a state prison, or pursuant to the California Penal Code for a period between two and five years or for both such fine and imprisonment.[40] With regard to civil liability, there are no private rights of action for the affected persons to recover their damages directly from those who commit commodities-based market manipulation offences.[41] However, any person who aids or assists another person to contravene any commodities-based market manipulation provisions will be jointly and severally liable with any such person for damages.[42]

Any person who wilfully engages in franchise-related touting and market manipulation will be liable to a fine not exceeding $100 000 or imprisonment in a state prison for a period not exceeding one year, or imprisonment pursuant to the California Penal Code,[43] or both such fine and imprisonment.[44] Such a person will also be liable to the franchisee, franchisor or any other affected person for compensatory damages.[45] A controlling person or every partner in a company who aids or abets another person to commit franchise-related touting and market manipulation offences will be jointly and severally liable with such person for actual damages suffered by the affected person and/or a temporary and permanent injunctive relief.[46]

The California Department of Corporations can also impose administrative penalties such as public censure, suspension, revocation of licenses, civil injunctions and administrative orders against any person who engages in fraudulent and manipulative Internet-based offering of investments and financial services.[47] The California Department of Corporations can further impose remedies such as rescission, restitution, civil penalties and

---

[38] S 25501 read with ss 25504 & 25504.1 of the California Corporations Code.

[39] S 29550 of the California Corporations Code.

[40] S 29550(b) & (c); read with s 29551 of the California Corporations Code which stipulates that the California State may also bring criminal charges against the offenders under any other statute. Also see s 1170(h) of the California Penal Code.

[41] S 29555 of the California Corporations Code.

[42] S 29552 read with ss 29553 & 29554 of the California Corporations Code.

[43] S 1170(h) of the California Penal Code.

[44] Ss 31410; 31411 read with s 31412 of the California Corporations Code.

[45] S 31300 read with 31301 of the California Corporations Code.

[46] Ss 31302 & 31302.5 of the California Corporations Code.

[47] Ss 25530 to 25534 of the California Corporations Code; also see Crandall 2001 *Legislation & Public Policy* 30 & related remarks by the California Department of Corporations "Fighting Internet 'Cyber Investment Fraud'" <http://www.corp.ca.gov/pub/ cyber.htm> (accessed 28-10-2013).

administrative penalties against any person who commits Internet-based market manipulation offences.[48] Lastly, the California Department of Corporations can issue investigation orders against Internet-based market manipulation offenders and/or refer any such related criminal matters to the relevant courts for further investigation or prosecution.[49] Be that as it may, it remains uncertain whether social media-related market manipulation activities are specifically and statutorily prohibited in California.

2 2 4 Analysis and Evaluation of the California Anti-Market Abuse Enforcement Framework

Various enforcement authorities are actively involved in the enforcement of the market abuse prohibition in California. For instance, the California Department of Corporations, the Commissioner of Corporations and the relevant courts are responsible for the enforcement of market abuse provisions in California.[50] As earlier stated,[51] California employs criminal, civil and administrative sanctions to curb market abuse activities.[52] These sanctions are enforced by the California Department of Corporations through the Commissioner of Corporations and the courts. However, there is no specific regulatory body established to oversee the enforcement of market abuse laws in California. Consequently, the Commissioner of Corporations has a variety of powers which include:

(a) imposing fees and penalties;
(b) cease and desist orders;
(c) revocation orders;
(d) restitution orders;
(e) civil injunction orders;
(f) investigation orders;
(g) public censure against the offenders; and
(h) issuing permits to all persons who seek to offer or sell investments, commodities or securities in California.[53]

The Commissioner of Corporations has further powers to make, amend or rescind any rules and/or orders for the purposes of effectively enforcing the securities and market abuse provisions.[54] Similarly, the Financial Services

---

[48] S 25535 of the California Corporations Code; also see Crandall 2001 *Legislation & Public Policy* 30.
[49] S 25533 of the California Corporations Code; also see Crandall 2001 *Legislation & Public Policy* 30.
[50] Crandall 2001 *Legislation & Public Policy* 28-30.
[51] See paragraph 2 *2 3* read with paragraphs 2 *2 1*; *2 2 2*.
[52] This is also the position in South Africa. See ss 78; 80; 81 & 82 of the Financial Markets Act.
[53] Ss 25111 to 25113 of the California Corporations Code; also see Crandall 2001 *Legislation & Public Policy* 28-30.
[54] Ss 31502 & 31503 of the California Corporations Code.

Board (FSB) is empowered to make market abuse rules in South Africa.[55] Notwithstanding the fact that the there is no specific regulatory body that polices the enforcement of market abuse laws in California, it is submitted that the Commissioner of Corporations has, from time to time, consistently exercised his/her powers to curb market abuse activities.[56]

With regard to Internet-based market manipulation, the California Department of Corporations relies on the Internet Compliance and Enforcement Team to investigate and prosecute any activities that amount to unlicensed securities, franchises or commodities offerings, fraud and market manipulation.[57] The Internet Compliance and Enforcement Team also ensures that there is extensive investigation and surveillance of Internet-based market manipulation.[58] Accordingly, if any violation is detected, it will be reported to the Commissioner of Corporations who then determines whether it was fair and justifiable.[59] In other words, when the Commissioner of Corporations receives some leads from the Internet Compliance and Enforcement Team's surveillance, junk mail and public complaints and referrals from other enforcement bodies, he may impose damages or other applicable remedies against the offenders.[60] On the contrary, there is no specific regulatory body that prohibits and investigates Internet-based market abuse practices in South Africa.[61] Moreover, it appears that social media-related market abuse activities are still not expressly and statutorily prohibited in both California and South Africa.

The district courts have to date enabled the California Department of Corporations to enforce the market abuse prohibition consistently in California. For example, the California Department of Corporations has successfully filed for a number of civil remedies such as the disgorgement of profits, damages and civil injunctions in the courts.[62]

---

[55] S 84(2)(f) of the Financial Markets Act.

[56] Crandall 2001 *Legislation & Public Policy* 29-30.

[57] Ss 25000 to 31516 of the California Corporations Code; also see Mariano "Stock Fraud Spurs Regulators to Look Online" (21-06-2000) <http://news.cnet.com/news/01-1005-200-2126256.html> (accessed 29-10-2013).

[58] Crandall 2001 *Legislation & Public Policy* 24.

[59] S 25140(c) of the California Corporations Code; Crandall 2001 *Legislation & Public Policy* 24.

[60] S 25535 of the California Corporations Code; also see paragraph *2 2 3* above. This has enabled California to curb Internet-based market manipulation successfully since 1998 to date, see Crandall 2001 *Legislation & Public Policy* 26-31.

[61] Internet-based market abuse practices are not expressly prohibited under the Financial Markets Act, see ss 78; 80; 81 & 82. Moreover, Internet-based market abuse practices are also not expressly outlawed in the Consumer Protection Act 68 of 2008.

[62] *Friese v Superior Court* 561, which held that the civil derivative cause of action for disgorgement of insider trading profits was also applicable to companies that were not incorporated in California; also see Langevoort 2006 *University of San Francisco Law Review* 886-887; *Medifast v Minkow* (2011) 10 CV 382 (JLS BGS), which held that defendants were not liable for civil remedies for their alleged

Likewise, South Africa also provides for civil,[63] criminal[64] and administrative[65] penalties for insider trading in terms of the Financial Markets Act. With regard to criminal penalties, the South African legislature has rigidly provided for a fixed maximum fine of R50 million, or imprisonment for a period not exceeding ten years, or both.[66] Although *prima facie* these penalties seem to be quite significant, it is submitted that Cassim[67] correctly argues that the currently available market abuse penalties might not be high enough for deterrence purposes. For example, some unscrupulous persons may take any fine for market abuse offences just like another cost of doing business. Furthermore, no distinction has been made in relation to the penalties imposed on natural and juristic persons to increase deterrence.[68] Moreover, in South Africa, civil and administrative penalties and remedies are mainly enforced by the FSB[69] and the Enforcement Committee (EC)[70] respectively. However, the Financial Markets Act does not expressly provide civil penalties and remedies for market manipulation offences.[71] This flaw could potentially weaken South Africa's anti-market abuse regime,[72] compared to similar foreign legislation in countries like the USA.

---

market manipulation; *Louisiana Pacific Corporation v Money Market 1Institutional Investment Dealer and others* (2011) 09-CV-03529 (JSW), where market manipulation damages were granted against the defendants; *Williams v Gaylord* (1902) 186 US 157, which, *inter alia*, held that a corporation that issues securities in any State is protected from possible market abuse liability that may arise from another State under the internal affairs doctrine; *Clothesrigger Inc v G T E Corporation* (1987) 191 Cal App 3d 605, which held that California's market abuse laws may be enforced whenever necessary to prevent fraud and other deceptive or manipulative practices; *Diamond Multimedia Systems Inc v Superior Court* (1999) 19 Cal 1036, the court held that California's securities and market abuse laws should be consistently enforced to promote financial markets that are fair and free from fraud and market abuse practices; *Desai, Lamb, Long and Christopher Long v Deutsche Bank Securities Limited, Deutsche Bank Securities Inc and others* (2009) 08-55081 US App Lexis 16704 (US App 9th Cir), which, *inter alia*, that the defendants were not liable for stock price manipulation because the appellants failed to establish a motion for class certification in terms of Rule 23(b)(3) of the federal rules.

[63] S 82.

[64] S 109(a).

[65] S 99.

[66] S 109 (a).

[67] Cassim "An Analysis of Market Manipulation under the Securities Services Act 36 of 2004 (Part 2)" 2008 *SA Merc LJ* 177 191-195.

[68] S 109(a) of the Financial Markets Act.

[69] S 84 of the Financial Markets Act.

[70] S 99 of the Financial Markets Act.

[71] Ss 80 & 81; also see Cassim 2008 *SA Merc LJ* 192. This suggests that persons who fall victim to market manipulation practices are left to find their own civil remedies. See further Cassim "An Analysis of Market Manipulation under the Securities Services Act 36 of 2004 (Part 1)" 2008 *SA Merc LJ* 33 36.

[72] For instance, there is no specific statutory civil remedy provision for market manipulation violations as outlawed under ss 80 & 81of the Financial Markets Act.

In a nutshell, one can conclude that California has managed to develop a relatively consistent anti-market abuse enforcement framework that discourages a number of market abuse practices (including franchise-related, capital markets-related as well as Internet-related market abuse violations).

2 2 5 Prohibition on Insider Trading in Delaware

In contrast to the Californian position,[73] insider trading is mainly outlawed as a breach of fiduciary duties by directors, officers or other employees (primary insiders) of an issuer who sell or purchase the issuer's securities or commodities on the basis of non-public inside information.[74] It appears that this fiduciary-related insider trading liability may be imposed upon any offenders who violate Delaware's securities and market abuse laws even if the issuer or any other affected persons did not suffer actual damages as result of the offender's alleged insider trading.[75] Moreover, a corporation may not repurchase its own shares if such repurchase will affect its payment of debts or cause capital impairment.[76]

Any sale or purchase of securities on the basis of non-public material information by a beneficial owner, director or officer of an insurer is also treated as insider trading.[77] This prohibition on insurance-related insider trading allows the insurer to recover any damages suffered within a period of less than six months unless the sale or purchase of the affected securities was done in good faith.[78] Intention on the part of the offenders is not required for the purposes incurring insurance-related insider trading liability.[79] On the

[73] See paragraph 2 2 1 above.

[74] See generally s 144 read with ss 160 to 162; 122(17); 271 & 174 under Title 8 of the Delaware General Corporation Law (Delaware General Corporation Law); s 73-202 read with ss 73-203 & 73-204 in Title 6 of the Delaware Code, under Chapter 73 of the Delaware Securities Act as amended (Delaware Securities Act); also see Langevoort 2006 *University of San Francisco Law Review* 881 & *Brophy v Cities Service Co* (1949) 70 A2d 5 (Del Ch), which, *inter alia*, held that the defendants' breach of fiduciary duty of loyalty was tantamount to insider trading.

[75] *Brophy v Cities Service Co* 5; *Kahn v Kohlberg, Kravis, Roberts & Co LP* (2010) CA No 436 (Del SC) & *Guth v Loft Inc* (1939) 5A2d 503 (Del) 510, which held that an employee occupying a position of trust and confidence towards his employer who nonetheless abuses non-public material information relating to the employer's securities to gain profit will be liable for insider trading regardless of whether the employer suffered actual loss.

[76] Put differently, a corporation may not repurchase its own shares while in possession of non-public material information that relates to any securities to prevent insider trading, see s 160 of the Delaware General Corporation Law.

[77] Ss 5104 & 5105 in Title 18, under Chapter 51 of the Delaware Insurance Code (Insurance Code).

[78] S 5104 (a) of the Insurance Code.

[79] S 5104 (a) read with 5104(b) & (c) of the Insurance Code.

contrary, in South Africa, there is no provision that specifically prohibits insurance-related insider trading in the Financial Markets Act.[80]

2 2 6 Prohibition on Market Manipulation in Delaware

Several practices may give rise to market abuse in Delaware. For instance, any person who employs a device, scheme or artifice to defraud or manipulate the offer, sale or purchase of a security will be liable for market manipulation.[81] Furthermore, any person who makes or omits to make a statement of a material fact in order to deceive or mislead others to purchase or sell a security will be liable for fraud and/or market manipulation.[82] Likewise, any persons who are not registered with the Securities Commissioner are prohibited from offering to sell or purchase any securities.[83] Moreover, misleading filings and unlawful purchase or sale of securities by broker-dealers, shareholders or any other person are prohibited.[84] This was probably targeted at preventing securities or stock price market manipulation by professional persons like broker-dealers, investment advisors, shareholders and other relevant stakeholders.

Contrary to the Californian position,[85] under the Delaware courts, a breach of fiduciary duty of disclosure by directors who issue misstated financial statements or misleading public statements to defraud, induce or manipulate others to purchase or sell any securities may give rise to monetary damages against such directors.[86]

Despite the fact that there is probably no statutory provision that expressly prohibits commodities-based market manipulation in Delaware, a number of

---

[80] Ss 78; 80; 81 & 82 & other relevant provisions under Chapter X entitled "Market Abuse" of the Financial Markets Act. Moreover, in South Africa, insurance-related insider trading is not expressly prohibited under both the Long-Term Insurance Act 52 of 1998 as amended and the Short-Term Insurance Act 53 of 1998 as amended.

[81] This shows that trade-based market manipulation practices are also prohibited in Delaware, see s 73-201(1) of the Delaware Securities Act.

[82] S 73-201(2) & (3) of the Delaware Securities Act.

[83] S 73-202 read with ss 73-203 & 73-204 of the Delaware Securities Act.

[84] Ss 73-209; 73-301of the Delaware Securities Act & s 610 read with ss 612 & 616 in Title 8 (Delaware General Corporation Law) under Chapter 6, which is also known as the Delaware Professional Service Corporations Act (Professional Service Corporations Act).

[85] See paragraph 2 2 2 above.

[86] See generally s 220(d) read with s 220(b) & (c) of the Delaware General Corporation Law, which gives shareholders the right to seek and/or inspect financial statements in order to, *inter alia*, prevent fraud and market manipulation; also see *Malone v Brincat* (1998) CA No 15510 WL 919123 (Del Supr. Ct); *Malone v Brincat* (1998) 722 A2d 5 (Del) which held that the director or defendant who filed or disseminated false information in a financial statement could be held liable for a breach of general fiduciary duties of care, loyalty or good faith and not for common law prohibited fraudulent and market abuse activities & *Seinfield v Verizon Communications Inc* (2006) 909 A2d 717 (Del), which held that shareholders are entitled to inspect or seek relevant information from a corporation to detect and prevent fraud and disclosure-based market manipulation.

deceptive or unfair commerce, trade and insurance practices are outlawed to *inter alia* combat market abuse activities.[87] Delaware also prohibits racketeering and other forms of organised crime in order to discourage all persons from engaging in market abuse activities.[88] In contrast to this, there is no provision that specifically prohibits racketeering and/or commerce and trade-related market abuse activities in South Africa, especially under the Financial Markets Act.[89]

2 2 7 Available Market Abuse Penalties and Remedies in Delaware

Illicit market abuse practices will give rise to various penalties and damages on the part of the offenders in Delaware. For example, any person who engages in fraudulent market manipulation which results in investors losing $50 000 or more will be liable per violation to a fine not exceeding $200 000 upon conviction, or imprisonment for a period not more than five years at level V incarceration, or both such fine and imprisonment.[90] Similarly, any person who engages in fraud or market manipulation which results in investors losing $10 000 or more but less than $50 000, will be liable per violation for a fine not more than $100 000 upon conviction, or imprisonment for a period not more than three years at level V incarceration, or both such fine and imprisonment.[91] Furthermore, any person who wilfully violates any related fraud or securities provisions of the Delaware Securities Act will be liable for a fine of not more than $100 000, or imprisonment for a period no more than two years, or both such fine and imprisonment.[92] The Securities Commissioner may impose injunctions, administrative remedies and stop orders to prohibit market abuse violations by the offenders by suspending or revoking the purchase or sale of any affected security.[93]

A broker-dealer, broker-dealer agent, issuer agent, investment advisor, investment advisor's representative or any other person who offers, sells or purchases securities by means of an untrue statement or any other market manipulation practices will be liable for civil compensatory damages.[94] Moreover, the courts may impose upon the insider trading offenders, orders

[87] Ss 2303 & 2304(1) to (12) in Title 18, under Chapter 23 of the Insurance Code; also see s 2532(a) to (c) in Title 6, under Chapter 25 of the Delaware Code which is also known as the Delaware Uniform Deceptive Trade Practices Act (Uniform Deceptive Trade Practices Act).

[88] S 1503 in Title 11, under Chapter 15 of the Delaware Criminal Code.

[89] See ss 78; 80; 81 & 82.

[90] S 73-604(a) of the Delaware Securities Act.

[91] S 73-604(b) of the Delaware Securities Act.

[92] S 73-604(c) of the Delaware Securities Act. The Supreme Court may also order the offenders to restitute any profits they obtained from the affected investors, see s 73-604(d) & (e) of the Delaware Securities Act.

[93] S 73-206 read with ss 73-601 & 73-602 of the Delaware Securities Act.

[94] S 73-605(a) & (b) of the Delaware Securities Act.

for damages, disgorgement of illicit profits and other applicable remedies.[95] The courts may further impose a fine of up to $5 million or imprisonment for a period not exceeding 20 years upon the insider trading offenders.[96]

Moreover, the offenders may be ordered by the relevant courts through an injunction to pay legal costs, compensatory damages or to disgorge any profits gained to the affected persons.[97] This is usually done to deter offenders and curb manipulative trading practices in the Delaware financial markets. Moreover, any persons who engage in insurance-related market abuse activities will be ordered by the courts to disgorge any profits they gained at the expense of the insurers.[98] The Commissioner of Insurance may also issue cease and desist orders and penalty orders against any person who commits insurance-related market abuse offences.[99]

2 2 8 Analysis and Evaluation of the Delaware Anti-Market Abuse Enforcement Framework

As is the position in California,[100] Delaware does not have a specific regulatory body that enforces its market abuse laws. Nonetheless, Delaware has established a consistent system of reliance on judicial law standards, well-developed common law principles and private enforcement measures to combat market abuse activities.[101] Consequently, the Delaware Supreme Court, the Delaware Chancery Court, the Delaware General Assembly, the Delaware Corporate Law Council, the Delaware Division of Securities and the Delaware Division Corporations bear the responsibility of enforcing the Delaware's securities and market abuse laws.[102]

---

[95] *Brophy v Cities Service Co* 5; *Kahn v Kohlberg, Kravis, Roberts & Co LP* 436, where the defendants were mandated to pay damages and to disgorge their insider trading profits to the affected persons (plaintiffs) even if such persons did not suffer actual damages.

[96] The United States Department of Justice District of Delaware "Newark Man Pleads Guilty to Insider Trading Charges" *Press Release* 25 March 2011, where Jeffery Temple of Newark DE was convicted of insider trading in March 2011 and was consequently liable for a fine not exceeding $5 million or imprisonment for a period of up to 20 years.

[97] S 2533(b) & (c) read with subsections (d) & (e) of the Uniform Deceptive Trade Practices Act.

[98] S 5104 of the Insurance Code.

[99] S 2308 read with s 2311 of the Insurance Code.

[100] Paragraph 2 2 4 above.

[101] Bebchuk & Hamdani "Federal Corporate Law: Lessons from History" 2006 *Harvard Law School John M Olin Center for Law, Economics & Business Discussion Paper Series 558* 35-37 <http://lsr.nellco.org/harvard_olin/558> (accessed 03-11-2013), for related remarks.

[102] Roe "Washington and Delaware as Corporate Lawmakers" 2009 *Harvard Law School John M Olin Center for Law, Economics & Business Discussion Paper Series 638* 8-12 <http://lsr.nellco.org/harvard_olin/638> (accessed 03-11-2013); Jones "Dynamic Federalism: Competition, Cooperation and Securities Enforcement" 2005 *Boston College Law School Faculty Paper 36* 2 <http://lawdigitalcommons.bc.edu/lsfp/36> (accessed 04-11-2013) & Wilson "Climate Change:

As highlighted above,[103] Delaware generally treats any securities dealing that is based on non-public inside information by primary insiders as a breach of fiduciary duties that also amounts to insider trading. Consequently, although Delaware does not have a statutory provision that expressly prohibits insider trading, it has to date successfully relied on common law principles on fiduciary duties to combat insider trading.[104] This success has prompted other commentators to conclude that Delaware was effectively combating insider trading and market manipulation because it cedes other areas of its laws that involve insider trading enforcement to the federal government.[105] For instance, Delaware's fiduciary-related insider trading remedies were controversially applied in some few cases.[106] Contrary this Delaware position, insider trading liability is not limited to instances where there is a breach of a fiduciary duty by primary insiders in South Africa.[107]

The Real Threat to Delaware Corporation Law, Why Delaware Must Keep A Watchful Eye on The Content of Political Change in the Air" 2010 *Entrepreneurial Business Law Journal* 481 484-490.

[103] Paragraph 2 2 5 above.

[104] *Brophy v Cities Service Co* 5, the defendants were ordered to pay compensatory insider trading remedies to the plaintiffs regardless of whether such plaintiffs suffered actual damages; *Kahn v Kohlberg, Kravis, Roberts & Co LP* 436, where the plaintiffs (stockholders) were allowed to institute a derivative action against the defendants (corporate fiduciaries) for their alleged insider trading violations without proof of any actual damages suffered by such plaintiffs or their corporation & *Guth v Loft Inc* 503-510, the court held that any breach of fiduciary duties through insider trading was against public policy.

[105] Hamermesh "How We Make Law in Delaware and What to Expect from Us in the Future" 2007 *Journal of Business & Technology Law* 409 413-414.

[106] *In re Oracle Corporation Derivative Litigation* (2003) WL 21396449 (Del Ch); *In re Oracle Corporation Derivative Litigation* (2004) 867 A2d 904 (Del Ch) 934; *In re Oracle Corporation Derivative Litigation* (2005) 872 A2d 960 (Del Ch), which held that the fiduciaries (defendants) should have traded on the basis of non-public inside information they possessed to the detriment of their corporation before any disgorgement of profits can be paid to the affected plaintiff. Nonetheless, the court denied the defendants' motion to dismiss the plaintiff's derivative action for breach of fiduciary duties and/or insider trading; *Guttman v Huang* (2003) 823 A2d 492 (Del Ch) 499-507; *In re American International Group Inc* (2009) 965 A2d 763 (Del Ch) 813; *Paddy Wood v Baum, Berndt, Brown & others* (2007) CA 621 (Del Supr. Ct); *Pfeiffer v Toll Brother Inc & others* (2010) 989 A2d 683 (Del Ch), where the court *inter alia* held that the plaintiff must prove that he suffered actual harm as a result of the defendant's breach of fiduciary duty through insider trading. This ruling was later reversed by the Delaware Supreme Court citing its unduly restricted approach and the defendants were ordered to pay compensatory damages regardless of whether the plaintiff suffered actual loss through breach of fiduciary duties or insider trading & Milbank Corporate Governance Group "Delaware Supreme Court Rejects Narrow Reading of Brophy" (27-07-2011) *Client Alert* 1-4 <http://www.milbank.com.cl/al.pdf> (accessed 27-07-2013), apparently, this so-called Brophy claim for insider trading damages is contingent upon the courts' interpretation of the violation in question. Similarly, in *Zapata Corporation v Maldonado* (1981) 430 A2d 779 (Del Ch), which held that affected persons will only recover their insider trading damages if prior investigations were objectively conducted and such objectivity is discretionally determined by the courts.

[107] Ss 78 & 82 of the Financial Markets Act.

Nevertheless, one fact which is certain is that Delaware relies heavily on its courts' judicial law standards and private enforcement to monitor and enforce its insider trading prohibition.[108]

In addition to the Delaware specialised corporate bar, courts and judicial law standards,[109] the Delaware Division Corporations' Securities Commissioner has powers to investigate, *subpoena* any suspects and issue stop orders, injunctions and other administrative remedies against any persons who commit insider trading or market manipulation.[110] Furthermore, the Commissioner of Insurance may issue investigation orders, cease and desist orders, penalty orders and judicial review orders against any market abuse offenders.[111] This has enabled Delaware Division Corporations to effectively complement the relevant courts in tackling and addressing market abuse challenges.[112] In contrast to the Californian position,[113] Delaware has a specialised commercial court and whistle-blower immunity provisions to encourage employees or any person to report any securities and market abuse violations without fear of reprisals from their employers or other offenders.[114] Nonetheless, South Africa relies mainly on the FSB rather than judicial law standards to enforce its market abuse prohibition. Moreover, South Africa's market abuse laws do not have a specific whistle-blower immunity provision to encourage all persons to report market abuse violations to the FSB or other relevant authorities without any fear of victimisation.[115] Furthermore, as

---

[108] Kahan & Rock "Symbiotic Federalism and The Structure of Corporate Law" 2005 *Vanderbilt Law Review* 1573 1604-1609 & 1620; Ott "Delaware Strikes Back: Newcastle Partners and The Fight for State Corporate Autonomy" 2007 *Indiana Law Journal* 159 171-173; Cary "Federalism and Corporate Law: Reflections upon Delaware" 1974 *Yale Law Journal* 663 666-670; Roe 2009 *Harvard Law School John M Olin Center for Law, Economics & Business Discussion Paper Series 638* 8-9 <http://lsr.nellco.org/ harvard_olin/638> (accessed 03-11-2013); Bebchuk & Hamdani 2006 *Harvard Law School John M Olin Center for Law, Economics & Business Discussion Paper Series 558* 23-25 <http://lsr.nellco.org/harvard_olin/558> (accessed 03-11-2013) & Roe "Delaware's Competition" 2003 *Harvard Law School John M Olin Center for Law, Economics & Business Discussion Paper Series 432* 3-4 <http://lsr.nellco.org/ harvard_olin/432> (accessed 03-11-2013).

[109] Wilson 2010 *Entrepreneurial Business Law Journal* 484; 486 & 490.

[110] Ss 73-206; 73-601; 73-602 & ss 73-401 to 73-404 of the Delaware Securities Act.

[111] Ss 2306 to 2309 & 2311 of the Insurance Code.

[112] *Nacco Industries Inc v Applica* (2009) 997 A2d 1 (Del Ch) 23, which held that common law remedies were available against those who engage in Schedule 13D misstatements filing and other related disclosure-based market manipulation practices.

[113] Paragraph *2 2 4* above.

[114] Ss 1703 & 1704 in Title 19, under Chapter 17 of the Delaware Code, also known as the Delaware Whistleblowers' Protection Act (Whistleblowers' Protection Act).

[115] Ss 78; 80; 81 & 82 of the Financial Markets Act. Put differently, although s 159 of the Companies Act 71 of 2008 (Companies Act 2008); the Protected Disclosures Act 26 of 2000; s 9 of the South African constitution & the Promotion of Equality and Prevention of Unfair Discrimination Act 4 of 2000 can be employed to protect shareholders, directors and other employees from occupational reprisals, there are no specific provisions in the Financial Markets Act that can be used to encourage and/or protect market abuse whistleblowers from such reprisals.

earlier stated,[116] the criminal penalties and/or available remedies for market abuse offences are still relatively few and little for deterrence purposes.

Against this background, one can conclude that Delaware has to date managed to flexibly and consistently develop effective and robust common law as well as judicial law standards to increase the private enforcement of its market abuse prohibition. Perhaps this explains why some commentators allude to the fact that Delaware is the "corporate haven" of the USA.[117]

2 2 9 Prohibition on Insider Trading in Washington

In contrast to the position in South Africa[118] and California,[119] Washington does not have a specific provision that directly and expressly prohibits insider trading. Nevertheless, insider trading is indirectly outlawed by discouraging directors, officers or employees from using non-public information filed with or obtained from the Department of Financial Institutions to deal in any security or commodity for personal gain.[120] Unlike the Delaware position,[121]

---

[116] See related remarks in paragraph 2 2 4 above.

[117] See Bebchuk & Hamdani 2006 *Harvard Law School John M Olin Center for Law, Economics & Business Discussion Paper Series 558* 1-5 <http://lsr.nellco.org/ harvard_olin/558> (accessed 03-11-2013); Wilson 2010 *Entrepreneurial Business Law Journal* 481-493; Ott 2007 *Indiana Law Journal* 159-162; Ahdieh "From 'Federalization' to 'Mixed Governance' in Corporate Law: A Defence of Sarbanes-Oxley" 2005 *Buff Law Review* 721 736; Cary 1974 *Yale Law Journal* 664-702; Pritchard "London as Delaware?" 2009 *University of Michigan Law School John M Olin Center for Law, Economics & Working Paper 09-008* 1-2 <http://www.law.umich.edu/ centersandprograms/olin/papers.htm> (accessed 04-11-2013) (seemingly, a John M Olin Center for Law & Economics is also established in the Harvard University Law School); Kahan & Rock 2005 *Vanderbilt Law Review* 1574 & 1620; Hamermesh 2007 *Journal of Business & Technology Law* 409-414; Jones 2005 *Boston College Law School Faculty Paper 36* 1-4 <http://lawdigitalcommons.bc.edu/lsfp/36> (accessed 04-11-2013); Roe 2003 *Harvard Law School John M Olin Center for Law, Economics & Business Discussion Paper Series 432* 2-44 <http://lsr.nellco.org/harvard_olin/432> (accessed 03-11-2013); Roe "Delaware's Politics" 2005 *Harvard Law School John M Olin Center for Law, Economics & Business Discussion Paper Series 511* 1-8 <http://lsr.nellco.org/ harvard_olin/511> (accessed 03-11-2013); Thompson "Collaborative Corporate Governance: Listing Standards, State Law and Federal Regulation" 2003 *Wake Forest Law Review* 961; Strine "The Delaware Way: How We Do Corporate Law and Some of the New Challenges We (and Europe) Face" 2005 *Del J.Corp.L* 673 673-683; Fisch "The Peculiar Role of the Delaware Courts in the Competition for Corporate Charters" 2000 *U.Cin.Law Review* 1061 1064; Rock "Saints and Sinners: How Does Delaware Corporate Law Work?" 1997 *UCLA Law Review* 1009 1024; Jones "Rethinking Corporate Federalism in Era of Corporate Reform" 2004 *Journal of Corp. Law* 625; Stevelman "Regulatory Competition, Choice of Forum and Delaware's Stake in Corporate Law" 2009 *Del J.Corp.L* 57 66 & Gorris, Hamermesh & Strine "Delaware Corporate Law and The Model Business Corporation Act: A Study in Symbiosis" 2011 *Law & Contemporary Problems* 107 112-116.

[118] Ss 78 & 82 of the Financial Markets Act.

[119] Paragraph *2 2 1* above.

[120] Ss 21.30.160 in Title 21, under Chapter 21.30 of the Revised Code of Washington Commodity Transactions 1986 c 14 as amended, s 46 (Commodity Transactions Act) & s 21.20.480 in Title 21, under Chapter 21.20 of the Revised Code of Washington 1951 c 5, s 2 as amended by 1959 c 282, s 69 (Securities Act of Washington); also see s 21.20.140 of the Securities Act of Washington, which re-

liability for insider trading is apparently not restricted only to instances where there is a breach of fiduciary duties by primary insiders in Washington. Moreover, Washington does not clearly provide whether it is required that the offenders should have profited or benefited from their alleged insider trading before incurring any liability.[122] The prohibition on insider trading is primarily restricted to directors, officers or other employees of a company.[123] Despite this, Washington prohibits broker-dealers, investment advisors and any other person from offering or selling any security or commodity without being registered to prevent insider trading and other related illicit practices.[124]

2 2 10 Prohibition on Market Manipulation in Washington

Washington state outlaws a number of illicit market abuse practices. For example, any person who employs a device, scheme or artifice to manipulate the offer, sale or purchase of securities will be liable for fraud and/or market manipulation.[125] Moreover, any person who received a consideration from another person is prohibited from employing a scheme, device, an act, practice or course of business and/or a dishonest practice for the purposes of influencing or advising other persons to purchase or sell any security.[126] Accordingly, an investment advisor, broker-dealer or any other person who knowingly and manipulatively purchases or sells any security for his own account or for another person will be liable for market manipulation.[127] This also indicates that trade-based market manipulation practices are statutorily outlawed in Washington.

Additionally, disclosure-based market manipulation practices such as the making of false or misleading statements of a material fact or omitting to make a material fact in relation to any filed documents for the purposes of influencing the purchase or sale of any securities are prohibited.[128] In relation to this, offering or selling unregistered securities by any person is expressly prohibited in Washington.[129] This prohibition is mainly aimed at discouraging

---

quires all persons to register with the Department of Financial Institutions before offering to sell any security or commodity.

[121] Paragraph 2 2 5 above.

[122] S 21.20.480 of the Securities Act of Washington & s 21.30.160 of the Commodity Transactions Act.

[123] Ss 21.20.480 read with s 21.20.140 of the Securities Act of Washington & s 21.30.160 of the Commodity Transactions Act.

[124] Ss 21.20.030; 21.20.035 & s 21.20.140 of the Securities Act of Washington & s 21.30.050 of the Commodity Transactions Act.

[125] S 21.20.010(1) & (3) of the Securities Act of Washington.

[126] S 21.20.020 of the Securities Act of Washington.

[127] S 21.20.020(2) read with ss 21.20.030 & 21.20.035 of the Securities Act of Washington.

[128] Ss 21.20.010(2) & 21.20.350 of the Securities Act of Washington.

[129] S 21.20.140 read with ss 21.20.040; 21.20.180 & 21.20.210 of the Securities Act of Washington.

all persons from deliberately engaging in unlawful fraudulent or market manipulation activities.

Commodity-based market manipulation is also prohibited in Washington. For example, no person may directly or indirectly employ a device, scheme or artifice to defraud or influence others to purchase or sell any commodity contract or commodity option.[130] Additionally, any person who engages in a transaction, act, practice, or course of business that will deceive others,[131] or who makes a false or misleading report, record or statement of a material fact by omission or otherwise[132] in order to induce others to purchase or sell any commodity or commodity option will be liable for market manipulation. Thus, any person who deliberately omits to state a material fact in relation to the purchase or sale of any commodity contract or commodity option will be liable for such omission and/or market manipulation.[133] Moreover, no person may purchase or sell a commodity contract or commodity option, or engage in a trade, business or other act as a commodity merchant unless he is registered, licensed or exempted by the Commodity Futures Trading Commission.[134] This preventative measure is employed to combat commodity-based market manipulation. In contrast to the position in Washington state, South Africa's market abuse laws do not have a specific provision that directly and expressly prohibits commodities-based market abuse practices.[135]

2 2 11 Available Market Abuse Penalties and Remedies in Washington

Notably, any person who commits insider trading, market manipulation or other related securities violations will be liable upon conviction for a fine not exceeding $5 000, or imprisonment for a period of not more than ten years, or both such fine and imprisonment.[136] Moreover, any person who alters, destroys, shreds or conceals a record or document and/or who knowingly attempts to make a false or misleading statement of a material fact will be liable for a class B felony or a fine not exceeding $500 000, or both such fine and class B felony.[137] The Director of Financial Institutions may refer any criminal matters to the attorney general for further investigation and prosecution.[138]

---

[130] S 21.30.060(1) of the Commodity Transactions Act.
[131] S 21.30.060(3) of the Commodity Transactions Act.
[132] S 21.30.060(2) of the Commodity Transactions Act.
[133] S 21.30.070 read with ss 21.30.080 & 21.30.090 of the Commodity Transactions Act.
[134] S 21.30.050 read with ss 21.30.020; 21.30.030 & 21.30.040 of the Commodity Transactions Act.
[135] Ss 78; 80; 81 & 82 of the Financial Markets Act.
[136] S 21.20.400 (as amended by 2003 c 53) of the Securities Act of Washington.
[137] S 21.20.400 (as amended by 2003 c 288) of the Securities Act of Washington & s 9A.20.021(1)(b) of the Revised Code of Washington which deals with the punishment of the class B felony.
[138] S 21.20.410 read with s 21.20.420 of the Securities Act of Washington.

Furthermore, any person who commits fraud, market manipulation or other related securities violations will be liable to the person buying or selling the affected securities for civil damages and reasonable legal costs plus 8% interest per annum.[139] Every person who directly or indirectly controls another person and who commits or aids another person to commit market manipulation and other related securities violations will be jointly and severally liable with such person for civil damages and reasonable legal costs plus 8% interest per annum.[140]

The Director of Financial Institutions may also institute administrative actions such as restraining orders, administrative fines, injunctions, orders for judicial review and stop orders against the securities and market abuse offenders.[141] Accordingly, any person who filed a false or misleading report or statement of a material fact in order to engage in market abuse activities or any other related securities violations will be liable to the affected persons for damages and reasonable legal costs.[142] The Director of Financial Institutions may further suspend the sale or trading of the affected securities by or through a broker-dealer, until the false or misleading statements or reports are corrected.[143]

Persons who perpetrate commodity-based market abuse and other related violations will be liable to a fine not exceeding $20 000 upon conviction, or imprisonment for a period not more than ten years, or both such fine and imprisonment.[144] However, no liability will be imputed upon any accused person if he proves that he had no knowledge of the violated rule or order or that he acted in good faith.[145] The prosecuting attorney may further impose criminal proceedings against any person who wilfully commits fraud, market manipulation or any other commodities-related violations.[146] The Director of Financial Institutions may, through the courts, issue compliance orders, declaratory judgments, cease and desist orders, summary orders, suspension orders, restitution orders, order for civil penalties, injunctions and other civil or administrative remedies against those who contravene the commodities provisions through fraud or market abuse practices.[147]

---

[139] S 21.20.430(1) & (2) of the Securities Act of Washington.

[140] S 21.20.430(3) of the Securities Act of Washington.

[141] S 21.20.280 read with ss 21.20.290; 21.20.390 & 21.20.395 of the Securities Act of Washington.

[142] S 21.20.745 of the Securities Act of Washington.

[143] S 21.20.750 of the Securities Act of Washington.

[144] S 21.30.140 of the Commodity Transactions Act.

[145] S 21.30.140 read with s 21.30.150 of the Commodity Transactions Act.

[146] S 21.30.360 read with s 21.30.370 of the Commodity Transactions Act.

[147] Ss 21.30.110; 21.30.120; 21.30.130; 21.30.200 & 21.30.350 of the Commodity Transactions Act.

2 2 12 Analysis and Evaluation of the Washington Anti-Market Abuse Enforcement Framework

The Director of Financial Institutions, courts (including the attorney general's office) and the Department of Financial Institutions share the responsibility of enforcing the market abuse prohibition in Washington.[148] As stated earlier,[149] Washington does not have a specific provision that prohibits insider trading. Accordingly, this could be creating some enforcement challenges for both the courts and the Department of Financial Institutions. For instance, it is extremely difficult to prove whether the accused person has knowingly committed any insider trading violations because the insider trading offence is not clearly defined.[150]

A number of civil, criminal and administrative penalties may be employed by the Director of Financial Institutions against any market abuse offenders. For example, the Director of Financial Institutions may impose administrative penalties such as public censure, suspension or revocation of the license of any broker-dealer, salesperson, investment advisor's representative, investment advisor or any other person who commits market abuse and other related securities violations.[151] Remarkably, unlike the position in Washington, the FSB is not statutorily and expressly empowered to use public censure against the market abuse offenders in South Africa.[152] The Director of Financial Institutions has further powers to investigate (publicly or privately) market abuse and other related violations.[153] In line with this, the Director of Financial Institutions may *subpoena* witnesses in relation to any ongoing investigation which pertains to securities or market abuse violations.[154] In contrast to Delaware,[155] Washington statutorily empowers its Director of Financial Institutions to publicly disseminate any information concerning an ongoing market abuse investigation and/or any other securities or commodities violations, if such dissemination is in the public interest.[156] The

[148] Conspicuously, unlike the position in South Africa, Washington does not have a specific regulatory body that enforces its market abuse prohibition.

[149] Paragraph 2 2 9 above.

[150] Notwithstanding the advantages of this broad and unrestricted insider trading enforcement approach, it is submitted that Washington should consider enacting an adequate provision that expressly define and prohibit the insider trading offence to enhance enforcement.

[151] S 21.20.110(1) read with (2) to (9); ss 21.20.120 & 21.20.130 of the Securities Act of Washington.

[152] See s 84 read with s 82 of the Financial Markets Act. Put differently, the Financial Markets Act merely provides that the FSB may publish the outcome of its market abuse investigations on its website or any other appropriate media if such publication is in the public interest, see s 84(2)(e).

[153] Ss 21.20.370 & 21.20.700 of the Securities Act of Washington.

[154] Ss 21.20.380 & 21.20.700 of the Securities Act of Washington; also see ss 21.30.100 & 21.30.110 of the Commodity Transactions Act.

[155] Paragraph 2 8 above.

[156] S 21.20.370(1) & (2) of the Securities Act of Washington & s 21.30.170 of the Commodity Transactions Act.

Director of Financial Institutions may also impose administrative sanctions like injunctions, mandamus, cease and desist orders, restraining orders and restitution orders against any person who commits market abuse offences or violates any provision of the Securities Act of Washington.[157]

The Director of Financial Institutions relies on the relevant courts to enforce its administrative sanctions or other court actions against the market abuse offenders and those who violate the relevant rules.[158] The courts play a key role in judicial review hearings involving any person aggrieved by an order or decision of the Director of Financial Institutions.[159] In contrast to the position in Delaware[160] and California,[161] Washington statutorily empowers the Director of Financial Institutions to cooperate with other State and federal enforcement authorities in order to effectively combat fraud, market abuse and other related securities or commodities violations.[162] Another advantage of Washington is the statutory availability of non-exclusive common law penalties and private rights of action for the prejudiced persons to claim their damages directly from the market abuse offenders.[163] This has enabled Washington to have some influence on corporate lawmaking (including the development and enforcement market abuse laws) both at State and federal levels in the USA.[164] Likewise, the Financial Markets Act now directly empowers the FSB to cooperate with other local and international regulatory bodies in order to enhance the enforcement of the market abuse prohibition in South Africa.[165] However, it remains to be seen whether this provision[166] will be successfully employed to investigate and combat cross-border market abuse activities in South Africa and elsewhere. In addition, as earlier stated,[167] the available penalties and/or available remedies for market abuse offences are still minimal and somewhat inconsistently[168] enforced in South Africa.

---

157 S 21.20.390 of the Securities Act of Washington.

158 Ss 21.30.120 & 21.30.140 of the Commodity Transactions Act.

159 S 21.20.440 of the Securities Act of Washington & s 21.30.400 of the Commodity Transactions Act, which states that the Director of Financial Institutions has powers to make, amend or rescind any rules, forms and orders relating to commodities transactions.

160 Paragraph 2 2 8 above.

161 Paragraph 2 2 4 above.

162 S 21.20.450 of the Securities Act of Washington & s 21.30.180 of the Commodity Transactions Act.

163 S 21.20.420 read with s 21.20.430 of the Securities Act of Washington & s 21.30.370 of the Commodity Transactions Act.

164 Roe 2009 *Harvard Law School John M Olin Center for Law, Economics & Business Discussion Paper Series 638* 5-9 <http://lsr.nellco.org/harvard_olin/638> (accessed 03-11-2013).

165 See s 84(2)(b) of the Financial Markets Act.

166 See s 84(2)(b) of the Financial Markets Act.

167 See related remarks in paragraphs 2 2 4 & 2 2 8 above.

168 For instance, and notwithstanding the fact that civil and administrative sanctions in respect of market manipulation may be imposed upon the offenders under the Financial Institutions (Protections of Funds) Act 28 of 2001 (Protections of Funds Act), no similar provisions are found in the

2 3 Concluding Remarks

As indicated above, the regulation and enforcement of the market abuse ban in the USA mainly involves the relevant different financial or corporation departments at the states level.[169] Although this state prohibition on market abuse is not uniform,[170] it has, to a great extent, relatively managed to consistently discourage market abuse practices in the USA.

On the contrary, the South African market abuse regime relies mainly on the FSB to oversee and enforce the market abuse ban. This approach has so far not been able to achieve more settlements and prosecutions in cases involving market abuse in South Africa.[171] This could be evidenced in part, by many delays in investigations, settlements and the inherent paucity of successful criminal prosecutions obtained in market abuse cases in South Africa to date.[172] Moreover, deficiencies such as the inconsistent application of the market abuse provisions and the use of few enforcement measures have directly impeded the curbing of market abuse in South Africa.[173] In light of these and other flaws indicated above, it is submitted that the Financial Markets Act should be amended to enact specific provisions for separate and distinct criminal penalties that can be imposed upon any juristic person or individual who commit or attempts to commit insider trading or market manipulation offences in South Africa (with higher criminal penalties being imposed on such juristic persons).

The Financial Markets Act should also be amended to provide specific market abuse whistle-blower immunity provisions and bounty rewards for the purposes of encouraging all the persons to report market abuse activities to the FSB and/or other relevant enforcement authorities in South Africa without the fear of reprisals. Furthermore, the Financial Markets Act should be amended to statutorily and expressly empower the FSB to use public censure against the market abuse offenders in South Africa. Additionally, the Financial Markets Act should be amended to enact provisions that specifically prohibit insurance-related as well as Internet-based (including social media-related) market abuse practices in South Africa.

Financial Markets Act except for s 99 which simply provides for the referral of any related contraventions to the EC.

[169] See the discussion in paragraphs (including sub-paragraphs) under 2 2 above.

[170] In relation to this, it is submitted that Delaware and other relevant states should enact specific and/or adequate statutory provisions that expressly prohibit insider trading and other related illicit activities and empower more regulatory authorities to enhance the combating of market abuse in the USA.

[171] Paragraphs 2 2 4; 2 2 8 & 2 2 12 above.

[172] See the FSB *Annual Report* 2011 4 99-101; the FSB *Annual Report* 2013 3 128-130.

[173] Generally see paragraphs 2 2 4; 2 2 8 & 2 2 12 above.

Furthermore, as is the position in Delaware (where there is a system in place for periodic revisions of the Delaware Codes), the South African policymakers should consider appointing a National Market Abuse Commission to examine and review all the matters and laws pertaining to market abuse in South Africa. In conclusion, another option is for the South African policymakers to consider introducing provincial market abuse statutes to: (a) create regulatory competition among the provinces to attract investors by effectively combating market abuse activities (b) promote dual or concurrent regulation and enforcement of the market abuse ban both at a provincial and national level. This should, however, be managed well to avoid creating potential problems such as balkanisation and/or violating the *autrefois* acquit or *autrefois* convict doctrine.

References

Books

Avgouleas E *The Mechanics and Regulation of Market Abuse: A Legal and Economic Analysis* (Oxford University Press Oxford 2005)

Lyon GJ & Du Plessis JJ *The Law of Insider Trading in Australia* (The Federation Press Sydney 2005)

Palmiter AR *Securities Regulation: Examples and Explanations* 3rd ed (Aspen Publishers New York 2005)

Journal articles

Ahdieh RB "From 'Federalization' to 'Mixed Governance' in Corporate Law: A Defence of Sarbanes-Oxley" 2005 *Buff Law Review* 721-756

Bhana N "Take-Over Announcements and Insider Trading Activity on the Johannesburg Stock Exchange" 1987 *South African Journal of Business Management* 198-208

Bhattacharya U & Daouk H "The World Price of Insider Trading" 2002 *Journal of Finance* 75-108

Botha D "Control of Insider Trading in South Africa: A Comparative Analysis" 1991 *SA Merc LJ* 1-18

Botha D "Increased Maximum Fine for Insider Trading: A Realistic and Effective Deterrent?" 1990 *SALJ* 504-508

Cary WL "Federalism and Corporate Law: Reflections upon Delaware" 1974 *Yale Law Journal* 663-707

Cassim R "An Analysis of Market Manipulation under the Securities Services Act 36 of 2004 (Part 1)" 2008 *SA Merc LJ* 33-60

Cassim R "An Analysis of Market Manipulation under the Securities Services Act 36 of 2004 (Part 2)" 2008 *SA Merc LJ* 177-199

Crandall MS "State Securities Regulation and the Internet" 2001 *Legislation & Public Policy* 23-31

Fisch JE "The Peculiar Role of the Delaware Courts in the Competition for Corporate Charters" 2000 *U.Cin.Law Review* 1061-1068

Gorris JM, Hamermesh LA & Strine LE "Delaware Corporate Law and The Model Business Corporation Act: A Study in Symbiosis" 2011 *Law & Contemporary Problems* 107-116

Hamermesh LA "How We Make Law in Delaware and What to Expect from Us in the Future" 2007 *Journal of Business & Technology Law* 409-414

Jones RM "Rethinking Corporate Federalism in Era of Corporate Reform" 2004 *Journal of Corp. Law* 625-664

Jooste R "A critique of the insider trading provisions of the 2004 Securities Services Act" 2006 *SALJ* 437-460

Kahan M & Rock E "Symbiotic Federalism and The Structure of Corporate Law" 2005 *Vanderbilt Law Review* 1573-1622

Langevoort DC "Federalism in Corporate/Securities Law: Reflections on Delaware, California, and State Regulation of Insider Trading" 2006 *University of San Francisco Law Review* 879-892

Luiz SM "Insider Trading Regulation – If at First You Don't Succeed…" 1999 *SA Merc LJ* 136-151

Osode PC "The new South African Insider Trading Act: Sound law reform or legislative overkill?" 2000 *Journal of African Law* 239-263

Ott MW "Delaware Strikes Back: Newcastle Partners and The Fight for State Corporate Autonomy" 2007 *Indiana Law Journal* 159-182

Rock EB "Saints and Sinners: How Does Delaware Corporate Law Work?" 1997 *UCLA Law Review* 1009-1107

Steinberg MI "Insider Trading Regulation–A Comparative Perspective" 2003 *The International Lawyer* 153-171

Stevelman F "Regulatory Competition, Choice of Forum and Delaware's Stake in Corporate Law" 2009 *Del J.Corp.L* 57-122

Strine LE "The Delaware Way: How We Do Corporate Law and Some of the New Challenges We (and Europe) Face" 2005 *Del J.Corp.L* 673-683

Thompson RB "Collaborative Corporate Governance: Listing Standards, State Law and Federal Regulation" 2003 *Wake Forest Law Review* 961-982

Van Deventer G "New Watchdog for Insider Trading" 1999 *FSB Bulletin* 1-3

Wilson DM "Climate Change: The Real Threat to Delaware Corporation Law, Why Delaware Must Keep A Watchful Eye on The Content of Political Change in the Air" 2010 *Entrepreneurial Business Law Journal* 481-490

Case law

South Africa

Pretorius and Another v Natal South Sea Investment Trust 1965 3 SA 410 (W)

United States of America

Brophy v Cities Service Co (1949) 70 A2d 5 (Del Ch)

Clothesrigger Inc v G T E Corporation (1987) 191 Cal App 3d 605

Desai, Lamb, Long and Christopher Long v Deutsche Bank Securities Limited, Deutsche Bank Securities Inc and others (2009) 08-55081 US App Lexis 16704 (US App 9th Cir)

Diamond Multimedia Systems Inc v Superior Court (1999) 19 Cal 1036

Friese v Superior Court (2005) 36 Cal Rptr 3d 558 (Cal Ct App)

Guth v Loft Inc (1939) 5A2d 503 (Del)

Guttman v Huang (2003) 823 A2d 492 (Del Ch)

In re American International Group Inc (2009) 965 A2d 763 (Del Ch)

In re Oracle Corporation Derivative Litigation (2003) WL 21396449 (Del Ch)

In re Oracle Corporation Derivative Litigation (2004) 867 A2d 904 (Del Ch)

In re Oracle Corporation Derivative Litigation (2005) 872 A2d 960 (Del Ch)

Kahn v Kohlberg, Kravis, Roberts & Co LP (2010) CA No 436 (Del SC)

Louisiana Pacific Corporation v Money Market 1Institutional Investment Dealer and others (2011) 09-CV-03529 (JSW)
Malone v Brincat (1998) CA No 15510 WL 919123 (Del Supr. Ct)
Malone v Brincat (1998) 722 A2d 5 (Del)
Medifast v Minkow (2011) 10 CV 382 (JLS BGS)
Nacco Industries Inc v Applica (2009) 997 A2d 1 (Del Ch)
Paddy Wood v Baum, Berndt, Brown & others (2007) CA 621 (Del Supr. Ct)
Pfeiffer v Toll Brother Inc & others (2010) 989 A2d 683 (Del Ch)
Williams v Gaylord (1902) 186 US 157
Seinfield v Verizon Communications Inc (2006) 909 A2d 717 (Del)
Zapata Corporation v Maldonado (1981) 430 A2d 779 (Del Ch)

Legislation

South Africa

Companies Act 71 of 2008
Consumer Protection Act 68 of 2008
Financial Markets Act 19 of 2012
Financial Institutions (Protections of Funds) Act 28 of 2001 as amended
Long-Term Insurance Act 52 of 1998 as amended
Promotion of Equality and Prevention of Unfair Discrimination Act 4 of 2000
Protected Disclosures Act 26 of 2000
Securities Services Act 36 of 2004
Short-Term Insurance Act 53 of 1998 as amended

United States of America

California Commodity Law of 1990
Commodity Exchange Act of 1936 7 USC 1 *et seq.* (1994)
Commodities Futures Modernization Act 2000 Public Law 106-554, 114 Stat.2763A-365
Commodity Futures Trading Commission Act of 1974 Public Law 93-64, 88 Stat 1398
Corporate Securities Law of 1968 (California Statutes 1968, Chapter 88)
Delaware General Corporation Law
Delaware Professional Service Corporations Act
Delaware Securities Act
Delaware Uniform Deceptive Trade Practices Act
Delaware Whistleblowers' Protection Act
Derivatives Market Manipulation Prevention Act of 2009
Public Company Accounting Reform and Investor Protection Act of 2002 Public Law 107-204, 116 Stat 745 (15; 28 USC)

Codes, bills and related instruments

California

California Corporations Code 1968
California Penal Code

Delaware

Delaware Code
Delaware Criminal Code
Delaware Insurance Code

Washington

Revised Code of Washington Commodity Transactions 1986 c 14, s 46
Revised Code of Washington 1951 c 5, s 2 as amended by 1959 c 282, s 69

Thesis and dissertations

Chitimira H *A Comparative Analysis of the Enforcement of Market Abuse Provisions* (LLD-thesis Nelson Mandela Metropolitan University 2012)

Chitimira H *The Regulation of Insider Trading in South Africa: A Roadmap for an Effective, Competitive and Adequate Regulatory Statutory Framework* (LLM-dissertation University of Fort Hare 2008)

Conference papers, media releases and other relevant material

The United States Department of Justice District of Delaware "Newark Man Pleads Guilty to Insider Trading Charges" *Press Release* 25 March 2011

Internet sources

Bebchuk LA & Hamdani A "Federal Corporate Law: Lessons from History" 2006 *Harvard Law School John M Olin Center for Law, Economics & Business Discussion Paper Series 558* <http://lsr.nellco.org/harvard_olin/558> (accessed 03-11-2013)

Bingham McCutchen Securities Litigation Group "California's Unique Treble Damages Insider Trading Law Applied to Corporations Incorporated Outside of California" 2006 *Securities Litigation Alert* <http://www.bingham.com.01.2006/03> (accessed 26-10-2013)

California Department of Corporations "Fighting Internet 'Cyber Investment Fraud'" <http://www.corp.ca.gov/pub/cyber.htm> (accessed 28-10-2013)

California Department of Corporations "Internet Investments Ordered to Stop Selling" *Press Release 98-11* (10-06-1998) <http://www.corp.ca.gov/pressrel/nr9811.htm> (accessed 27-10-2013);

California Department of Corporations "Department of Corporations Files Internet Market Manipulation Actions" *Press Release 00-11* (20-06-2000) <http://www.corp.ca.gov/pressrel/nr0011.htm> (accessed 27-10-2013)

Jones RM "Dynamic Federalism: Competition, Cooperation and Securities Enforcement" 2005 *Boston College Law School Faculty Paper 36* <http://lawdigitalcommons.bc.edu/lsfp/36> (accessed 04-11-2013)

Mariano G "Stock Fraud Spurs Regulators to Look Online" (21-06-2000) <http://news.cnet.com/news/01-1005-200-2126256.html> (accessed 29-10-2013)

Milbank Corporate Governance Group "Delaware Supreme Court Rejects Narrow Reading of Brophy" (27-07-2011) *Client Alert* <http://www.milbank.com.cl/al.pdf> (accessed 27-07-2013)

Myburgh A & Davis B "The Impact of South Africa's Insider Trading Regime: A Report for the Financial Services Board" (25-03-2004) <http://www.genesis-analytics.com/public/FSBReport.pdf> (accessed 09-02-2013)

Pritchard AC "London as Delaware?" 2009 *University of Michigan Law School John M Olin Center for Law, Economics & Working Paper 09-008* <http://www.law.umich.edu/centersandprograms/olin/papers.htm> (accessed 04-11-2013)

Roe MJ "Washington and Delaware as Corporate Lawmakers" 2009 *Harvard Law School John M Olin Center for Law, Economics & Business Discussion Paper Series 638* <http://lsr.nellco.org/harvard_olin/638> (accessed 03-11-2013)

Roe MJ "Delaware's Competition" 2003 *Harvard Law School John M Olin Center for Law, Economics & Business Discussion Paper Series 432* <http://lsr.nellco.org/harvard_olin/432> (accessed 03-11-2013)

Roe MJ "Delaware's Politics" 2005 *Harvard Law School John M Olin Center for Law, Economics & Business Discussion Paper Series 511* <http://lsr.nellco.org/harvard_olin/511> (accessed 03-11-2013)

Van Deventer G "Anti-Market Abuse Legislation in South Africa" (10-06-2008) <http://www.fsb.co.za/public/marketabuse/FSBReport.pdf> (accessed 05-05-2013)

Chapter 3

The Federal Regulation of Market Abuse in the United States of America: Lessons for South Africa?

3 1 Introduction

The United States of America (USA) is one of the few countries that has successfully enacted some relatively adequate anti-market abuse laws to, *inter alia*, curb the negative effects of illicit market abuse activities in its financial markets. Accordingly, the USA has a relatively broad and adequate market abuse prohibition in place at a federal level. For instance, insider trading, market manipulation and other related illicit activities such as tipping and short selling[1] are regulated at a federal level in the USA. This approach has to date relatively culminated in greater deterrence, compliance and curbing of market abuse practices across the USA financial markets.[2] Given this background, this chapter provides a brief overview analysis of the federal regulation and enforcement of the market abuse[3] prohibition in the USA.[4] Consequently, the development, prohibition and the available penalties and remedies for insider trading are discussed first. Secondly, a similar analysis will be done in respect of market manipulation. Additionally, relevant federal provisions and cases from the USA will be contrasted with similar provisions[5] and cases in South Africa in order to recommend, where appropriate, possible

---

* This chapter is influenced in part, by an article that was initially published in the *Mediterranean Journal of Social Sciences*, see Chitimira "Overview of the Federal Prohibition on Market Abuse in the United States of America" 2014(5)(7) *Mediterranean Journal of Social Sciences* 119-135. This was done with legal permission from the editors of the *Mediterranean Journal of Social Sciences*.

[1] Notably, short selling has been regulated at a federal level in the USA as early as 1938 through the price test prohibition (uptick rule). This prohibition was formerly referred to as Rule 10a-1 of the Securities Exchange Act of 1934 15 USC 78i(a)(2)-(5) (2006) as amended by PL-111-257. See further Rule 10b-21 (a naked short selling anti-fraud Rule) which is also a final Rule under the aforesaid Act.

[2] Steinberg "Insider Trading Regulation–A Comparative Perspective" 2003 *The International Lawyer* 153 169-171; see further Bhattacharya & Daouk "The World Price of Insider Trading" 2002 *Journal of Finance* 75 75-108; Lyon & Du Plessis *The Law of Insider Trading in Australia* (2005) 159-168 & Avgouleas *The Mechanics and Regulation of Market Abuse: A Legal and Economic Analysis* (2005) 75-502, for further analysis on the regulation and enforcement of anti-market abuse laws in other countries.

[3] Market abuse includes insider trading and market manipulation in this book.

[4] Steinberg 2003 *The International Lawyer* 169.

[5] Ss 78; 80; 81 & 82 of the Financial Markets Act 19 of 2012 (Financial Markets Act).

anti-market abuse measures that could be employed to enhance the combating of market abuse practices in South Africa.[6]

3 2 Historical Overview of the Federal Prohibition on Market Abuse

3 2 1 Overview Development of the Insider Trading Prohibition

Notably, the regulation of insider trading at a federal level in the USA was introduced by the Securities Exchange Act of 1934.[7] Before the Securities Exchange Act, cases dealing with insider trading were reportedly inconsistently decided on the basis of existing common law.[8] The Securities Exchange Act discouraged insider trading and other related practices in the USA both directly[9] and indirectly.[10] Nonetheless, its direct prohibition on insider trading applied only to directors or officers (primary insiders) of a company who held more than a 10% stake in the company.[11] In other words, this direct prohibition on insider trading did not expressly apply to other persons like tippees. Moreover, the Securities Exchange Act's indirect prohibition on insider trading was generally employed as an anti-fraud provision which prohibited insiders from defrauding other innocent investors

---

[6] See related remarks by Van Deventer "Anti-Market Abuse Legislation in South Africa" (10-06-2008) 1-5 <http://www.fsb.co.za/public/marketabuse/ FSBReport.pdf> (accessed 05-05-2013) & see further Myburgh & Davis "The Impact of South Africa's Insider Trading Regime: A Report for the Financial Services Board" (25-03-2004) 8-33 <http://www.genesis-analytics.com/public/FSBReport.pdf> (accessed 09-02-2013); Chanetsa B "Insider Trading is Notoriously Hard to Prosecute" (2004-04-26) *Business Report*; *Pretorius and Another v Natal South Sea Investment Trust* 1965 3 SA 410 (W), were the court failed to convict the suspected insider trading offenders; Chitimira *A Comparative Analysis of the Enforcement of Market Abuse Provisions* (Unpublished thesis, Nelson Mandela Metropolitan University) 2012, 210-257; Botha "Control of Insider Trading in South Africa: A Comparative Analysis" 1991 *SA Merc LJ* 1 1-18; Botha "Increased Maximum Fine for Insider Trading: A Realistic and Effective Deterrent?" 1990 *SALJ* 504 504-508; Chitimira *The Regulation of Insider Trading in South Africa: A Roadmap for an Effective, Competitive and Adequate Regulatory Statutory Framework* (LLM dissertation, University of Fort Hare) 2008, 41–72; Osode "The New South African Insider Trading Act: Sound Law Reform or Legislative Overkill?" 2000 *Journal of African Law* 239 239-263; Jooste "A Critique of the Insider Trading Provisions of the 2004 Securities Services Act" 2006 *SALJ* 437 441–460; Van Deventer "New Watchdog for Insider Trading" 1999 *FSB Bulletin* 2 3 & Luiz "Insider Trading Regulation – If at First You Don't Succeed…" 1999 *SA Merc LJ* 136 136-151.

[7] Public Law 73-291, 48 Stat 881 15 USC 78a-78ll as amended (Securities Exchange Act). See s 16(a) & (b) as well as s 10(b); also see Hazen *Federal Securities Law* (2003) 1-4.

[8] *Godwin v Agassiz* (1933) 186 NE 659 (Mass), where the plaintiff who had ignorantly sold his own shares to his detriment after having read a newspaper report stating that the company had stopped operating as a result of insider trading was denied relief by the Supreme Court of Massachusetts.

[9] S 16(b) prohibited short-swing profits (profits obtained in less than 6 months) by corporate insiders in the corporation's stock except when it was in the best interests of that corporation or its shareholders.

[10] S 10(b) prohibited any person to use or to employ in the purchase or sale of any securities registered on a securities exchange or any unregistered securities, a deceptive device for the purpose of contravening any rules and regulations of the United States Securities and Exchange Commission (SEC).

[11] S 16(b) read with subsection (a).

by trading in their own company's stock while in possession of advance knowledge of a forthcoming earnings disclosure.[12] Notably, the Securities Exchange Act imposed a mandatory disclosure requirement on all insiders.[13] They had to file with the SEC any requested statements and/or transactions, including those that could amount to insider trading, within ten days after they were concluded.

The initial insider trading provisions of the Securities Exchange Act were, however, flawed in some respects. For example, they did not give sufficient authority to the SEC[14] to enforce and recover profits that were illegally obtained by those who practised insider trading.[15] This function was merely left to a company's own managers, directors and shareholders.[16] Additionally, the SEC introduced other anti-fraud provisions such as Rule 10b-5[17] but they nonetheless remained deficient. Neither section 10(b) nor Rule 10b-5 expressly prohibited illicit insider trading by insiders or other unscrupulous persons. The successful prosecution or settlement of insider trading cases was contingent upon the interpretation of the courts.[18] It is clear that non-disclosure by an insider of material facts that were not known to the other party during the negotiations could probably amount to other market abuse practices like market manipulation. In 2000 the SEC adopted Rule 10b5-1[19] in an attempt to define insider trading and provide defences to any person charged with insider trading if such person purchases or sells securities before acquiring material non-public information.[20] The SEC further adopted Rule 10b5-2[21] to provide clarity on when a breach of a fiduciary duty or otherwise gives rise to liability under the misappropriation theory of insider trading in order to increase the consistent enforcement of the federal insider trading prohibition.[22]

---

[12] S 10(b) read with subsection (a); also see *SEC v Lipson* (2001) No 97–CV-2661 129F Supp.2d 1148, for related remarks.

[13] S 16(a).

[14] This body was established in 1934 as an independent board to enforce the federal securities laws so as to combat market practices like insider trading in the USA.

[15] S 16(a) & (b).

[16] Steinberg 2003 *The International Lawyer* 169-171.

[17] 17 CFR, s 240.10b-5 (2007); Rule 10b-5 can be downloaded at <http://www.sec.gov> (accessed 01-02-2014).

[18] As demonstrated in *Cady, Roberts and Company* [1961-1964 Transfer Binder] CCH *Fed Sec L Rep* 76. 803 81. 016 & *Chiarella v United States* (1980) 445 US 222-230.

[19] 17 CFR, 240.10b5-1; Rule 10b5-1 can be downloaded at <http://www.sec.gov> (accessed 01-02-2014).

[20] Horwich "The Origin, Application, Validity and Potential Misuse of Rule 10b5-1" 2007 *The Bus. Lawyer* 913 922-923.

[21] 17 CFR, 240.10b5-2; Rule 10b5-2 can be downloaded at <http://www.sec.gov> (accessed 01-02-2014).

[22] Pearson "When Hedge Funds Betray A Creditor Committee's Fiduciary Role: New Twists on Insider Trading in the International Financial Markets" 2009 *Review of Banking & Financial Law* 165 204.

Likewise, the SEC adopted Rule 100 and Regulation Fair Disclosure[23] in a bid to discourage companies from selectively disclosing material non-public information to market professionals and favoured shareholders in another attempt to combat insider trading.

The Securities Exchange Act was amended and introduced provisions that granted the SEC the authority to make rules that are appropriate and necessary[24]for the enforcement of the securities laws.[25] Therefore, the SEC adopted Rule 14e-3[26] which applied only in tender offer situations. Rule 14e-3 prohibited "any person who has obtained directly or indirectly, material confidential information" regarding a tender offer from the offeror (bidder), target company or an intermediary, to trade or tip another person to trade in that offer before making an adequate public disclosure of such information. Furthermore, a tippee who knew or should have known that such information had come from an insider was prohibited from trading with it until an adequate public disclosure was made. Rule 14e-3 applied to all persons (even juristic persons) but nevertheless it was not easily enforced in practice. Besides being a basis for some of the SEC's enforcement actions, Rule 14e-3 has been very difficult to enforce and in some instances it is confusingly interpreted to create an implied private action against the offenders.[27]

Various shortcomings of the Securities Exchange Act led the Congress to enact the Insider Trading Sanctions Act of 1984[28] at the request of the SEC. This Act for the first time empowered the SEC to bring a civil action in the federal districts courts against persons who engage in insider trading activities.[29] Therefore, the SEC could impose civil penalties on anyone who practised insider trading through tipping or other related practices to pay an amount of

---

[23] Securities Exchange Act Release Number 43154 [2000 Transfer Binder] Fed Sec L Rep CCH 86 319. These rules and regulations can be downloaded at <http://www.sec.gov> (accessed 01-02-2014); also see <http://www.sec.gov/ rules/final/33-7881.htm#P22_3882> (accessed 01-02-2014); also see related analysis by Palmiter *Securities Regulation: Examples and Explanations* (2005) 371 & Morrison & Foerster "Insider Trading" 2010 *Year End Review* 1 1-6.

[24] S 23(a)(1).

[25] S 14(e).

[26] 17 CFR, s 240.14e-3 (2007); Rule 14e-3 can be downloaded at <http://www.sec.gov> (accessed 01-02-2014). See further Arshadi & Eyssell *The Law and Finance of Corporate Insider Trading: Theory and Evidence* (1993) 46; Gaillard (ed) *Insider Trading: The Laws of Europe, the United States and Japan* (1992) 296; Palmiter *Securities Regulation* 368; Ryan "Rule14e-3's Disclose or Abstain Rule and Its Validity under Section 14(e)" 1991 *U. Cin. Law Review* 449 453-454 & Pearson 2009 *Review of Banking & Financial Law* 191-204.

[27] Palmiter *Securities Regulation* 368. Also see *United States v O'Hagan* (1997) 117 (SCt) 2199; *United States v Chestman* (1991) 947 F2d 551 (2d Cir).

[28] Public Law 98-376, 98 Stat.1264 (1984) (Insider Trading Sanctions Act).

[29] Gilson & Kraakman "The Mechanisms of Market Efficiency" 1984 *VA.L.REV* 549 550-644 & Friedman "The Insider Trading and Securities Fraud Enforcement Act of 1988" 1990 *North Carolina Law Review* 465 466-494.

up to three times the profit made or loss avoided for the benefit of all the persons who were prejudiced by it. The Insider Trading Sanctions Act further empowered the courts to impose a criminal penalty on any person who violated the insider trading provisions.[30] Despite these developments, the Insider Trading Sanctions Act still failed to provide a lasting solution to the enforcement problems in the USA. It did not expressly define insider trading and its provisions applied only to a few persons (primary insiders); other persons like "controlling persons"[31] were not specifically prohibited from committing insider trading offences.[32]

In another attempt to enhance the regulation of insider trading, the Congress passed the Insider Trading and Securities Fraud Enforcement Act of 1988.[33] This Act stipulated that public companies, broker-dealers and investment advisors should adopt appropriate policies to monitor and prohibit their employees from practising insider trading.[34] Moreover, the Securities Fraud Enforcement Act modified the wording of section 21A to make it clear that tippers could be liable for civil penalties when their tip resulted in insider trading, even if they are not technically aiders and abettors.[35] The Securities Fraud Enforcement Act broadened the treble penalty for insider trading[36] and further imposed liability on "controlling persons" for insider trading activities of their employees.[37] This Act also permitted the SEC to pay bounties to informants of up to 10% of the civil penalties recovered in order to promote and enhance the enforcement of insider trading in the USA.[38] These bounties were not paid to members, officers or employees of federal regulatory agencies, Department of Justice and self-regulatory organisations.[39] The Securities Fraud Enforcement Act further empowered the SEC to investigate upon the request of similar regulatory bodies elsewhere any insider trading practices, regardless of whether such practices violated the SEC's federal insider trading

---

[30] S 21A.

[31] A "controlling person" includes not only employers but also any person with the power to influence or control the direction or the management policies or activities of another person. Gaillard *Insider Trading: The Laws of Europe, the United States and Japan* 308.

[32] Pearson 2009 *Review of Banking & Financial Law* 194.

[33] Public Law 100-704, 102 Stat. 4677 (Securities Fraud Enforcement Act).

[34] Arshadi & Eyssell *The Law and Finance of Corporate Insider Trading* 51 & Pearson 2009 *Review of Banking & Financial Law* 195.

[35] S 21A(d).

[36] Pearson 2009 *Review of Banking & Financial Law* 195.

[37] S 21A as amended.

[38] Kaswell "An Insider's View of the Insider Trading and Securities Fraud Enforcement Act" 1989 *Bus.Law* 145 152-164 & Fisher, Harshman, Gillespie, Ordower, Ware & Yeager "Privatizing Regulation: Whistle-blowing and Bounty Hunting in the Financial Services Industries" 2000 *Dick.J. Int'L. L* 117 135-136 & Pearson 2009 *Review of Banking & Financial Law* 195.

[39] Friedman 1990 *North Carolina Law Review* 466-494.

laws.[40] Despite the notable improvements brought by the Securities Fraud Enforcement Act, some persons were still able to contravene its insider trading provisions. For example, as a result of poor auditing and insider trading activities on the part of Enron's directors, its net income was reduced by $600 million and its debt increased to about $628 million.[41]

In 2000, the Commodities Futures Modernization Act[42] was enacted to *inter alia* repeal the ban on single-stock futures, enhance the regulation futures exchanges and empower both the Commodity Futures Trading Commission (CFTC) and the SEC to share the responsibility of regulating insider trading in the single-stock futures markets.[43] This Act, unlike the Commodity Exchange Act of 1936,[44] further enabled the CFTC to prohibit insider trading by discouraging market regulators' employees and other professionals like brokers from trading ahead of a client or other investors while in possession of non-public material information.[45] The aforementioned insider trading prohibition was, however, not extended to other persons who are not market professionals or employees *per se*.[46]

In 2002 the Congress enacted the Public Company Accounting Reform and Investor Protection Act of 2002[47] in response to several landmark corporate scandals like *World Com* and *Enron*.[48] This Act brought a more rigorous regulatory and enforcement structure for accounting companies and professionals to combat corporate fraud, insider trading and other market abuse practices.[49] For example, in order to prevent insider trading, the Sarbanes-Oxley

---

[40] S 6(b)(2) of the Securities Fraud Enforcement Act, which amended s 21(a)(2) of the Securities Exchange Act; also see Pearson 2009 *Review of Banking & Financial Law* 195.

[41] Palmiter *Securities Regulation* 24.

[42] Public Law 106-554, 114 Stat.2763A-365 (Commodities Futures Modernization Act).

[43] Knepper "Examining the Merits of Dual Regulation for Single-Stock Futures: How the Divergent Insider Trading Regimes for Federal Futures and Securities Markets Demonstrate the Necessity for (and Virtual Inevitability of) Dual CFTC-SEC Regulation for Single-Stock Futures" 2004 *Pierce Law Review* 33 34-45.

[44] 7 USC 1 *et seq.* (1994), (Commodity Exchange Act) and it came into effect on 15 June 1936.

[45] See the CFTC Regulation 1.59, 17 CFR, 1.59 (2004); also see Markham "'Front-Running'-Insider Trading under the Commodity Exchange Act" 1988 *Cath.U.Review* 69 94; 110 & Knepper 2004 *Pierce Law Review* 40--45.

[46] Knepper 2004 *Pierce Law Review* 42-45; also see the CFTC & the SEC "A Joint Report of the SEC and the CFTC on Harmonization of Regulation" *Report* 16 October 2009 1 6-7; 59-61.

[47] Public Law 107-204, 116 Stat 745 (as codified in scattered sections of 15; 28 USC) (Sarbanes-Oxley Act). See further Palmiter *Securities Regulation* 23.

[48] Avgouleas *The Mechanics and Regulation of Market Abuse* 449.

[49] This heading discusses mainly the US's federal statutes on insider trading. Other statutes that specifically regulate and prohibit fraud such as the Racketeer Influenced and Corrupt Organization Act of 1970 (RICO) will not be discussed for purposes of this thesis because it is limited only to the enforcement of the insider trading and market manipulation prohibition.

Act prohibits employees (primary insiders) from trading in their company's stock relating to its pension plan funds during closed periods.[50]

In the wake of the 2007-2008 global financial crisis, the Congress recently enacted the Dodd-Frank Wall Street Reform and Consumer Protection Act of 2010[51] to *inter alia* enhance and broaden the SEC's ability to enforce insider trading and other securities laws.[52] For instance, this Act now allows the SEC and/or the CFTC to institute appropriate proceedings against any employee or agent of an agency or department of the federal government who purchases or sells a commodity while in possession of non-public material information which relates to that commodity.[53] In relation to this, the Dodd-Frank Act empowers the SEC to enforce the federal anti-fraud securities and insider trading prohibition extra-territorially.[54] The Dodd-Frank Act now provides incentives of up to 30% and immunity to whistleblowers who report insider trading and related violations to the SEC or the CFTC.[55]

In contrast to the early developments of the regulation and enforcement of the insider trading ban in the USA,[56] the legislature in South Africa only introduced a prohibition on insider trading in 1973.[57] Nonetheless, like the position in the US,[58] the South African regulatory framework also prohibits any person (including juristic persons) from practising insider trading and related activities like tipping.[59] For instance, the Financial Markets Act merely enumerates and prohibits four types of practices, namely, (a) dealing (directly or indirectly) in securities listed on a regulated market by an insider who knows that he has inside information which relates to such securities for his own personal benefit;[60] (b) dealing (directly or indirectly) in securities listed on a regulated market by an insider who knows that he has inside information which relates to such securities for the benefit of another person;[61] (c) improper disclosure of inside information to another person by an insider who

---

[50] S 306(a).
[51] Public Law 111-203, 124 Stat.1376 (codified at 12 USC, s 5301 *et seq.*) (Dodd-Frank Act).
[52] Morrison & Foerster 2010 *Year End Review* 11-13.
[53] S 746 of the Dodd-Frank Act.
[54] S 929P(b) read with (c) of the Dodd-Frank Act; also see Morrison & Foerster 2010 *Year End Review* 14-15.
[55] See s 922 of the Dodd-Frank Act which enacted s 21F to repeal and replace s 21A(e) of the Securities Exchange Act; see further Morrison & Foerster 2010 *Year End Review* 12-14.
[56] See earlier remarks above.
[57] S 224 & ss 229 to 233 of the now repealed Companies Act 61 of 1973 (Companies Act). See further the *Explanatory Memorandum to the Objects of the Companies Second Amendment Bill* of 1990 B 119-90 (GA); Botha 1991 *SA Merc LJ* 4.
[58] See earlier remarks above.
[59] Ss 78 & 82 read with ss 77 & 79 of the Financial Markets Act.
[60] S 78(1)(a) read with subsection (3)(a) & s 82.
[61] S 78(2)(a) read with subsection (3)(a) & s 82.

knows that he has such information;[62] and (d) the encouraging or discouraging of another person by an insider, to deal in securities listed on a regulated market.[63] Despite these similarities, there is no express provision that prohibits dealing in securities on unregulated over the counter markets through agents in South Africa.[64] Over and above, unlike the situation in the USA,[65] the Financial Markets Act does not expressly prohibit other related illicit activities such as naked short selling.[66]

3 2 2 Available Penalties for Insider Trading

Various penalties are employed against the market abuse offenders in the USA. For instance, the USA's enforcement framework uses civil, criminal and administrative penalties to discourage insider trading. This can be traced back to the Securities Act of 1933[67] which provided that any person who contravened its provisions was criminally liable for a fine of $10 000, or imprisonment for a period not exceeding five years, or both such fine and imprisonment.[68] Moreover, the Securities Exchange Act allows the SEC to impose any other appropriate administrative penalties on broker-dealers who involve themselves in insider trading practices.[69] As indicated above,[70] the SEC was empowered to impose treble civil penalties on insider trading offenders for the profit made or loss avoided as a result of their illicit trading.[71] Nonetheless, these sanctions were still insufficient for deterrence purposes and it was generally assumed that many persons benefited from insider trading without

---

[62] S 78(4)(a).

[63] S 78(5).

[64] Put differently, although the current South African insider trading ban has extra-territorial application, it is mainly limited to securities listed on a regulated market in South Africa or elsewhere. Moreover, this extra-territorial application is still to be successfully enforced in South Africa and/or elsewhere because it is, *inter alia*, not restricted to instances where a territorial link is present by virtue either of the fact that the offender is at the time physically present in South Africa, or was acting through an agent who is in South Africa or by virtue of the prohibited conduct occurring in South Africa. S 77 read with ss 78 & 82 of the Financial Markets Act.

[65] See related remarks above.

[66] In relation to this, there are no incentives, bounty rewards and/or whistleblowers immunity provisions to encourage all the relevant persons to timeously report insider trading and related violations to the Financial Services Board (FSB) and/or the Johannesburg Stock Exchange Limited (JSE). Furthermore, the available defences for insider trading offences are still relatively insufficient.

[67] Public Law 22, 48 Stat.74 15 USC 77a-77mm *et seq.* (2000) as amended (Securities Act).

[68] S 24 of the Securities Act; see further Kaswell 1989 *Bus.Law* 169-170 & Friedman 1990 *North Carolina Law Review* 466-494.

[69] For example the SEC was permitted to impose the so-called "watchdog" penalties on offenders. Palmiter *Securities Regulation* 370.

[70] See paragraph *3 2 1* above.

[71] S 21A of the Securities Exchange Act.

any fear of incurring liability. This might have been influenced by the fact that insider trading activity is inherently difficult to detect and enforce.[72]

Additionally, the Congress introduced the Insider Trading Sanctions Act to improve *inter alia* the enforcement of the insider trading ban. The Insider Trading Sanctions Act imposed separate criminal penalties for natural and juristic persons. This Act further increased the criminal penalties for insider trading to a fine of $100 000 for natural persons and $500 000 for juristic persons.[73] The maximum imprisonment term for natural persons remained five years and the civil penalties were unchanged, in spite of the broad powers conferred upon the SEC to claim treble damages from the offenders. These penalties did not deter all persons from knowingly practising insider trading. It remained possible for some unscrupulous persons to benefit from their insider trading practices after paying the stipulated fine or after serving their imprisonment terms.

The Securities Fraud Enforcement Act was adopted and a further amendment, especially to criminal sanctions, was made in order to improve the enforcement of the insider trading prohibition.[74] The maximum criminal penalties were increased to a fine of $1 million for natural persons and to $2, 5 million for juristic persons.[75] Furthermore, the imprisonment sentence was significantly increased to a period not exceeding ten years.[76] Notably, the prior version of the criminal fines for insider trading applied only to matters relating to stock exchanges.[77] The Securities Fraud Enforcement Act enabled the SEC to continue paying bounty rewards to anyone who *bona fide* provided information leading to civil penalties in order to encourage all persons to expose insider trading activities.[78] The Securities Fraud Enforcement Act further expanded civil penalties to cover not only insiders or tippers, but also to apply to "controlling persons" to prevent potential insider trading and tipping by their employees.[79] In other words, this Act empowered the SEC to impose civil penalties on "controlling persons" who are not broker-dealers *per se* or

---

[72] Steinberg 2003 *The International Lawyer* 169-171; Kaswell 1989 *Bus.Law* 169-170; Friedman 1990 *North Carolina Law Review* 466-494 & Palmiter *Securities Regulation* 370.

[73] Hazen *Federal Securities Law* 134-136.

[74] Hazen *Federal Securities Law* 137-138; also see s 32(a) of the Securities Exchange Act as amended.

[75] Palmiter *Securities Regulation* 370.

[76] Palmiter *Securities Regulation* 370.

[77] Friedman 1990 *North Carolina Law Review* 466-494; Hazen *Federal Securities Law* 134-136 & also see s 32(a) of the Securities Exchange Act as amended.

[78] S 21A(e) which was later repealed and replaced by s 21F of the Securities Exchange Act as amended. Also see Palmiter *Securities Regulation* 370; Hazen *Federal Securities Law* 137-138 & Morrison & Foerster 2010 *Year End Review* 12-14.

[79] S 21A(a)(3) read with subsection (2) of the Securities Exchange Act as amended; see further Friedman 1990 *North Carolina Law Review* 466-494 & Hazen *Federal Securities Law* 137-138.

investment advisors like banks, accounting firms and financial publishers.[80] Civil penalties imposed on "controlling persons" could differ to some extent from those that may be imposed on "controlled persons".[81] The civil or administrative penalties that could be imposed on "controlling persons" were generally limited to a fine not exceeding $1 million.[82] Furthermore, the Sarbanes-Oxley Act[83] increased the insider trading sanctions to a maximum fine of $5 million for natural persons and up to $25 million for juristic persons and a maximum imprisonment sentence of 20 years.[84] The criminal sanctions and the civil remedies are enforced by the Department of Justice and the SEC respectively. This resulted in more successful criminal prosecutions and civil settlements to be obtained by the courts and the SEC respectively.[85]

In 2010, the Dodd-Frank Act empowered the SEC to recover monetary penalties in cease-and-desist administrative proceedings involving commodities or securities (including insider trading) violations.[86] Nonetheless, the Dodd-Frank Act does not have specific penalties for insider trading practices.[87]

Notably, South Africa also provides for civil,[88] criminal[89] and unlimited administrative[90] penalties for insider trading under the Financial Markets Act. The aforesaid civil and unlimited administrative penalties are mainly

---

[80] S 21A(a)(1); (2) & (3) read with s 21A(b) of the Securities Exchange Act as amended; see further Friedman 1990 *North Carolina Law Review* 466-494 & Hazen *Federal Securities Law* 137-138.

[81] This usually refers to employees or any other persons influenced or managed by another person.

[82] See Friedman 1990 *North Carolina Law Review* 466-494; Hazen *Federal Securities Law* 137-138 & also see s 21A(a)(3) of the Securities Exchange Act as amended.

[83] Notably, this Act was named after its sponsors Senator Paul Sarbanes and the United States of America Representative, Michael G Oxley. Moreover, the Sarbanes-Oxley Act was enacted in response to major corporate and accounting scandals involving companies such as Enron, Tyco International, Adelphia, Peregrine Systems and WorldCom. In addition, the Sarbanes-Oxley Act was enacted in bid to restore public investor confidence, especially after the aforesaid scandals had caused the share prices of the affected companies to collapse, giving rise to a number of investors losing their profits. See Anonymous "History and Context of the Events Contributing to the Adoption of the Sarbanes-Oxley Act" http://en.wikipedia.org/wiki/Sarbanes%E2%80%93Oxley_Act#History_and_context:_events_contributing_to_the_adoption_of_Sarbanes.E2.80.93Oxley (accessed 12-06-2012), for further related analysis.

[84] S 306(a); s 1348 to s 1350; also see Palmiter *Securities Regulation* 369-370.

[85] The increase in settlements and prosecutions were also enhanced in part by the fact that the courts have the discretion to impose, in light of the facts and relevant circumstances other additional penalties. See for example *SEC v Texas Gulf Sulphur Company* (1968) 401 F2d 833 (2d Cir); *Dirks v SEC* (1983) 463 US 646-655; *United States v O'Hagan* 2199; *United States v Falcone* [2001 Transfer Binder] 91 489 Fed Sec L Rep CCH (2d Cir) & *SEC v Yun* (2003) 327 F3d 1263 (11th Cir).

[86] Morgan Lewis "2009 Year in Review: SEC and SRO Selected Enforcement Cases and Developments Regarding Broker-Dealers" 2010 14 <http://www.morganlewis.com/lit_SECandYearlyReviewWP_Jan2010.pdf> (accessed 10-06-2013).

[87] See s 746 of the Dodd-Frank Act.

[88] S 82.

[89] S 109(a).

[90] S 99.

enforced by the FSB[91] and the Enforcement Committee (EC)[92] respectively.[93] Nevertheless, the Financial Markets Act only provides a few criminal penalties, namely, a fixed maximum fine of R50 million, or imprisonment for a period not exceeding ten years, or both such fine and imprisonment against the offenders.[94] Furthermore, no distinction has been made in relation to the penalties imposed on natural and juristic persons to increase deterrence.[95] In a nutshell, more may still need to be done to increase the successful investigation, prosecution and settlement of insider trading cases in South Africa.[96]

3 2 3 Available Remedies for Insider Trading

One of the most far-reaching insider trading regulatory developments in the USA is the availability of a wide range of remedies to all the affected persons.[97] For example, a private right of action is available to contemporaneous purchasers or sellers of securities against insider trading offenders.[98] The affected persons may claim damages not exceeding the profit gained or loss avoided by the defendant (offender) or his tippees.[99] It is clear that tippers and tippees are jointly and severally liable for insider trading damages.[100] Nevertheless, any losses incurred or amounts used in a SEC injunction action relating to any civil penalty transaction for contemporaneous traders are deducted from the damages recovered.[101] No limit or condition is imposed on any person who

---

[91] S 84 of the Financial Markets Act.

[92] S 99 of the Financial Markets Act.

[93] These bodies have relatively similar regulatory and enforcement roles as those of the SEC.

[94] S 109(a).

[95] S 109(a) of the Financial Markets Act.

[96] See the FSB *Annual Report* 2011 4 99-101; the FSB *Annual Report* 2013 3 128-130; *Pather and Another v Financial Services Board and Others (57617/10)* [2014] 3 All SA 208 (GP), for related discussion on the role of the EC; *Zietsman v Director of Market* Abuse 2016 1 SA 218 (GP), for further discussion on the meaning of "inside information" for the purposes of the insider trading offence in South Africa; the Directorate of Market Abuse (DMA) "Past Investigations" *DMA Media Release* 23 June 2015, 1-11.

[97] Palmiter *Securities Regulation* 369-370 & Friedman 1990 *North Carolina Law Review* 466-494.

[98] S 20A of the Securities Exchange Act as amended by s 5 of Securities Fraud Enforcement Act; see further *Blue Chip Stamps v Manor Drug Stores* (1975) 421 US 723, where the actual affected persons were allowed to bring a private action in terms of Rule 10b-5 against the insider trading offenders.

[99] *Elkind v Liggett and Myers Inc* (1980) 635 F2d 156(2d Cir) 172-173; *FMC Corp v Boesky* (1988) 852 F2d 981 (7th Cir), the court held that the affected company was entitled to claim its damages from the insider trading offenders, but nevertheless the tippee was controversially not found guilty because such company did not suffer actual loss. Also see Friedman 1990 *North Carolina Law Review* 466-494.

[100] S 20A(c) of the Securities Exchange Act; also see Friedman 1990 *North Carolina Law Review* 466-494.

[101] S 20A(b)(2) of the Securities Exchange Act; also see Friedman 1990 *North Carolina Law Review* 466-494 & Palmiter *Securities Regulation* 369.

brings an action to enforce the provisions of the Securities Exchange Act or on the availability of any implied right of action under the same Act.[102]

Moreover, the SEC can bring a judicial enforcement action seeking a court order that enjoins insiders or tippees from indulging in insider trading activity and that mandates them to return or disgorge all the profits gained or losses avoided.[103]

Another remedy available in the USA is the civil action for recovery or compensation for "defrauded" owners of non-public confidential information. Such persons are statutorily allowed to take a private action against any persons who practise insider trading and other similar activities.[104] The entities like companies are also allowed to recover any losses suffered as a result of insider trading from the offenders.[105] There is no explicit statutory limitation that applies to the period on which private actions may be instituted under Rule 10b-5. Instead, the courts have been required to determine the appropriate limitation periods on private civil actions giving regard to any other relevant factors.[106]

The SEC may also claim treble civil damages from any person who violates its insider trading rules.[107] These damages, like any other remedies, are usually paid into the federal treasury. It is possible for offenders to disgorge their profits in a private or SEC action and still pay a treble damage penalty without any concerns of double jeopardy violation.[108] The Dodd-Frank Act further allows the SEC to pay bounty rewards to whistle-blowers who report insider trading and related violations that results in the successful disgorgement of profits, monetary penalties and prejudgment interest exceeding $1 million in any judicial or administrative proceedings.[109]

Similarly, as is the position in the USA,[110] the enforcement of the civil remedies and penalties in South Africa is mainly a responsibility of an independent

---

[102] Kaswell 1989 *Bus.Law* 167-169.

[103] *SEC v Texas Gulf Sulphur Company* 833, which, *inter alia*, postulated that a separate fund be established from which the prejudiced shareholders and other contemporaneous traders could recoup their losses or be compensated from any money recovered from the offenders. Also see generally Palmiter *Securities Regulation* 369-370.

[104] Rule 10b-5. See further Palmiter *Securities Regulation* 369.

[105] Palmiter *Securities Regulation* 369. Also see *FMC Corp v Boesky* 981.

[106] Friedman 1990 *North Carolina Law Review* 466-494.

[107] Rules 10b-5 & 14e-3.

[108] Palmiter *Securities Regulation* 370. See further *SEC v Levine* (1986) 86 Civ 3726 (SDNY) (RO) & *SEC v Boesky* (1986) 86 Civ 8767.

[109] S 922(a) of the Dodd-Frank Act; also see Morrison & Foerster 2010 *Year End Review* 13-14 & Morgan Lewis 2010 14 <http://www.morganlewis.com/lit_SEC andYearlyReviewWP_Jan2010.pdf> (accessed 10-06-2013).

[110] See related remarks above.

board, the FSB.[111] However, administrative remedies are generally administered by the EC, which is a committee of the FSB. For instance, the EC may impose against the insider trading offender, an administrative sanction not exceeding the profit made or loss avoided by that offender.[112]

Moreover, the Financial Markets Act also provides compensatory damages for an amount of up to three times the profit made or loss avoided by the offender,[113] to those prejudiced by insider trading activities. Thus, any person affected by insider trading activities may institute a claim for part of the proceeds and/or compensatory damages from the FSB under the Financial Markets Act.[114] Moreover, the Financial Markets Act now allows the affected persons to claim extra-compensatory damages proceeds for an amount of up to R1 million[115] from the FSB.[116] Likewise, insider trading victims may also recover part of the proceeds obtained by the FSB from the offenders, in relation to any interests, investigation costs, legal costs and commission[117] as determined by the EC under the Financial Markets Act.[118] The Financial Markets Act also provides actual calculable damages which may be utilised by those who fall victim to insider trading practices.[119] However, unlike the position in the US,[120] the Financial Markets Act does not provide any new measures or statutory guidelines that could be employed by the EC and/or the claims officer when determining the actual calculable damages that will be given to the affected persons.[121] Furthermore, the Financial Markets Act's insider trading remedies are still very few, and they could also be less dissuasive for deterrence purposes.[122] For instance, unlike the situation in the USA,[123] other alternative remedies such as specific civil pecuniary penalties, punitive damages, bounty rewards, class actions and private rights of action are not expressly provided under the Financial Markets Act.[124]

---

[111] S 84 read with s 82 of the Financial Markets Act.
[112] S 82(1)(a); (2)(a).
[113] S 82(1)(b); (2)(b).
[114] S 82(4)(b) read with subsections 5 & 6.
[115] S 82(1)(b); (2)(b).
[116] S 82(1)(b); (2)(b).
[117] S 82(2)(e).
[118] S 82(1)(c) & (d); (2)(c) & (d).
[119] See s 82(6)(a) and (b).
[120] See related analysis above.
[121] See further s 82(6)(a) & (b) read with subsection (5)(b).
[122] See s 82.
[123] See earlier related remarks above.
[124] See s 82.

3 2 4 Prohibition on Market Manipulation

3 2 4 1 Prohibition on Trade-Based and Disclosure-Based Market Manipulation

Notwithstanding the fact that the concept of market abuse is not expressly and statutorily defined in the USA,[125] the regulation and prohibition of market abuse practices can be traced back to the so-called "New Deal" legislation that was enacted after a heavy crash occurred in its stock markets in 1929.[126] The most important "New Deal legislation" was the Securities Act and the Securities Exchange Act.

The Securities Act prohibits the making of corporate misstatements that will lead to the defrauding of innocent investors.[127] This is mainly done to protect investors against corporate false or misleading statements in the context of new issues and to safeguard the adequate and continuous flow of issuer-specific information.[128]

In addition, the Securities Exchange Act expressly prohibits market manipulation. This Act, for instance, prohibits any person from willingly creating misleading appearances of active trading in securities listed on a stock exchange.[129] Put differently, the Securities Exchange Act discourages and prohibits a number of activities that create or that might create a misleading appearance of trading in listed securities like wash sales and matched orders (when the same person or affiliate is essentially both the buyer and the seller of the securities in question), a series of transactions to induce the purchase or sale by others and the false or reckless "touting" or spreading of rumours by broker-dealers or other traders to induce trading in such securities.[130]

The Securities Exchange Act further prohibits any person from directly or indirectly using manipulative and other deceptive devices to purchase or sell any listed securities to the detriment of investors.[131] In addition, any such persons who violate the rules and regulations prescribed by the SEC will also be liable for an offence.[132] In relation to this, the SEC is authorised to make any other appropriate rules and regulations to combat market manipulation

---

[125] Avgouleas *The Mechanics and Regulation of Market Abuse* 104.
[126] Avgouleas *The Mechanics and Regulation of Market Abuse* 174-175.
[127] S 17.
[128] Avgouleas *The Mechanics and Regulation of Market Abuse* 174.
[129] S 9(a). Also see Palmiter *Securities Regulation* 266.
[130] S 9(a).
[131] S 10(b) read with subsection (a). See further Friedman 1990 *North Carolina Law Review* 466-494; Avgouleas *The Mechanics and Regulation of Market Abuse* 104.
[132] S 9(b) & (c) read with subsection (a) of the Securities Exchange Act.

in the USA.[133] The SEC introduced a rule that discourages any person from employing any device, scheme or artifice to defraud or to engage in an act, practice or course of business that will deceive other persons.[134] This rule further prohibits all persons from making untrue and misleading statements relating to the material facts of any securities.[135]

Moreover, the SEC introduced Regulation M[136] which, among other aspects, prohibits market manipulation during a public distribution (public offering of securities) and allows price-stabilisation activities only in some specific circumstances. The SEC further adopted Rule 10a-1 (the so-called up-tick rule) to prevent market manipulation and free falls in stock prices due to short selling in a falling market.[137] This rule has been criticised as too narrow because it did not cover short sales and other manipulative activities in over the counter markets and in sales of derivatives. Regulation SHO was then enacted to combat naked short selling and market manipulation in all the USA's financial markets and in broker-dealer transactions.[138]

The Securities Exchange Act further prohibits the making of false or misleading statements of any material fact or engagement in any fraudulent, deceptive or manipulative practices in connection with tender offers.[139] Additionally, the Securities Exchange Act allowed the SEC to define "fraudulent, deceptive or manipulative practices" and to make appropriate rules designed to prevent such manipulative practices.[140] This Act does not expressly prohibit market manipulation in over the counter markets.[141]

---

[133] For example, the SEC promulgated Rule 10b-5 in order to effectively enforce the provisions of s 10(b) of the Securities Exchange Act. See further Avgouleas *The Mechanics and Regulation of Market Abuse* 104.

[134] See Rule 10b-5 which prohibits three types of market manipulation, namely false dissemination of material information relating to securities, distortion and misleading behaviour and the use of manipulative devices that negatively affect the price of securities and create a false appearance in the market activity. Also see Palmiter *Securities Regulation* 316-317 & Barnes *Stock Market Efficiency, Insider Dealing and Market Abuse* (2009) 132.

[135] Rule 10b-5. Also see Palmiter *Securities Regulation* 306; 308-309.

[136] 17 CFR, s 241.100-240.105 (2007). The SEC normally relies on its wide powers as conferred by s 10(b) of the Securities Exchange Act. See further Palmiter *Securities Regulation* 267-268 & Hazen *Federal Securities Law* 89-91.

[137] Palmiter *Securities Regulation* 268-269.

[138] Palmiter *Securities Regulation* 269.

[139] S 14(e) of the Securities Exchange Act.

[140] For example the SEC adopted Rule 14e-3 to enhance the enforcement of the provisions of s 14(e) of the Securities Exchange Act and a number of measures that discourage market manipulation were introduced. Rule 14e-3(a) & (d). Also see Friedman 1990 *North Carolina Law Review* 466-494.

[141] Nelemans "Redefining Trade-Based Market Manipulation" 2008 *Valparaiso University Law Review* 1169 1171-1172.

In an effort to avoid the recurrence of corporate scandals[142] and to reassure investors that the USA financial markets will be free from market abuse practices, the Sarbanes-Oxley Act was enacted.[143] This Act prohibits any person (including a juristic person) or employee from engaging in an act or practice that will improperly influence the conduct of audits or the falsification of books, records and accounts.[144] The Sarbanes-Oxley Act further prohibits senior officers of a company from selling stocks during certain pension "black-out" periods if they received that stock as compensation during their employment with the company in question in order to prevent possible market abuse activities like insider trading and market manipulation.[145] Additionally, the SEC enacted a specific rule that prohibits officers, directors and persons acting under their direction from knowingly coercing, manipulating, misleading or fraudulently influencing the auditor of the issuer's financial statements.[146]

Interestingly, the Financial Markets Act, like its USA counterpart, the Securities Exchange Act, prohibits any person from knowingly engaging or participating in trade-based market manipulation practices that interfere with the normal market mechanisms of supply and demand for securities.[147] Notably, the Financial Markets Act employs the term "knowingly" in its trade-based market manipulation provision[148] and this could imply that proof of intention is mandatorily required before any liability can be imposed upon the offenders. Furthermore, the Financial Markets Act's disclosure-based market manipulation provisions,[149] like similar provisions in the USA,[150] prohibit all persons from making or publishing false, misleading or deceptive statements,

---

[142] *SEC v WorldCom Inc* (2003) 02 Civ 4963(JSR).

[143] Mossos "Sarbanes-Oxley goes to Europe: A Comparative Analysis of United States and European Union Corporate Reforms after Enron" 2004 *Currents International Trade Law Journal* 9 9-10; Anonymous
<http://en.wikipedia.org/wiki/Sarbanes%E2%80%93Oxley_Act#History_and_context:_events_contributing_to_the_adoption_of_Sarbanes.E2.80.93Oxley> (accessed 12-06-2012), who also submits that the Sarbanes-Oxley Act was *inter alia* enacted in bid to restore public investor confidence in the aftermath of several corporate and accounting scandals which affected companies such as Enron, Tyco International, Adelphia, Peregrine Systems and WorldCom in the USA.

[144] S 303(a).

[145] S 306(a)(1).

[146] The Sarbanes-Oxley Act empowers the SEC to make further rules that it may deem necessary for the purposes of enforcing the market abuse provisions, see Rule 13b-2; Rule 13b2-2(b)(1). Also see Mossos 2004 *International Trade Law Journal* 9-11.

[147] S 80(1). Moreover, the provisions of s 80(3) goes a bit wider than s 10(b) of the Securities Exchange Act by deeming a number of trading practices to be regarded as manipulative in South Africa. Also see Cassim "An Analysis of Market Manipulation under the Securities Services Act 36 of 2004 (Part 1)" 2008 *SA Merc LJ* 33 52-60.

[148] S 80(1).

[149] S 81.

[150] S 9(a)(4) of the Securities Exchange Act.

promises or forecasts that relate to any security.[151] Nonetheless, the Financial Markets Act does not expressly prohibit a person who inadvertently aided or abetted another person to make or publish a false, misleading or deceptive statement, promise or forecast that relate to any security.[152] For instance, where a printing company inadvertently aided or abetted an offender by ignorantly printing and/or publishing his misleading or deceptive materials pertaining to listed securities, to the detriment of other uninformed investors. In other words, it was *inter alia* held in *Central Bank of Denver NA v First Interstate Bank of Denver NA*[153] that the words "directly or indirectly" do not apply to secondary actors who are not directly involved in market manipulation practices like aiders and abettors. Therefore, if we are to follow the approach employed in this case, the words "directly or indirectly" as stated in the Financial Markets Act's disclosure-based market manipulation provisions[154] could be interpreted to exclude aiders and abettors.

3 2 4 2 Prohibition on Commodity Market Manipulation

Market manipulation with respect to commodities futures and other kinds of derivatives is principally regulated under the Commodity Exchange Act.[155] Thus, the CFTC, and not the SEC, is the main regulatory body that deals with the enforcement of commodity market manipulation in the USA.[156] Actual or attempted market manipulation of any commodity or future or option is prohibited under the Commodity Exchange Act as amended.[157] Consequently, any conduct or practice that results in the misleading of investors and the creation of an artificial price of commodities is prohibited.[158] The Commodity Exchange Act further prohibits intentional aiding, abetting and inducement of other persons to commit market manipulation offences.[159] Under this Act, the CFTC could bring a civil action or any other appropriate action against the offenders if it has a reason to believe that such offenders have a specific intent to create an artificial price or to influence the price of the commodities or that

---

[151] See s 81; also see Cassim "An Analysis of Market Manipulation under the Securities Services Act 36 of 2004 (Part 2)" 2008 *SA Merc LJ* 177 179-180.

[152] S 81 & also see Cassim 2008 *SA Merc LJ* 178.

[153] (1994) 511 US 164 (US SC) 170-171.

[154] S 81 & also see Cassim 2008 *SA Merc LJ* 178.

[155] See the CFTC & the SEC *Report* 16 October 2009 56-57.

[156] The CFTC was established pursuant to the Commodity Futures Trading Commission Act of 1974 (Public Law 93-64, 88 Stat. 1398). Avgouleas *The Mechanics and Regulation of Market Abuse* 106.

[157] S 9(a)(2).

[158] All persons are prohibited from entering into or confirming the execution of a transaction that is misleading in nature (wash sales) to create a fictitious sale of any commodities, see s 4(c). Also see Swan *Market Abuse Regulation* (2006) 192-194.

[159] Ss 13(a); 6(c) to (d) & 9(a)(2); also see Avgouleas *The Mechanics and Regulation of Market Abuse* 104.

an artificial price that exists has been caused by their manipulative practices.[160]

The Commodities Futures Modernization Act prohibits commodities-based market manipulation in the single-stock futures markets and over the counter derivative transactions.[161] Accordingly, under this Act both the CFTC and the SEC have the authority to institute appropriate proceedings against any person who commits market manipulation and other related activities.[162] Notably, the SEC's authority is only limited to violations relating to single-stock futures transactions, not "broad-based" security futures transactions which are exclusively covered by the CFTC.[163] Nonetheless, if there is a rule violation or market manipulation in the sale or purchase of a single-stock future, either the CFTC or the SEC may, after consultation, bring an enforcement action against the offenders.[164]

Recently, the Dodd-Frank Act broadened the authority of the CFTC to make appropriate rules[165] and prohibit both trade-based market manipulation and disclosure-based market manipulation practices.[166] Moreover, the Dodd-Frank Act introduced the prohibition on fraud-based market manipulation practices in relation to any purchase or sale of a swap or commodity contract in interstate commerce or for future delivery and/or subject to the rules of any registered entity.[167] The Dodd-Frank Act further introduced a broad prohibition on direct or indirect swap or commodity-based market manipulation as well as attempted swap or commodity-based market manipulation.[168]

---

[160] Avgouleas *The Mechanics and Regulation of Market Abuse* 104; Swan *Market Abuse Regulation* 192-194.

[161] Knepper 2004 *Pierce Law Review* 36-37.

[162] See generally s 251 of the Commodities Futures Modernization Act; also see Knepper 2004 *Pierce Law Review* 36.

[163] S 201 of the Commodities Futures Modernization Act; also see Knepper 2004 *Pierce Law Review* 37.

[164] Ss 204; 251 of the Commodities Futures Modernization Act; also see Knepper 2004 *Pierce Law Review* 37-38.

[165] See the CFTC Proposed Rules 180.1 & 180.2; also see Morrison & Foerster 2010 *Year End Review* 15.

[166] S 753 of the Dodd-Frank Act which amended s 6(c) of the Commodity Exchange Act. It is stated that s 753 of the Dodd-Frank Act was originally modelled upon the Derivatives Market Manipulation Prevention Act of 2009 which was introduced by Senator Cantwell in 2009. Cantwell "Senate Passes Cantwell Anti-Manipulation Amendment" (06-05-2010) <http://cantwell.senate.gov/news/record.cfm?id=324761> (accessed 26-11-2013), for generally related remarks.

[167] S 753 of the Dodd-Frank Act which amended s 6(c) of the Commodity Exchange Act.

[168] S 753 of the Dodd-Frank Act which amended s 6(c) of the Commodity Exchange Act; also see Morrison & Foerster 2010 *Year End Review* 15.

In contrast to the status quo in the USA,[169] the Financial Markets Act does not have provisions that specifically prohibit commodity-based market manipulation in South Africa.[170] Apparently, commodity-based market manipulation practices are prohibited and enforced by both the JSE and the FSB. Nonetheless, in contrast with the CFTC,[171] it remains to be seen whether the JSE and the FSB will consistently increase the prohibition and surveillance of commodity-based market manipulation practices in South Africa.[172] Furthermore, it is uncertain whether the FSB prohibits Internet-based and/or social media-related market manipulation activities. For instance, unlike the SEC, the FSB does not have a specific unit that prohibits Internet-based market abuse activities.[173]

3 2 5 Available Penalties for Market Manipulation

Several penalties such as criminal, civil and administrative sanctions are used to combat market manipulation practices in the USA. The Securities Act imposes criminal penalties of up to five years imprisonment and a $10 000 fine on any person who knowingly violates its anti-fraud and market manipulation provisions.[174] Furthermore, the Securities Exchange Act imposes a maximum criminal penalty fine of $100 000, or imprisonment for a period not exceeding five years, or both on natural persons who wilfully engage in prohibited trade practices and other related market manipulation offences.[175] The Securities Exchange Act further imposes a separate fine not exceeding $5 million, or imprisonment for a period of up to 20 years on individuals as well as a $25 million fine for juristic persons (companies and other entities) that intentionally engage in disclosure-based market manipulation and other related practices.[176] This distinction is believed to have been made to increase deterrence and improve the general enforcement of the market abuse provisions in the USA.[177] Importantly, both the Securities Act and the Securities Exchange Act

---

[169] See the earlier discussion in paragraphs above.

[170] Ss 80 & 81.

[171] See the earlier discussion in paragraphs above.

[172] See Myburgh & Davis (25-03-2004) 13 <http://www.genesis-analytics.com/public/ FSBReport.pdf> (accessed 09-02-2013).

[173] On the other hand, the SEC introduced the Office of Internet Enforcement to *inter alia* combat Internet-based market abuse practices. See further Cassim 2008 *SA Merc LJ* 182-183.

[174] S 24. Also see Palmiter *Securities Regulation* 452.

[175] S 32(c)(2)(A) read with subsection (a) of the Securities Exchange Act; also see Palmiter *Securities Regulation* 451-454.

[176] These criminal penalties are mainly enforced by the Department of Justice. S 32(a) of the Securities Exchange Act as amended by the Sarbanes-Oxley Act.

[177] Palmiter *Securities Regulation* 451-455.

criminalised false and misleading registration statements and the filing of misleading documents with the SEC respectively.[178]

With regard to civil penalties, the Securities Exchange Act has empowered the SEC to impose civil penalties on any person who wilfully or recklessly aided, abetted, counseled, commanded or induced another person to commit market abuse practices like filing false and misleading documents with the SEC.[179] Although there is no explicit provision for a civil penalty for the contravention of Rule 10b-5, a private right of action for such contravention is available to all prejudiced actual purchasers and sellers of securities on the basis of equity.[180]

In relation to administrative penalties, the SEC is further authorised to administer and impose unlimited administrative penalties upon the market manipulation offenders. The SEC may also issue a refusal or stop order (cease and desist orders) to prevent an already existing registration statement from being effective or to stop the filing of a false or misleading statement.[181] The SEC may also claim the disgorgement of any profits made by a person who violates the securities and market abuse provisions.[182] Additionally, the SEC may impose a judicial order for civil monetary penalties on the alleged offenders if it reasonably believes that such penalties will be in the public interest.[183]

On the other hand, the Commodities Futures Modernization Act provides criminal penalties against any commodities-based market manipulation offenders in the single-stock futures markets, over the counter commodities derivatives and other related markets in the USA. Similarly, the Commodity Exchange Act imposes a criminal penalty fine of up to $100 000 on individuals and up to $500 000 on entities that indulge in fraudulent and/or other prohibited commodities-based market manipulation practices. Individuals could also be liable to imprisonment for up to five years, or both such fine and imprisonment.[184] In addition, the Commodity Exchange Act imposes civil penalties against any commodities-based market manipulation offenders. This Act

---

[178] S 32 of the Securities Exchange Act & s 24 of the Securities Act; also see Palmiter *Securities Regulation* 452- 453.

[179] S 21(d)(3) of the Securities Exchange Act; see further s 20(d) of the Securities Act.

[180] Cassim 2008 *SA Merc LJ* 192-193.

[181] For example, the SEC may impose a cease and desist order compelling any alleged offender to stop committing further market abuse violations. Ss 8A; 8(b) & (d) of the Securities Act & s 21C of the Securities Exchange Act. Also see Palmiter *Securities Regulation* 436-444.

[182] S 8A(e) of the Securities Act; s 21B(e) of the Securities Exchange Act. Also see further Palmiter *Securities Regulation* 438.

[183] S 21(d)(3) of the Securities Exchange Act; see further s 20(d) of the Securities Act; also see Palmiter *Securities Regulation* 441-442.

[184] See generally s 13(a) read with subsection (c)(a) of the Commodity Exchange Act.

allows the CFTC to take appropriate civil action against any persons who aids, abets, counsels, induces or procures the commission of market manipulation offences.[185] The CFTC may, therefore, claim any disgorgement profits and civil monetary penalties of up to $1 million or three times the profits gained by offenders and distribute them to the affected persons.[186]

Additionally, the Sarbanes-Oxley Act introduced significantly higher criminal penalties for market manipulation and other related offences. It imposes a maximum criminal fine of $5 million and imprisonment sentence of up to 20 years for individuals.[187] A separate maximum criminal fine not exceeding $25 million is also imposed on entities that are involved in market manipulation and other related activities.[188] The Sarbanes-Oxley Act further provides civil penalties against any person who knowingly executes or attempts to execute a scheme or artifice to defraud or to manipulate by means of false pretenses, representations or promises, any money or property in connection with the securities of a public company.[189] This suggests that there is an attempted market manipulation offence in the USA. The Sarbanes-Oxley Act permits the SEC to seek civil compensatory penalties against any person who presents manipulative, fraudulent, false or misleading statements with regard to the conduct of audits, books, records and accounts of a company.[190] The SEC may impose other civil and administrative penalties necessary to enforce and discourage market manipulation activities.[191]

As is the position in the USA,[192] the Financial Markets Act also imposes criminal[193] and unlimited administrative[194] penalties against any person who indulges in trade-based market manipulation[195] and disclosure-based market manipulation[196] practices in South Africa. These criminal and unlimited

---

[185] S 25(a)(1).

[186] S 6(c)(10)(C) as amended by s 753(a) of the Dodd-Frank Act. The profits disgorged and the penalties recovered are normally kept in a fund or trust controlled by the CFTC for purposes of offering compensatory aid to all the prejudiced persons.

[187] S 807.

[188] Palmiter *Securities Regulation* 452.

[189] Avgouleas *The Mechanics and Regulation of Market Abuse* 458.

[190] S 303(a). See further Rule 13b2-2(b)(1) & Rule 13b2-2(b)(2).

[191] There is no express statutory limitation on SEC's enforcement actions. Palmiter *Securities Regulation* 436-444.

[192] See earlier remarks in paragraphs above.

[193] S 109(a).

[194] Notably, these administrative sanctions are provided for in terms of the Financial Institutions (Protection of Funds) Act 28 of 2001 as amended (Protection of Funds Act), but no similar provisions are found in the Financial Markets Act, generally see s 99.

[195] S 80.

[196] S 81; see further Cassim 2008 *SA Merc LJ* 193-195.

administrative penalties are generally enforced by the courts and the EC[197] respectively. Nevertheless, as stated earlier,[198] the Financial Markets Act still imposes a few and minimal criminal penalties of a fixed maximum fine of R50 million, or imprisonment for a period not exceeding ten years, or both such fine and imprisonment[199] against the market manipulation offenders. Contrary to the position in the USA, relatively few investigations[200] and criminal prosecutions involving market manipulation cases have been obtained in the relevant courts in South Africa to date.[201] As previously indicated,[202] this could be aggravated by the fact that the Financial Markets Act does not impose sufficient, separate and distinct criminal penalties against the natural and juristic persons that commit market manipulation offences to increase deterrence.[203]

Moreover, the Financial Markets Act does not expressly provide civil penalties for market manipulation offences.[204] This flaw could be negatively affecting the curbing of market manipulation practices in South Africa,[205] compared to similar foreign legislation in countries like the USA.

Additionally, unlike the situation in the USA,[206] little or no consideration was given to the introduction of specific civil penalties for commodities-

---

[197] Despite this, the EC does not have more discretionary powers with regard to the enforcement of administrative penalties for market abuse. For instance, unlike the position in the US, the EC does not have discretionary powers to impose administrative penalties on the persons who attempt to commit market manipulation offences in South Africa. S 99 of the Financial Markets Act; see further Cassim 2008 *SA Merc LJ* 195.

[198] See related remarks in paragraph 3 2 2 above.

[199] S 109(a). Cassim 2008 *SA Merc LJ* 191-195.

[200] For example, during the period between January 1999 and June 2011 only about 14 market manipulation cases were investigated and successfully completed by the Directorate of Market Abuse, see the FSB *Annual Report* 2011 4 99-101; generally see further the FSB *Report* (28-06-2011) <http://www.fsb.co.za/ftp://ftp.fsb.co.za/public/ documents/AReport2011.pdf> (accessed 22-11-2013); the Financial Services Board "List of Current Investigations of the Directorate of Market Abuse" *Media Release* (28-06-2011) <http://www.fsb.co.za/ftp://ftp.fsb.co.za/public/documents/AReport2011.pdf> (accessed 22-11-2013), indicates that during the period between March 2007 and April 2010 only four cases involving disclosure-based market manipulation and twelve cases of trade-based market manipulation were investigated and such investigations were still ongoing.

[201] See the FSB *Annual Report* 2013 128-130.

[202] See related remarks in paragraph 3 2 2 above.

[203] S 109(a).

[204] See ss 80 & 81 read with ss 109(a) & 82; also see Cassim 2008 *SA Merc LJ* 192. This suggests that persons who fall victim to market manipulation practices are left to find their own civil remedies. See Cassim 2008 *SA Merc LJ* 36.

[205] Put differently, there is no specific statutory civil penalty provision for market manipulation violations under the Financial Markets Act, see ss 80 & 81 read with ss 109(a) & 82. However, it is generally submitted that the civil penalties for market manipulation may be enforced in terms of the Protection of Funds Act.

[206] See earlier remarks above.

based market manipulation practices in South Africa.[207] Moreover, although it appears that the enforcement of the commodities-based market manipulation ban vests with both the FSB and the JSE, not many settlements involving such cases have been obtained in the South African courts to date.[208] It is not clear whether the FSB and the JSE have the statutory authority to impose their own civil penalties and appropriate rules to prevent commodity-based market manipulation. Furthermore, neither the Protection of Funds Act nor the Financial Markets Act has a statutory provision that expressly empowers the EC to make or enact its own rules to enhance the combating of market manipulation practices in South Africa.[209]

3 2 6 Available Remedies for Market Manipulation

A wide range of remedies such as criminal, civil and administrative remedies are available to all the persons affected by market manipulation in the USA. Apart from these remedies, a private right of action, damages, injunctions, disciplinary sanctions and suspension orders may be employed by the victims of market manipulation to recover their losses from the offenders.

Criminal remedies may be obtained from any person who contravenes market manipulation provisions or the SEC rules, including the making of a false or misleading statement in a filing submitted to the SEC.[210] If the offenders refuse or delay to pay up their fines, the SEC will refer such cases to the Department of Justice for further criminal prosecution.[211]

Furthermore, a statutory derivative civil remedy for market manipulation violations is permitted in the USA on grounds of equity.[212] The SEC may,

---

[207] Ss 80 & 81 read with ss 109(a) & 82 of the Financial Markets Act.

[208] See generally the FSB *Annual Report* 2011 99-102; the FSB *Annual Report* 2013 128-130; also see the FSB "Enforcement Committee Actions" *Media Release* (28-06-2011) <http://www.fsb.co.za/ftp://ftp.fsb.co.za/ public/documents/AReport2011.pdf> (accessed 22-11-2013), which shows that the EC successfully obtained administrative penalties in only about sixteen cases of market manipulation during the period between December 2006 and July 2011 & see further related remarks in paragraph 3 2 4 2 above.

[209] S 99 read with ss 80 & 81 of the Financial Markets Act & ss 6A to 6I of the Protection of Funds Act. See further the FSB *Annual Report* 2011 101-102 & Van Deventer "Harnassing Administrative Law in Encouraging Compliance" 2009 *FSB Bulletin* 3 4. One can argue that the EC, like the SEC, must have express statutory authority to make additional administrative rules and to take any other action which it reasonably believe will improve the enforcement of the market abuse administrative sanctions in South Africa.

[210] The affected persons may obtain criminal remedies of up to $5 million and $25 million fines for individuals and entities respectively from the offenders. See s 32(a) of the Securities Exchange Act (as amended); s 24 of the Securities Act. Also see Palmiter *Securities Regulation* 452-454.

[211] The fines or monetary remedies recovered by the SEC or the Department of Justice are paid into the treasury account for distribution to all the persons who fall victim to market manipulation and other related market abuse practices. Palmiter *Securities Regulation* 370; 441.

[212] Cassim 2008 *SA Merc LJ* 192-193.

therefore, claim disgorgement of profits and other civil compensatory remedies from any person who contravenes its rules or other market manipulation provisions.[213] Likewise, the CFTC may institute court orders for civil monetary fines, restitution, disgorgement of profits, rescission and actual damages against any commodities-based market manipulation offenders.[214]

The SEC and the CFTC are further empowered to take appropriate administrative action against any persons who violate the relevant market manipulation provisions in the USA. In relation to this, the SEC may issue cease and desist orders compelling any alleged offenders to stop or refrain from violating its market abuse rules.[215] If the alleged offender fails to comply with the cease and desist order, the SEC may enforce the order in a federal court.[216] Furthermore, the SEC may impose a compliance order with regard to any misleading tender offer statements or where a registrant's filing is defective, manipulative or misleading.[217] The SEC can further suspend trading and offering of securities traded publicly for up to ten days pending a hearing.[218] In line with this, the SEC can take disciplinary action against broker-dealers and other persons who contravene the market abuse provisions.[219] In the same way, the CFTC may seek rescission or permanent injunction orders against persistent commodities-based market manipulation offenders.[220]

As stated earlier,[221] a private right of action is available to all the persons who are prejudiced by market manipulation, insider trading and other related

---

[213] The offenders will be liable to pay the SEC civil remedies of up to three times the profit gained or loss avoided as a result of their illicit practices. See s 308 of the Sarbanes-Oxley Act. Also see *FMC Corp v Boesky* (1987) 673 F2d 272 (ND I11); *Blue Chip Stamps v Manor Drug Stores* 723; also see Palmiter *Securities Regulation* 369-370.

[214] S 13a-1(a); (b) & (d)(1) read with s 22 & 25 of the Commodity Exchange Act; see further s 6(c)(10)(C) as amended by s 753(a) of the Dodd-Frank Act.

[215] S 8A of the Securities Act; s 21C of the Securities Exchange Act. Also see *WHX Corp v SEC* (2004) 362 F3d 854 (DC Cir); Palmiter *Securities Regulation* 437.

[216] The federal courts may impose their own additional civil monetary penalties for non-compliance. The SEC may further impose a cease and desist order to prevent the registration or filing of any documents which contains false, deceptive or misleading statements, see Palmiter *Securities Regulation* 437.

[217] S 15(c)(4) read with ss 15(b)(1)(B) & 15(b)(4) of the Securities Exchange Act.

[218] S 12(k) of the Securities Exchange Act. The SEC can suspend trading in the affected securities for up to twelve months or revoke the registration of the alleged offender in cases of persistent market abuse violations and non-compliance, see s 12(j) of the Securities Exchange Act; also see *SEC v Sloan* (1978) 436 US 103 & Palmiter *Securities Regulation* 437.

[219] Such action includes claiming monetary administrative fines, revocation of registration and temporary suspension. See further s 21B read with s 21C of the Securities Exchange Act. The SEC may also seek temporary restraining orders, preliminary injunctions, temporary judicial asset freeze of up to 45 days as well as permanent asset freeze against any alleged offenders. See generally s 21(a) to (i) of the Securities Exchange Act. Also see Palmiter *Securities Regulation* 438-439; 441.

[220] Ss 13a-1(a) & (b); 13a-1(d)(1) of the Commodity Exchange Act.

[221] See paragraph 3 2 5 above; also see related analysis in paragraph 3 2 3 above.

practices to claim their damages directly from the offenders.[222] For instance, any prejudiced person may have a private right of action against brokers, exchanges and related organisations that commit commodities-based market manipulation offences. Nonetheless, where the costs of bringing such action are too high, the CFTC may claim remedies on behalf of the prejudiced persons.[223] It is possible that the offenders who engage in trade-based or disclosure-based market manipulation and/or commodities-based market manipulation may be subjected to the SEC or CFTC action as well as another private action from the actual prejudiced persons.[224]

In contrast to the position in the USA,[225] there are no specific civil remedies for commodities-based and other related forms of market manipulation practices that are provided in the Financial Markets Act.[226] In other words, the Financial Markets Act falls short when it comes to the statutory provision and policing of commodities-based market manipulation remedies in South Africa.[227] On the other hand, the EC may recover administrative damages from the trade-based and/or disclosure-based market manipulation offenders in terms of the Protection of Funds Act.[228] However, the Financial Markets Act does not expressly empower the EC to provide civil monetary administrative remedies and/or sanctions to compensate persons who fall victim to market manipulation.[229] Consequently, the EC is currently able to bring only a few administrative actions such as compensatory orders, cost orders and disciplinary orders against the market manipulation offenders.[230]

---

[222] S 20A read with s 21A; s 27A & s 28 of the Securities Exchange Act; s 22 & s 25 of the Commodity Exchange Act. Also see Cassim 2008 *SA Merc LJ* 192-193.

[223] S 25(a) of the Commodity Exchange Act. Although the actual damages that may be imposed against the offenders are not clearly stipulated, it is generally believed that such offenders will be liable to pay the CFTC compensatory damages for the actual loss avoided or profit gained. Therefore, in successful cases, the affected persons will recover their damages from offenders through the CFTC. See *Comm`n v Heffernan* (2003) 274 FSupp2d 1375 (SDGa); also see Pearce "Broadening Actual Damages in the Context of the Commodities Exchange Act" 2007 *Journal of Law and Policy* 449 449; 480 & 483.

[224] This is not viewed as a violation to the double jeopardy clause of the US constitution which asserts that no person may be subjected to multiple prosecutions or punishment of the same conduct. See Palmiter *Securities Regulation* 460-461.

[225] See earlier related remarks above.

[226] Ss 80 & 81 read with ss 109(a) & 82. See related discussion in paragraph 3 2 5 above; also see related analysis in paragraph 3 2 3 above

[227] Ss 80 & 81 read with ss 109(a) & 82. The JSE and the FSB should be statutorily empowered to have more discretionary powers to combat and discourage all the types of market manipulation activities in South Africa.

[228] Ss 6A to 6I; read with s 99 of the Financial Markets Act.

[229] Such compensatory money is only available in matters involving insider trading, see s 82 read with ss 80 & 81 of the Financial Markets Act. This may indicate that the EC, unlike the SEC and the CFTC, does not have express statutory authority to make its own appropriate additional administrative remedies for market manipulation.

[230] See the FSB (28-06-2011)

Furthermore, there is no express statutory provision for a private right of action for market manipulation victims in South Africa.[231]

3 3 Concluding Remarks

As discussed above, both the USA, at a federal level,[232] and South Africa[233] have market abuse legislation which mainly discourages insider trading and market manipulation. However, as earlier stated,[234] the prohibitions, penalties and remedies for market abuse in the USA are relatively broader than those available in South Africa. For instance, unlike the position in the USA,[235] Internet-based and commodities-based market manipulation practices are not expressly outlawed in South Africa, especially, under the Financial Markets Act.[236] Furthermore, the Financial Markets Act still does not impose sufficient, separate and distinct criminal penalties against the natural and juristic persons that commit market abuse offences in South Africa.[237] Over and above, other alternative remedies such as specific civil pecuniary penalties, punitive damages, bounty rewards, class actions and private rights of action are not expressly provided under the Financial Markets Act.[238]

Given this background, it is submitted that the Financial Markets Act should be reviewed to enact specific provisions for separate and distinct criminal penalties that can be imposed upon any juristic person[239] or individual who commits or attempts to commit market abuse offences in South Africa for deterrence purposes. Additionally, the Financial Markets Act should be amended to enact adequate provisions that prohibit Internet-based market abuse practices in South Africa. The Financial Markets Act should also be reviewed to enact provisions that expressly prohibit a person who

---

<http://www.fsb.co.za/ftp://ftp.fsb.co.za/public/documents/AReport2011.pdf> (accessed 22-11-2013); also see the FSB *Annual Report* 2011 101-102; Van Deventer 2009 *FSB Bulletin* 4 & related discussion in paragraph 3 2 5 above.

[231] See ss 80 & 81 read with ss 109(a) & 82 of the Financial Markets Act. Moreover, the Consumer Protection Act 68 of 2008 (Consumer Protection Act), also does not expressly provide for any private of action for the persons affected by market manipulation. See generally ss 115 & 116 read with Part C of the Consumer Protection Act. It is accordingly submitted that a private right of action provision should be enacted to give equal opportunity to all the affected persons to claim their own damages straight from the perpetrators of market abuse practices in South Africa.

[232] Generally see the sub-paragraphs under paragraph 3 2 above.

[233] See related discussion in the sub-paragraphs under paragraph 3 2 above.

[234] Generally see the sub-paragraphs under paragraph 3 2 above.

[235] See the discussion in the sub-paragraphs under paragraph 3 2 above.

[236] See ss 78; 80; 81; 82 read with ss 79 &109(a).

[237] See related remarks in paragraphs 3 2 2 & 3 2 5 above.

[238] See s 82; also see related remarks in paragraphs 3 2 3 & 3 2 6 above.

[239] It is submitted that a minimum fine of R750 million, or a much higher penalty should be imposed on juristic persons to increase deterrence and/or compliance with the market abuse prohibition in South Africa.

inadvertently aided or abetted another person to commit market abuse practices from making or publishing a false, misleading or deceptive statement, promise or forecast that relates to any security in South Africa. It is also recommended that the Financial Markets Act should be reviewed to enact provisions that expressly prohibit commodity-based market manipulation and provide civil penalties for all market manipulation offences in South Africa.

References

Books

Arshadi N & Eyssell TH *The Law and Finance of Corporate Insider Trading: Theory and Evidence* (Kluwer Academic Publishers Massachusetts 1993)

Avgouleas E *The Mechanics and Regulation of Market Abuse: A Legal and Economic Analysis* (Oxford University Press Oxford 2005)

Barnes P *Stock Market Efficiency, Insider Dealing and Market Abuse* (Gower Publishing Limited Surrey England 2009)

Beuthin RC and Luiz SM *Beuthin's Basic Company Law* 3rd ed (Butterworths Durban 2000)

Gaillard E (ed) *Insider Trading: The Laws of Europe, the United States and Japan* (Kluwer Law & Taxation Publishers Deventer Netherlands 1992)

Hazen TL *The Law of Securities Regulation: Handbook Series Student Edition* (West Publishing Company St Paul, MN 1985)

Hazen TL *Federal Securities Law* 2nd ed (Federal Judicial Center United States of America 2003)

Lyon GJ & Du Plessis JJ *The Law of Insider Trading in Australia* (The Federation Press Sydney 2005)

Palmiter AR *Securities Regulation: Examples and Explanations* 3rd ed (Aspen Publishers New York 2005)

Swan EJ *Market Abuse Regulation* 1st ed (Oxford University Press United States of America 2006)

Journal articles

Bhattacharya U & Daouk H "The World Price of Insider Trading" 2002 *Journal of Finance* 75-108

Botha D "Control of Insider Trading in South Africa: A Comparative Analysis" 1991 *SA Merc LJ* 1-18

Botha D "Increased Maximum Fine for Insider Trading: A Realistic and Effective Deterrent?" 1990 *SALJ* 504-508

Cassim R "An Analysis of Market Manipulation under the Securities Services Act 36 of 2004 (Part 1)" 2008 *SA Merc LJ* 33-60

Cassim R "An Analysis of Market Manipulation under the Securities Services Act 36 of 2004 (Part 2)" 2008 *SA Merc LJ* 177-199

Fisher J, Harshman E, Gillespie W, Ordower H, Ware L & Yeager F "Privatizing Regulation: Whistle-blowing and Bounty Hunting in the Financial Services Industries" 2000 *Dick.J. Int'L. L* 117-143

Friedman HM "The Insider Trading and Securities Fraud Enforcement Act of 1988" 1990 *North Carolina Law Review* 465-494

Gilson RJ & Kraakman RH "The Mechanisms of Market Efficiency" 1984 *VA.L.REV* 549-644

Horwich A "The Origin, Application, Validity and Potential Misuse of Rule 10b5-1" 2007 *The Bus. Lawyer* 913-954

Jooste R "A critique of the insider trading provisions of the 2004 Securities Services Act" 2006 *SALJ* 437-460

Kaswell SJ "An Insider's View of the Insider Trading and Securities Fraud Enforcement Act" 1989 *Bus.Law* 145-180

Knepper ZT "Examining the Merits of Dual Regulation for Single-Stock Futures: How the Divergent Insider Trading Regimes for Federal Futures and Securities Markets Demonstrate the Necessity for (and Virtual Inevitability of) Dual CFTC-SEC Regulation for Single-Stock Futures" 2004 *Pierce Law Review* 33-47

Luiz SM "Insider Trading Regulation – If at First You Don't Succeed..." 1999 *SA Merc LJ* 136-151

Markham JW "'Front-Running'-Insider Trading under the Commodity Exchange Act" 1988 *Cath. U.Review* 69-127

Mossos E "Sarbanes-Oxley goes to Europe: A Comparative Analysis of United States and European Union Corporate Reforms after Enron" 2004 *Currents International Trade Law Journal* 9-22

Nelemans M "Redefining Trade-Based Market Manipulation" 2008 *Valparaiso University Law Review* 1169-1220

Osode PC "The New South African Insider Trading Act: Sound Law Reform or Legislative Overkill?" 2000 *Journal of African Law* 239-263

Pearce BD "Broadening Actual Damages in the Context of the Commodities Exchange Act" 2007 *Journal of Law and Policy* 449-483

Pearson TC "When Hedge Funds Betray A Creditor Committee's Fiduciary Role: New Twists on Insider Trading in the International Financial Markets" 2009 *Review of Banking & Financial Law* 165-220

Ryan L "Rule14e-3's Disclose or Abstain Rule and Its Validity under Section 14(e)" 1991 *U. Cin. Law Review* 449-465

Steinberg MI "Insider Trading Regulation–A Comparative Perspective" 2003 *The International Lawyer* 153-171

Van Deventer G "New Watchdog for Insider Trading" 1999 *FSB Bulletin* 2-3

Van Deventer G "Harnassing Administrative Law in Encouraging Compliance" 2009 *FSB Bulletin* 3-4

Case law

South Africa

Pather and Another v Financial Services Board and Others (57617/10) [2014] 3 All SA 208 (GP)

Pretorius and Another v Natal South Sea Investment Trust 1965 3 SA 410 (W)

Zietsman v Director of Market Abuse 2016 1 SA 218 (GP)

United States of America

Blue Chip Stamps v Manor Drug Stores (1975) 421 US 723

Cady, Roberts and Company [1961-1964 Transfer Binder] CCH Fed Sec L Rep 76. 803

Cargil Inc v Hardin case (1971) 452 F2d 1154
Central Bank of Denver NA v First Interstate Bank of Denver NA (1994) 511 US 164 (US SC)
Chiarella v United States (1980) 445 US 222
Comm`n v Heffernan (2003) 274 FSupp2d 1375 (SDGa)
Dirks v SEC (1983) 463 US 646
Elkind v Liggett and Myers Inc (1980) 635 F2d 156(2d Cir)
FMC Corp v Boesky (1988) 852 F2d 981 (7th Cir)
FMC Corp v Boesky (1987) 673 F2d 272 (ND I11)
Godwin v Agassiz (1933) 186 NE 659 (Mass)
SEC v Boesky (1986) 86 Civ 8767
SEC v Levine (1986) 86 Civ 3726 (SDNY) (RO)
SEC v Lipson (2001) No 97–CV-2661 129F Supp.2d 1148
SEC v Sloan (1978) 436 US 103
SEC v Texas Gulf Sulphur Company (1968) 401 F2d 833 (2d Cir)
SEC v WorldCom Inc (2003) 02 Civ 4963(JSR)
SEC v Yun (2003) 327 F3d 1263 (11th Cir)
WHX Corp v SEC (2004) 362 F3d 854 (DC Cir)
United States v Chestman (1991) 947 F2d 551 (2d Cir)
United States v Falcone [2001 Transfer Binder] 91 489 Fed Sec L Rep CCH (2d Cir)
United States v O'Hagan (1997) 117 (SCt) 2199

Legislation

South Africa

Companies Act 61 of 1973
Companies Act 71 of 2008
Consumer Protection Act 68 of 2008
Financial Markets Act 19 of 2012
Financial Institutions (Protection of Funds) Act 28 of 2001 as amended
Securities Services Act 36 of 2004

United States of America

Commodity Exchange Act of 1936 7 USC 1 *et seq.* (1994)
Commodities Futures Modernization Act 2000 Public Law 106-554, 114 Stat.2763A-365
Commodity Futures Trading Commission Act of 1974 Public Law 93-64, 88 Stat 1398
Derivatives Market Manipulation Prevention Act of 2009
Dodd-Frank Wall Street Reform and Consumer Protection Act of 2010, Public Law 111-203, 124 Stat.1376 (12 USC; s 5301 *et seq.*)

Insider Trading and Securities Fraud Enforcement Act of 1988 Public Law 100-704, 102 Stat 4677

Insider Trading Sanctions Act of 1984 Public Law 98-376, 98 Stat.1264 (1984)

International Securities Enforcement Cooperation Act of 1990

Investment Advisors Act of 1940

Investment Company Act of 1940

Public Company Accounting Reform and Investor Protection Act of 2002 Public Law 107-204, 116 Stat 745 (15; 28 USC)

Public Utility Holding Company Act of 1935

Racketeer Influenced and Corrupt Organization Act of 1970

Securities Act of 1933 Public Law 22 48 Stat 74 15 USC77a-77mm (1994)

Securities Act of 1933, Public Law 22 48 Stat.74 15 USC 77a-77mm *et seq.* (2000)

Securities Act of 1933 15 USC 77q(a) (2006) as amended by PL-111-229 (approved 11-08-2010)

Securities Exchange Act of 1934 Public Law 73-291, 48 Stat 881 15 USC 78a-78II

Securities Exchange Act of 1934 15 USC 78i(a)(2)-(5) (2006) as amended by PL-111-257 (approved 05-10-2010)

Securities Exchange Act Release Number 43154 [2000 Transfer Binder] Fed Sec L Rep CCH 86.319

Trust Indenture Act of 1939

Commissions, committees and reports

South Africa

Financial Services Board *Annual Report* 2011

Financial Services Board *Annual Report* 2013

The King Task Group into Insider Trading Legislation *Minority Report on Insider Trading* 1997

The King Task Group into the Insider Trading Legislation *First Report* 15 May 1997

The King Task Group into the Insider Trading Legislation *Final Report* 21 October 1997

Van Wyk de Vries Commission of Inquiry into the *Companies Act* of 1973

United States of America

The Commodity Futures Trading Commission & the United States Securities and Exchange Commission "A Joint Report of the SEC and the CFTC on Harmonization of Regulation" *Report* 16 October 2009

Thesis and dissertations

Chitimira H *A Comparative Analysis of the Enforcement of Market Abuse Provisions* (LLD-thesis Nelson Mandela Metropolitan University 2012)

Chitimira H *The Regulation of Insider Trading in South Africa: A Roadmap for an Effective, Competitive and Adequate Regulatory Statutory Framework* (LLM-dissertation University of Fort Hare 2008)

Conference papers, media releases and other relevant material

Morrison & Foerster "Insider Trading" 2010 *Year End Review* 1

The United States Department of Justice District of Delaware "Newark Man Pleads Guilty to Insider Trading Charges" *Press Release* 25 March 2011

Newspaper reports

Chanetsa B "Insider Trading is Notoriously Hard to Prosecute" *Business Report* (2004-04-26)

Internet sources

Cantwell M "Senate Passes Cantwell Anti-Manipulation Amendment" (06-05-2010) <http://cantwell.senate.gov/news/record.cfm?id=324761> (accessed 26-11-2013)

Financial Services Board "Enforcement Committee Actions" *Media Release* (28-06-2011) <http://www.fsb.co.za/ftp://ftp.fsb.co.za/public/documents/AReport2011.pdf> (accessed 22-11-2013)

Financial Services Board "List of Current Investigations of the Directorate of Market Abuse" *Media Release* (28-06-2011) <http://www.fsb.co.za/ftp://ftp.fsb.co.za/public/documents/AReport2011.pdf> (accessed 22-11-2013)

Morgan Lewis "2009 Year in Review: SEC and SRO Selected Enforcement Cases and Developments Regarding Broker-Dealers" 2010 <http://www.morganlewis.com/lit_SECandYearlyReviewWP_Jan2010.pdf> (accessed 10-06-2013)

Myburgh A & Davis B "The Impact of South Africa's Insider Trading Regime: A Report for the Financial Services Board" (25-03-2004) <http://www.genesis-analytics.com/public/FSBReport.pdf> (accessed 09-02-2013)

Van Deventer G "Anti-Market Abuse Legislation in South Africa" (10-06-2008) <http://www.fsb.co.za/public/marketabuse/ FSBReport.pdf> (accessed 05-05-2013)

Chapter 4

The Enforcement of the Market Abuse Prohibition in the United States of America and South Africa

4 1 Introduction

Notwithstanding the fact that various market abuse practices such as insider trading, front running and market manipulation are still posing some challenges to the United States of America (USA)'s regulated financial, derivative and commodity markets, the USA has developed one of the most progressive and effective anti-market abuse enforcement frameworks in recent years.[1] For example, its federal anti-market abuse enforcement framework involves self-regulatory organisations as well as private actions that enhance compliance with the law and facilitate the levying of sanctions against offenders.[2] In other words, rigorous enforcement is the key component of the USA's market abuse regulation that makes it unique from similar regulation in other countries.[3] As a result, the USA's anti-market abuse enforcement approaches have influenced the regulation of market abuse in a number of countries, including South Africa.[4] Given this background, the detection, prosecution and enforcement measures adopted in the USA will be briefly discussed and, where

---

* This chapter is influenced in part, by an article that was initially published in the *Mediterranean Journal of Social Sciences*, see Chitimira "An Analysis of the Market Abuse Prohibition Enforcement in the United States of America" 2014(5)(7) *Mediterranean Journal of Social Sciences* 188-199. This was done with legal permission from the editors of the *Mediterranean Journal of Social Sciences.*

[1] Steinberg "Insider Trading Regulation–A Comparative Perspective" 2003 *The International Lawyer* 153 169-171; Clifford Chance "Overview of United States and United Kingdom Derivative and Commodity Market Enforcement Regimes" 2016 *Clifford Chance Markets Publication Series* 1 8-226.

[2] Clifford Chance 2016 *Clifford Chance Markets Publication Series* 8-226; Steinberg 2003 *The International Lawyer* 169.

[3] Clifford Chance 2016 *Clifford Chance Markets Publication Series* 8-226; Steinberg 2003 *The International Lawyer* 169. For related comparative analysis in other jurisdictions, see Bhattacharya & Daouk "The World Price of Insider Trading" 2002 *Journal of Finance* 75 75-108; Lyon & Du Plessis *The Law of Insider Trading in Australia* (2005) 159-168 & Avgouleas *The Mechanics and Regulation of Market Abuse: A Legal and Economic Analysis* (2005) 75-502.

[4] Chitimira *The Regulation of Insider Trading in South Africa: A Roadmap for an Effective, Competitive and Adequate Regulatory Statutory Framework* (Unpublished LLM dissertation, University of Fort Hare) 2008, 41–72; Botha "Control of Insider Trading in South Africa: A Comparative Analysis" 1991 *SA Merc LJ* 1 1-18; Botha "Increased Maximum Fine for Insider Trading: A Realistic and Effective Deterrent?" 1990 *SALJ* 504 504-508.

applicable, contrasted with similar enforcement methods in South Africa in order to recommend possible anti-market abuse enforcement measures that could be employed to increase the curbing of market abuse (market manipulation and insider trading) activities in South Africa.[5] This is done by, first, examining the role of the United States Securities and Exchange Commission (SEC) in relation to the enforcement of the market abuse prohibition in the USA. Secondly, the role of the Department of Justice (DOJ) and the courts in relation to the enforcement of the market abuse ban in the USA will be analysed. Lastly, a similar analysis in respect of other selected self-regulatory organisations will be provided.

4 2 Detection, Prosecution and the Enforcement of the Market Abuse Prohibition

4 2 1 The Role of the United States Securities and Exchange Commission

The SEC and the Commodity Futures Trading Commission (CFTC) are both empowered to enforce the federal anti-market abuse laws in the USA. Accordingly, the responsibility for civil and administrative enforcement of the market abuse prohibition rests primarily with the SEC.[6] On the other hand, the Commodity Futures Trading Commission (CFTC) has the prerogative to oversee and enforce the prohibition relating to commodities derivatives and futures market abuse practices. The CFTC plays a key role in the regulation of commodities derivatives and futures markets in order to combat market

---

[5] Chitimira *A Comparative Analysis of the Enforcement of Market Abuse Provisions* (Unpublished LLD thesis, Nelson Mandela Metropolitan University) 2012, 230-257; Van Deventer "Anti-Market Abuse Legislation in South Africa" (10-06-2008) 1-5 <http://www.fsb.co.za/public/marketabuse/FSB Report.pdf> (accessed 05-05-2013); Myburgh & Davis "The Impact of South Africa's Insider Trading Regime: A Report for the Financial Services Board" (25-03-2004) 8-33 <http://www.genesis-analytics.com/public /FSBReport.pdf> (accessed 09-02-2013); Chanetsa "Insider Trading is Notoriously Hard to Prosecute" (2004-04-26) *Business Report* page number unknown; *Pather and Another v Financial Services Board and Others (57617/10)* [2014] 3 All SA 208 (GP); *Zietsman v Director of Market Abuse* 2016 1 SA 218 (GP); *Pretorius and Another v Natal South Sea Investment Trust* 1965 3 SA 410 (W), were the courts failed to convict the suspected insider trading offenders; Osode "The New South African Insider Trading Act: Sound Law Reform or Legislative Overkill?" 2000 *Journal of African Law* 239 239-263; Jooste "A Critique of the Insider Trading Provisions of the 2004 Securities Services Act" 2006 *SALJ* 437 441–460; Van Deventer "New Watchdog for Insider Trading" 1999 *FSB Bulletin* 2 3; Beuthin & Luiz *Beuthin's Basic Company Law* (2000) 235–238; Luiz "Market Abuse and the Enforcement Committee" 2011 *SA Merc LJ* 151 151-172; Luiz "Insider Trading Regulation – If at First You Don't Succeed…" 1999 *SA Merc LJ* 136 136-151; Henning & Du Toit "The Regulation of False Trading, Market Manipulation and Insider Trading" 2000 *Journal for Juridical Science* 155 155-165 & Osode "The Regulation of Insider Trading in South Africa: A Public Choice Perspective" 1999 *African Journal of International and Comparative Law* 688 688-708, for related comments.

[6] Anonymous "The Regulation of Insider Trading in the United States of America" (09-03-2008) <http://www.sec.gov> (accessed 08-06-2016); Ashe & Counsell *Insider Trading: The Tangled Web* (1990) 7-12; Langevoort & Gulati "The Muddled Duty to Disclose under Rule 10b-5" 2004 *Vand L Rev* 1639 1639-1680.

abuse practices such as fraud-based market manipulation, false reporting-based market manipulation, intentional spoofing, wash trades, layering, accommodation trades, fictitious trades and attempted market manipulation.[7] Nonetheless, for the purposes of this sub-heading, the discussion will be mainly focused on the roles of the SEC regarding the enforcement of the federal anti-market abuse prohibition in the USA.

Despite the fact that there are several other regulatory bodies,[8] the SEC was established as an independent quasi-judicial and legislative regulatory board responsible for the enforcement of federal securities laws through the regulation of the stock market and securities industry in the USA.[9] The SEC's legislative powers include promulgating rules and regulations that have the force of law.[10] The SEC may, for instance, issue interpretive letters and the so-called no-action letters to express its views and provide guidance to all the relevant persons regarding any market abuse violations.[11] Moreover, the SEC's judicial functions include acting as an original tribunal regarding disciplinary actions

---

[7] Notably, in 2015, the CFTC filed 69 enforcement actions against the offenders and this culminated into a total of about 419 of such actions that were successfully brought by the CFTC against the offenders in the recent years. The CFTC imposed civil monetary penalties of about $3, 144 billion against the offenders in 2015 and over $2, 8 billion was deposited at the USA Treasury. The CFTC also received $59 million in respect of its restitution and disgorgement orders in 2015. Thus, the CFTC obtained over $3.2 billion monetary sanctions against the market abuse and related offenders in 2015. See the CFTC "Releases Annual Enforcement Results for Fiscal Year 2015" *CFTC Press Release* 6 November 2015. For example, the recent cases that were successfully prosecuted and settled include, *inter alia, BP America Inc.* (2016) 156 FERC 61,031; *Carpenters Pension Trust Fund of St. Louis v Barclays PLC,* (2014) 750 F.3d 227 (2d Cir); *Commodity Futures Trading Comm'n v Moncada* (2014) No. 12-cv-8791 (SDNY) and *Ashmore v CGI Group Inc.* (2015) 138 F. Supp. 3d 329 (SDNY). In addition, wholesale commodities and derivative markets are regulated by the Federal Energy Regulatory Commission (FERC) in respect of energy products and the Federal Trade Commission (FTC) in terms of the Energy Policy Act of 2005, the Commodity Exchange Act of 1936 7 USC 1 *et seq.* (1994) as amended (CEA), see ss 6(c); 9(a)(2) & 13(a)(2) and the Commodities Futures Modernization Act 2000 Public Law 106-554, 114 Stat.2763A-365. See Clifford Chance 2016 *Clifford Chance Markets Publication Series* 6-10; see further Avgouleas *The Mechanics and Regulation of Market Abuse* 104; 106.

[8] Such regulatory bodies include the CFTC and other self-regulatory organisations.

[9] Securities Exchange Act of 1934 15 USC 78i(a)(2)-(5) (2006) as amended by PL-111-257 (approved 05-10-2010) (Securities Exchange Act), see s 4. Apart from enforcing the provisions of the Securities Exchange Act, the SEC enforces the relevant provisions of the Securities Act, the Trust Indenture Act of 1939, the Investment Company Act of 1940, the Investment Advisors Act of 1940, the Public Utility Holding Company Act of 1935, the Public Company Accounting Reform and Investor Protection Act of 2002 Public Law 107-204, 116 Stat 745 (as codified in scattered sections of 15; 28 USC) (Sarbanes-Oxley Act) and other related statutes. The SEC does not work in isolation. Other institutions under its authority include the New York Stock Exchange (NYSE) as well as self-regulatory organisations like the National Association of Securities Dealers (NASD) and the Municipal Securities Rule Making Board (MSRMB). Palmiter *Securities Regulation: Examples and Explanations* (2005) 402-415.

[10] Ss 4; 4A & 4C of the Securities Exchange Act, also see Hazen *Federal Securities Law* (2003) 4-7.

[11] Generally see s 14(a) to (e) of the Securities Exchange Act. Also see Palmiter *Securities Regulation* 29; 415; 433-444.

against securities professionals subject to its supervision who violate securities laws or commit market abuse offences.[12]

Moreover, the SEC exercises administrative and supervisory authority over the key participants in the securities industry to prevent and combat market abuse activities in the USA.[13] The SEC is also responsible for protecting investors, maintaining fair, orderly and efficient financial markets through facilitating capital formation and effectively enforcing securities laws to curb fraud, insider trading, market manipulation and other related market abuse practices. For purposes of effectiveness, the SEC is divided into four main divisions, namely the Corporate Finance, Market Regulation, Investment Management and Enforcement Divisions.

The Corporate Finance Division polices compliance with the mandatory disclosure requirement as well as registration by public companies of transactions such as mergers. It additionally operates an online Electronic Data Gathering Analysis and Retrieval system (EDGAR system) to ensure equal access to non-public inside information for all relevant persons. This system has been successfully utilised to prevent possible insider trading and market manipulation in the USA's financial markets.[14]

Moreover, the Market Regulation Division regulates the NYSE, the NASD, the MSRMB and other self-regulatory organisations. In this regard, the Market Regulation Division interprets any proposed changes to regulations, publicises investment-related topics for public education and monitors operations of the industry. In practice, the SEC delegates most of its enforcement and rule-making authority to the NYSE and the NASD.[15] Notably, these two self-regulatory organisations merged to form the Financial Industry Regulatory Authority in 2007.[16]

The Investment Management Division oversees investment companies and their advisory professionals. It further administers federal security laws to

[12] Furthermore, the SEC may act as an appellate tribunal to review disciplinary decisions or actions taken by the stock exchanges, the NASD and other self-regulatory organisations against their members. Palmiter *Securities Regulation* 29; 415; 433-444.

[13] Palmiter *Securities Regulation* 29.

[14] The EDGAR system has been used in a number of instances to assess, review and obtain misleading, manipulative or deceptive information regarding any filings with the SEC. Palmiter *Securities Regulation* 31.

[15] Consequently, all trading persons or companies not regulated by other self-regulatory organisations are obliged to be registered with the NASD in order to curb all possible market abuse activities.

[16] Notwithstanding the existence of this merger, it is stated that the New York Stock Exchange still maintains its autonomous oversight and enforcement responsibility regarding any securities and market abuse violations which are effected on its facilities and systems by the offenders. See generally Morgan Lewis "2009 Year in Review: SEC and SRO Selected Enforcement Cases and Developments Regarding Broker-Dealers" (2010) 4-6 <http://www.morganlewis.com/lit_SECandYearly ReviewWP_Jan2010.pdf> (accessed 10-06-2013).

improve the disclosure of non-public inside information and to minimise prejudice to investors without imposing an undue burden on regulated companies. Therefore, the SEC can interpret such laws and make rules to curb the occurrence of market abuse practices in the relevant financial markets as much as possible.[17]

Furthermore, the Enforcement Division investigates any violation of the laws and rules that govern insider trading, market manipulation and other related practices. Its extensive investigatory powers include issuing *subpoenae* for the production of relevant evidence such as documents, and compelling suspects and others to testify in the courts. Furthermore, it has powers to:

(a) enforce civil remedies;
(b) institute administrative orders;
(c) recover any illegally obtained profits from guilty persons (disgorgement of profits);
(d) extra-territorially enforce the federal anti-fraud securities and market abuse prohibition;[18]
(e) provide greater incentives and immunity to whistle-blowers who report market abuse violations to the SEC;[19] and
(f) impose punitive penalties on such persons and refer criminal matters to the Department of Justice.[20]

In 2009, the Enforcement Division created the Office of Market Intelligence, the Asset Management Unit, the Market Abuse Unit, the Structured and New Products Unit, the Foreign Corrupt Practices Act Unit and the Municipal Securities and Public Pensions Unit. This enabled the Enforcement Division to successfully minimise securities law violations by *inter alia* analysing and monitoring tips, complaints or referrals received by the SEC each year, especially after 2009, and to obtain enforcement actions and/or settlements consistently in a number of market abuse cases between 2005 and 2014 as indicated in the table 1 below.[21]

---

[17] Palmiter *Securities Regulation* 28-31.

[18] S 929P(b) read with (c) of the Dodd-Frank Wall Street Reform and Consumer Protection Act of 2010, Public Law 111-203, 124 Stat.1376 (12 USC; s 5301 *et seq.*) (Dodd-Frank Act); also see Morrison & Foerster "Insider Trading" 2010 *Year End Review* 1 14-15.

[19] S 922 of the Dodd-Frank Act which enacted s 21F to repeal and replace s 21A(e) of the Securities Exchange Act; see further Morrison & Foerster 2010 *Year End Review* 12-14.

[20] Dooley "Enforcement of Insider Trading Restrictions" 1980 *Virginia Law Review* 1 60-83; Carlton & Fischel "The Regulation of Insider Trading" 1983 *Stanford Law Review* 857 857-895 & Bainbridge *Corporation Law and Economics* (2002) 571-573.

[21] Notably, this table was adapted from the SEC website <https://www.sec.gov/news/newsroom/images/enfstats.pdf> (accessed 14-10-2017). Moreover, the aforesaid consistent enforcement of the market abuse prohibition is supported, in part, by the fact that the SEC has established eighteen offices and eleven of these offices are regional and district

Table 1: Overview of the SEC's annual anti-market abuse enforcement statistics from 2005 to 2014.

Enforcement Actions by Fiscal Year	2005	2006	2007	2008	2009	2010	2011	2012	2013	2014
Broker-Dealer	94	75	89	67	109	70	112	134	121	166
Delinquent Filings	n/a	91	52	113	92	106	121	127	132	107
FCPA	n/a	n/a	n/a	n/a	n/a	n/a	* 20	15	5	7
Insider Trading	50	46	47	61	37	53	57	58	44	52
Investment Adviser/ Investment Co.	97	87	79	87	76	113	146	147	140	130
Issuer Reporting and Disclosure	185	138	219	154	143	126	** 89	79	68	99
Market Manipulation	46	27	36	53	39	34	35	46	50	63
Securities Offering	60	61	68	115	141	144	124	89	103	81
Other	98	49	65	21	27	35	31	39	13	50
Total Enforcement Actions	**630**	**574**	**655**	**671**	**664**	**681**	**735**	**734**	**676**	**755**

Adapted from the SEC website.[22]

Additionally, the SEC continues to play a crucial role in the combating of market abuse and related illicit activities in the USA. For instance, several offenders were successfully investigated and charged with insider trading, front running, layering, running illicit Ponzi schemes and other market manipulation-related offences by the SEC in 2017.[23] Nonetheless, the SEC is

offices throughout the USA with approximately 3100 competent staff. Over half of the estimated 3100 SEC employees are in the Enforcement Division. This could indicate that the SEC gives top priority to the effective enforcement of securities laws and combating of market abuse practices. As a result a significant number of settlements and prosecutions have to date been obtained in some landmark market abuse cases like *SEC v Texas Gulf Sulphur Company* (1968) 401 F2d 833 (2d Cir); *Dirks v SEC* (1983) 463 US 646 646-655; *Chiarella v United States* (1980) 445 US 222; *US v Martha Stewart and Peter Bacanovic* (2006) 433 F3d 273; *SEC v Galleon Management & others* (2009) 09 Civ 8811(SDNY); *SEC v Arthur J Cutillo & others* (2009) 09 Civ 9208 (SDNY) & *SEC v Anthony Fareri & others* (2009) 09 Civ 80360 (SDFla); generally see further related analysis and/or discussion of the SEC's enforcement statistics as summarised in Morgan Lewis 2010 2-4 & 7-13 <http://www.morganlewis.com/lit_SECandYearlyReviewWP_Jan2010.pdf> (accessed 10-06-2013).

[22] <https://www.sec.gov/news/newsroom/images/enfstats.pdf> (accessed 14-10-2017).

[23] SEC "SEC Files Fraud Charges in Bitcoin and Office Space Investment Schemes" *Press Release 2017-123* 30 June 2017; SEC "Law Firm Partner and Neighbor Charged in $1 Million Insider Trading

currently grappling with several market abuse regulatory challenges that are perpetrated in the USA's regulated financial markets through disruptive technology such as automated financial services, computerised trading, algorithms and artificial intelligence.[24]

In order to combat cross-border market abuse activities, the SEC entered into non-binding co-operative agreements (Memoranda of Understanding) with similar foreign securities regulatory bodies. These Memoranda of Understanding (MOUs) permit the SEC to request such foreign regulators to investigate and provide it with certain information in circumstances in which the SEC will not be able to do so itself.[25]

Likewise, the SEC can also aid other foreign regulators' investigations even when no USA legislation would have been violated by the occurrence of the illicit conduct in question in the USA's financial markets.[26] The SEC may further sanction market participants who engage in activities that are deemed illegal in other countries, even if such activities are not illegal or deemed manipulative, misleading or deceptive in the USA.[27] Additionally, the SEC's international co-operation and extra-territorial enforcement powers are enhanced by the fact that it is a member of the International Organisation of Securities Commissions (IOSCO).[28]

Scheme" *Press Release 2017-100* 11 May 2017; SEC "SEC Freezes Brokerage Accounts Behind Alleged Insider Trading" *Press Release 2017-80* 14 April 2017; SEC "Investment Bank VP Charged With Insider Trading" *Press Release 2017-83* 24 April 2017; SEC "SEC Announces Charges in Hamilton Ticket Resale Ponzi Scheme" *Press Release 2017-37* 27 January 2017; SEC "Brokerage Firm Charged With Gatekeeper Failures Related to Pump-and-Dump Scheme" *Press Release 2017-33* 25 January 2017; SEC "Morgan Stanley, Citigroup Charged With Misleading Investors About Forex Trading Program" *Press Release 2017-30* 24 January 2017; SEC "SEC Charges Fake Filer With Manipulating Fitbit Stock" *Press Release 2017-107* 19 May 2017 and SEC "SEC Charges Brokerage Firm With Failing to Comply With Anti-Money Laundering Laws" *Press Release 2017-112* 5 June 2017.

[24] Brummer "Disruptive Technology and Securities Regulation" 2015 *Fordham Law Review* 977 997-1003; see further related comments in paragraph 1 1 of Chapter One of this book.

[25] This co-operative enforcement at an international level has allowed the SEC to track down illicit trading and market abuse practices like offshore insider trading, secret and manipulative bank accounts in other foreign jurisdictions. SEC "Overseas Traders Paying Back All Profits Plus Penalties in Insider Trading Case" *Press Release 2017-70* 24 March 2017; also see Palmiter *Securities Regulation* 501-502.

[26] S 21(a)(2) of the Securities Exchange Act.

[27] See generally the International Securities Enforcement Cooperation Act of 1990; s 15(b)(4)(G) of the Securities Exchange Act. Also see Palmiter *Securities Regulation* 502.

[28] The IOSCO was founded in 1974 and is an organisation which provides guidelines on various aspects of securities enforcement and regulation to its more than 170 members. The SEC's IOSCO membership has equipped it to investigate and combat Internet-based fraud, insider trading, market manipulation and other illicit cross-border market abuse practices. See Palmiter *Securities Regulation* 502.

As indicated above, the SEC has been very instrumental in the enforcement of the market abuse ban in the USA. For instance, apart from being tasked with the responsibility to enforce the civil and administrative sanctions, the SEC supervises other participants in the securities industry and the self-regulatory organisations. This enabled the SEC to score a number of victories in the civil enforcement of market abuse in the USA to date.[29] Moreover, the SEC recently tightened and improved its enforcement in the aftermath of the World Com, Enron and other related market abuse cases. For example, it imposed a civil monetary fine of $2, 25 billion on World Com in 2005 for the misuse of inside information and other related securities law violations, like corporate financial fraud.[30] The SEC further imposed civil monetary fines of $250 million on Qwest Communications, $100 million on the Royal Dutch/Shell company and $100 million in the Bristol-Myers Squibb case for insider trading and other related securities law violations like financial misrepresentation.[31] The SEC further imposed 987 administrative sanctions (cease or desist orders, censures and suspension orders) against market abuse offenders during the period between 1978 and 2004.[32] The SEC has also successfully and consistently managed to bring several enforcement actions against the insider trading offenders during the period between 2004 and 2010 as evidenced in figure 1 below.[33]

[29] The SEC recovered civil penalties and disgorgement fines of about $3.3 billion from the market abuse offenders in 2006. During the period between 2002 and 2005, the SEC recovered total monetary sanctions in civil cases for market abuse ranging from approximately $5.3 billion to $11.5 billion. Coffee "Law and the Market: The Impact of Enforcement" 2007 *University of Pennsylvania Law Review* 229 230-311.

[30] *In re World Com Inc Sec. Litig* (2005) 388 F Supp 2d 319 (SDNY) 322-335, where the total settlement amount for market abuse and other related securities law violations was approximately $6 133 000 000 plus interest. See further Coffee 2007 *University of Pennsylvania Law Review* 230-311.

[31] Coffee 2007 *University of Pennsylvania Law Review* 230-311.

[32] As earlier stated, the SEC has, on a number of instances, relied on its MOUs and help from fellow IOSCO member countries to track and impose appropriate sanctions against market abuse offenders in the US and other jurisdictions. See Coffee 2007 *University of Pennsylvania Law Review* 230-311 & Karpoff, Lee & Martin "The Legal Penalties for Financial Misrepresentation" (2007) <http://www.ssrn.com/abstract =933333> (accessed 28-09-2013).

[33] Figure 1 was adapted from <http://www.sec.gov/spotlight/insidertrading.shtml> (accessed 30-11-2013).

Figure 1: Overview of the SEC's annual anti-insider trading enforcement statistics from 2004 to 2010.

Adapted from the SEC website.[34]

On the other hand, the Financial Services Board (FSB)[35] has almost similar functions as those of the SEC.[36] Put differently, the FSB, like the SEC, bears the main responsibility to oversee and enforce the securities and market abuse laws in South Africa. It is not very clear whether the FSB is also statutorily responsible for enforcing the prohibition on commodities-based market manipulation in South Africa. Moreover, there is no specific regulatory body like the CFTC[37] which is statutorily authorised to deal effectively and exclusively with the commodities-based market manipulation violations in South Africa.[38] Strikingly, this flaw has still not been corrected by the Financial

---

[34] <http://www.sec.gov/spotlight/insidertrading.shtml> (accessed 30-11-2013); notably, figure 1 indicates a relatively high number of insider trading enforcement actions that were successfully and consistently instituted against the offenders each year, from 2004 to 2010. Also see Fons & Rowe "The SEC Speaks: Aggressive Enforcement to Intensify in 2011" *Morrison & Foerster Client Alert* 09 February 2011 1-5 & Morgan Lewis 2010 7-13 http://www.morganlewis.com/ lit_SECandYearly ReviewWP_Jan2010.pdf (accessed 10-06-2013).

[35] S 84 of the Financial Markets Act 19 of 2012 (Financial Markets Act). Notably, the FSB is set to be replaced by the Financial Sector Conduct Authority (FSCA) when the Financial Sector Regulation Act 9 of 2017 (Financial Sector Regulation Act) comes into effect, see ss 56 to 72 of the same Act.

[36] S 84 of the Financial Markets Act.

[37] See related remarks above.

[38] See generally ss 78; 80; 81 & 82 of the Financial Markets Act. In relation to this, it is submitted that either the FSB or the JSE should be statutorily empowered to exclusively deal with the enforcement and prohibition of commodities-based market abuse practices in the relevant South African financial markets.

Markets Act.[39] Like the SEC,[40] the FSB also has quasi-legislative (rulemaking) authority.[41] The FSB may, for instance, make market abuse rules after consulting with the Directorate of Market Abuse (DMA).[42]

In addition, the FSB exercises administrative and supervisory authority over the DMA, the Enforcement Committee (EC) and other relevant securities market participants. In spite of these positive developments, most of the market abuse rules that could be made by the FSB are only limited to the general manner in which its administrative powers and roles should be conducted.[43] To ensure more compliance and to enhance the enforcement of the market abuse ban, the FSB delegates some of its roles to the DMA, the Johannesburg Stock Exchange Limited (JSE) and the EC. The DMA[44] deals primarily with the market abuse investigations, the JSE offers surveillance support for the detection of market abuse activity and the EC oversees the enforcement of the administrative sanctions.[45] Nevertheless, the FSB does not have its own surveillance systems or other mechanisms like the SEC's EDGAR[46] to detect and prevent market abuse activity in the South African financial markets.[47] In contrast with the SEC,[48] the FSB is still to employ other additional relevant measures to discourage and curb cross-border market abuse activities.[49] Additionally, unlike the SEC,[50] the FSB has not been able to investigate and/or successfully obtain timeous enforcement settlements consistently in market abuse cases as evidenced in figure 2 and table 2 below.

[39] See ss 78; 80; 81; 82 & 84.

[40] See related remarks above.

[41] S 84(2)(f) of the Financial Markets Act.

[42] S 84(2)(f) of the Financial Markets Act.

[43] In contrast to the SEC, the FSB does not have express or actual authority to make (quasi-judicial powers) additional binding rules that it reasonably believe are necessary for the effective enforcement of the market abuse prohibition in South Africa. S 84(2)(f) of the Financial Markets Act.

[44] S 85 of the Financial Markets Act.

[45] S 99 of the Financial Markets Act & ss 6A to 6I of the the Financial Institutions (Protection of Funds) Act 28 of 2001 as amended (Protection of Funds Act).

[46] See related remarks above.

[47] In relation to this, the FSB should consider following the SEC approach of devoting more competent persons to deal specifically with the enforcement of the market abuse prohibition in South Africa.

[48] See related remarks above.

[49] Generally see the FSB *Annual Report* 2011 4 99-101; the FSB *Annual Report* 2013 3 128-130.

[50] See related remarks above.

Figure 2: The FSB's anti-market abuse enforcement statistics from 1999 to 2010.

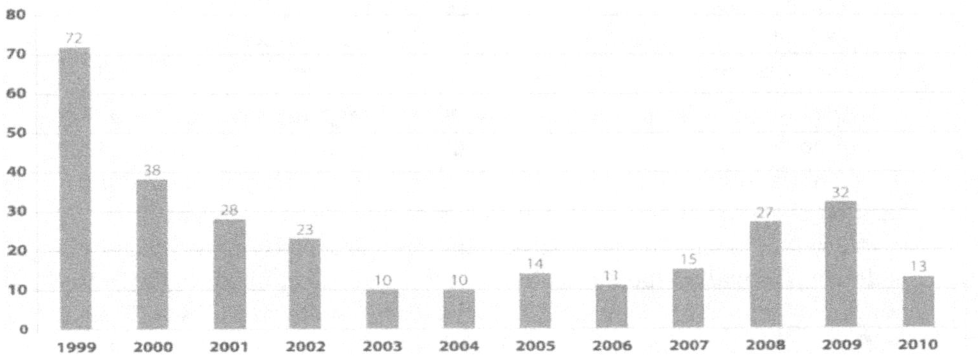

Adapted from the FSB's 2011 Annual Report.[51]

Table 2: The FSB's annual anti-market abuse enforcement statistics of new cases from 1999 to 2010.

	1999	2000	2001	2002	2003	2004	2005	2006	2007	2008	2009	2010	Total
Brought forward	-	37	26	32	17	12	12	22	14	15	13	22	222
New cases	66	35	25	21	19	8	11	20	16	19	21	23	284
Completed cases	(29)	(46)	(19)	(36)	(24)	(8)	(1)	(28)	(15)	(21)	(12)	(20)	(259)
Carried forward	**37**	**26**	**32**	**17**	**12**	**12**	**22**	**14**	**15**	**13**	**22**	**25**	**247**

Adapted from the FSB's 2011 Annual Report.[52]

The FSB has continued to obtain relatively minimal successful prosecutions and settlements in market abuse-related cases from the period between 2011 and 2017.[53]

---

[51] See the FSB *Annual Report* 2011 99-101. Notably, figure 2 indicates a sharp and inconsistent decline in new cases of market abuse that were successfully investigated each year, from 1999 to 2010. See further the FSB *Annual Report* 2013 128-130.

[52] See the FSB *Annual Report* 2011 99-101. Table 2 indicates that very few cases were successfully investigated while many cases were either brought forward or carried forward each year, from 1999 to 2010. Also see the FSB *Annual Report* 2013 128-130.

[53] *Pather and Another v Financial Services Board and Others (57617/10)* 208; *Zietsman v Director of Market Abuse* 218; the DMA "Past Investigations" *DMA Media Release* 23 June 2015, 1 1-11; the DMA "Report by the Directorate of Market Abuse" *FSB Media Release* 30 March 2016, 1 1-3; the DMA "Report by the Directorate of Market Abuse" *FSB Press Release* 31 March 2017, 1 1-3.

4 2 2 The Role of the Department of Justice and the Courts

Notably, the DOJ or the federal courts have the prerogative to enforce the criminal sanctions for market abuse in the USA.[54] Nevertheless, the DOJ may only prosecute any criminal cases for market abuse referred to it by the SEC.[55]

In spite of this referral procedure, the DOJ and the federal courts play a very important role in the enforcement of the market abuse prohibition in the USA. This is supported in part by the current rigorous enforcement and prosecution of such practices in the USA's competent courts. In other words, the significant number of reported cases indicates that such courts are effectively enforcing the market abuse prohibition in the USA. For example, in the Drexel Burnham Lambert scandal of 1990, Kimba Wood J sentenced Michael Milken to ten years imprisonment or a criminal fine of $200 million and ordered him to pay a $400 million civil disgorgement of profits fine. Dennis Levine was sentenced to two years in prison, or a fine of $11, 5 million while Ivan F. Boesky was sentenced to three years imprisonment, or a fine of $50 million. Milken eventually paid the criminal fine of $200 million and $400 million civil disgorgement profits fine. Dennis Levine paid the $11, 5 million civil disgorgement of profits fine and Ivan F. Boesky later paid the $50 million civil disgorgement fine and an additional $50 million civil penalty.[56]

In *US v O'Hagan*[57] the accused person's plea of not guilty to insider trading charges was rejected and it was held that the breach of a fiduciary duty by corporate insiders could further involve the breach of a duty of trust and confidence on the part of such insiders or other shareholders of a corporation whose securities are traded. Moreover, in *The Trane Company v O'Connor Securities*[58] it was held that market manipulation should be discouraged and prohibited to promote open and free markets which allow natural forces of supply and demand to determine the prices of securities. This was also

---

[54] Put differently, the DOJ oversees the enforcement of the criminal sanctions for market abuse by the competent federal courts. Such competent courts include the US's federal district courts, High courts and Supreme courts. Palmiter *Securities Regulation* 370.

[55] This implies that the DOJ may only institute criminal proceedings against any person who knowingly engages in market abuse practices on a referral basis. See further s 32(a) of the Securities Exchange Act.

[56] Tomasic "Insider Trading in the USA and United Kingdom" 1991 *Australian Studies in Law, Crime and Justice Series* 31 35-39.

[57] (1997) 521 US 642, O'Hagan was convicted on all counts of fraud, securities violation and money laundering and sentenced to prison. Nonetheless, this conviction was later reversed by the Supreme Court on the basis that misappropriation did not violate Rule 10b-5; see further Palmiter *Securities Regulation* 361-362.

[58] (1983) 561 F Supp 301 (SDNY) 304. See further Cassim "An Analysis of Market Manipulation under the Securities Services Act 36 of 2004 (Part 1)" 2008 *SA Merc LJ* 33 37.

echoed in *United States v Brown,*[59] which postulated that market manipulation negatively affects the price of listed securities and, in so doing, it misleads and prejudices outside investors.

The successful prosecution of market abuse practices involving World Com, Martha Stewart, Tyco, Parmalat and Enron cases is further testimony of the effectiveness and competence of the USA's federal courts.[60] For example, the former Enron Executives, Jeffrey Skilling and Ken Lay, were convicted for insider trading and other market abuse violations. On 26 May 2006 Ken Lay was convicted on six counts of conspiracy and fraud and sentenced to 45 years in prison while Jeffrey Skilling was found guilty on 19 counts of conspiracy, fraud, making false statements and insider trading and sentenced to 185 years in prison.[61] On 23 October 2006, Skilling was criminally convicted on further counts of insider trading and sentenced to an additional imprisonment term of 25 years. The effectiveness of these courts has been made possible, in part, by the necessary government support and the available resources, as well as the fact that competent personnel was allocated to them.[62]

As stated above, the DOJ and the competent courts play a major role in enforcing the market abuse ban in the USA. Federal courts have to date managed to radically and rigorously prosecute a number of cases involving market abuse practices like insider trading and market manipulation.[63] The courts have further imposed about 2262 permanent injunctions against individuals and another 321 injunctions against companies (juristic persons) between the years 1978 and 2004.[64] About 574 executive persons were barred from working as officers and directors of public corporations and 415 were barred from serving as financial professionals by both the SEC and the courts during the same period.[65] Furthermore, about 755 individuals and 40 companies were indicated, 543 of the individuals were convicted and only ten were acquitted. Moreover, the DOJ formed the Corporate Fraud Task Force (CFTF) and conse-

---

[59] (1933) 5 F Supp 81 (SDNY) 85; 325. It was further held that the use of "wash sales" should be discouraged because it usually involves the publication of information regarding the buyer and the seller's securities transactions (share prices) which would be deceptive, false or misleading. See further *Santa Fe Industries Inc v Green* (1977) 430 US 462 476.

[60] Avgouleas *The Mechanics and Regulation of Market Abuse* 171; 210.

[61] See the judgement of the US District Court SD Texas Houston Division in the case of in *re Enron Corporation Securities Derivative and "ERISA"Litigation Plaintiffs v Enron Corp Oregon Corporation Defendants* (2006) WL 2795321 (SD Tex).

[62] The federal courts have also successfully prosecuted market manipulation practices. See *US v Milken (1990) 759 F Supp 109 (SDNY); US v Mulheren (1991) 938 F2d 364 (2nd Cir).*

[63] This is evidenced in part, by the successful criminal prosecution of the World Com case, where the DOJ recovered a criminal fine of $27 million and prosecuted its CEO (Bernard Ebbers), its CFO (Scott Sullivan) and four others, resulting in combined in imprisonment terms of 32.4 years and $49.2 million in restitution.

[64] *Coffee 2007 University of Pennsylvania Law Review* 230-311.

[65] *Coffee 2007 University of Pennsylvania Law Review* 230-311.

quently, a number of market abuse activities have been successfully detected and prosecuted to date.[66] In light of this, one can conclude that the USA has so far been fairly successful in combating market abuse and other illicit practices. However, there is no empirical evidence that explicitly indicates that market abuse activities have either been significantly reduced or completely eradicated in the USA's financial markets as a result of deterrence and/or effective enforcement.[67]

Contrary to the position in the USA,[68] it has already been pointed out that very few cases of market abuse have, to date, been successfully prosecuted and settled in South Africa.[69] Moreover, unlike the USA's DOJ and courts,[70] the Director of Public Prosecutions (DPP) and the competent courts in South Africa have, to some extent, struggled to obtain more convictions in market abuse cases to date.[71] Notwithstanding the efforts being made by the FSB to refer the criminal cases of market abuse to the DPP for prosecution, only a few competent courts[72] have jurisdiction to hear such cases. This has, to some extent, restricted or resulted in delays in the prosecution of some market abuse cases in South Africa.[73] Moreover, some of the market abuse cases that were referred to the DPP by the FSB are still pending while others have either

[66] The CFTF was formed in 2002 and since its inception over 1300 persons have been charged with insider trading, fraud or other related market abuse activities and about1000 were convicted. Coffee 2007 *University of Pennsylvania Law Review* 230-311; also see related comments and analysis contained in the press release by the DOJ "US Department of Justice, Fact Sheet: Corporate Fraud Task Force" (2006) <http://www.usdoj.gov.opa/pr/2006/August/06_odag_525.html> (accessed 12-02-2014).

[67] Coffee 2007 *University of Pennsylvania Law Review* 230-311.

[68] See related comments above.

[69] Cassim 2008 *SA Merc LJ* 33-37.

[70] See related comments above.

[71] Notwithstanding the fact that Bloomberg News published a story on 11 April 2007, stating that the FSB was investigating and/or has reported to the DPP the alleged market manipulation caused by an unknown American business consortium after making a substantial offer of $12, 5 billion for Gold Fields Limited resulting in 11% increase in its shares and adding about R10 billion to the market value of Gold Fields Limited shares. See Brown "Gold Fields Zooms 11% on Bid Talk" *Business Report* 12 April 2007 1. This story was unfortunately somewhat false and misleading, for example, as at 13 April 2007, the JSE had since the enactment of the now repealed Securities Services Act 36 of 2004 only referred about seven cases of market manipulation to the FSB and/or the DPP for further investigation and possible prosecution by the courts. No convictions were obtained by the South African competent courts in all these cases. This may further indicate that market abuse practices are still difficult to investigate and prosecute in South Africa. See report by Brown "FSB may Probe Bloomberg Story on Gold Fields" *Business Report* 13 April 2007 1; also see Cassim 2008 *SA Merc LJ* 34.

[72] S 84(10) & other relevant provisions of the Financial Markets Act.

[73] This could be worsened by the fact that the Financial Markets Act does not have provisions that empower or establish more courts to specifically adjudicate or deal with market abuse cases in South Africa. See generally s 84(10) & other relevant provisions under Chapter X of the Financial Markets Act.

been withdrawn or abandoned, possibly because of insufficient evidence and the backlog of other cases in the relevant courts.[74]

4 2 3 The Role of Other Selected Self-Regulatory Organisations

Although individual persons are entitled to claim their damages directly from the offenders in private litigation, the self-regulatory organisations have to date played a key role in the civil enforcement of the market abuse prohibition and speedy provision of appropriate remedies to all the affected persons in the USA.

As stated above,[75] the SEC, through its Market Regulation Division, has a broad Congressional mandate to oversee the day-to-day regulation of securities market participants by the self-regulatory organisations like the NYSE, the NASD, the MSRMB and other broker-dealer companies and investment houses.[76] Therefore, the SEC inspects the self-regulatory organisations and performs targeted oversight examinations of their broker-dealer members to determine whether such self-regulatory organisations are effectively supervising the financial regulations and business practices of their members.[77]

The NASD administers the registration of new issuers of securities and has the authority to promulgate rules governing voluntary membership of broker-dealers in over the counter markets such as the NASD Automated Quotation System.[78] In order to improve the enforcement of securities laws and to curb market abuse activity among its members, the NASD divided itself into two subsidiaries, namely the NASD Regulation Inc[79] and the NASD Automated Quotation System Public Market Inc.[80] Each of these subsidiaries has its own independent board of directors.[81] The NASD s has further authority to make

---

[74] See the FSB *Annual Report* 2011 99-101; the FSB *Annual Report* 2013 128-130; the DMA *FSB Press Release* 31 March 2017 1-3. Moreover, the DPP is still to ensure that the competent courts are manned by sufficient people with the relevant expertise in order to obtain more prosecutions and settlements in market abuse cases referred to them by the FSB.

[75] See paragraph 4 2 1 above.

[76] Palmiter *Securities Regulation* 31; Hazen *Federal Securities Law* 5-9.

[77] Put differently, the SEC may approve or amend the rules of the self-regulatory organisations in accordance with the public interest and/or to enhance the combating of illicit market abuse activities like insider trading, market manipulation and the deceptive or misleading filing with the SEC, of any statements, documents or accounts. Palmiter *Securities Regulation* 433-434 & 439.

[78] S 15(b)(8) read with s 15A of the Securities Exchange Act (as amended). Also see Palmiter *Securities Regulation* 404.

[79] The NASD Regulation Inc oversees the regulatory functions of the NASD.

[80] Likewise, the NASD Automated Quotation System Public Market Inc runs the NASD Automated Quotation System.

[81] Palmiter *Securities Regulation* 404; Lastra "The Governance Structure for Financial Regulation and Supervision in Europe" 2003 *Colum J Eur L* 49 53.

rules aimed at preventing market abuse activities by market participants like research and financial market analysts.[82]

Moreover, the NYSE is the largest securities exchange in the USA responsible for monitoring the public trading of listed securities to minimise the occurrence of potential market abuse practices in the USA's financial markets. This is done by operating special computerised devices and surveillance systems to detect and prevent market abuse practices. The NYSE is further empowered to make rules or to take other action reasonably necessary to discourage market abuse activities in the USA's financial markets.[83]

The NYSE and the NASD merged to form the Financial Industry Regulatory Authority (FINRA) in 2007.[84] In 2009, the FINRA created the Office of Fraud Detection and Market Intelligence, the Office of the Whistle-blower, the Office of Disciplinary Affairs and the Central Review Group for the speedy investigation of any suspected violations and to review tips from whistle-blowers in order to root out fraud, insider trading, market manipulation and other related market abuse practices in the USA's financial markets.[85]

The MSRMB was established in 1975 to supervise the companies involved in the underwriting and trading of municipal securities. Although its rules are usually monitored and enforced by the SEC, the MSRMB is authorised to make its own additional market abuse enforcement rules and to impose any appropriate action against the securities laws (including State Blue Sky Laws) and market abuse violators.[86]

Against this background, it is evident that the self-regulatory organisations have contributed immensely towards the effective enforcement of securities laws to curb market abuse and other illicit trading practices in the USA. In addition to the self-regulatory organisations, there are currently more than ten federal, state and industry regulatory bodies in the USA. This suggests that there is good competition among the regulators to regulate certain securities products and the industry effectively and efficiently.[87] Accordingly, self-

[82] See the NASD Rule 2711; also see Palmiter *Securities Regulation* 414.
[83] See the NYSE Rule 472; also see Palmiter *Securities Regulation* 414; 492.
[84] See generally related analysis and comments by Morgan Lewis 2010 4-6 & 65-68 http://www.morganlewis.com/lit_SECandYearlyReviewWP_Jan2010.pdf (accessed 10-06-2013).
[85] Accordingly, about 1103 enforcement actions were successfully instituted against the offenders; 20 companies were expelled; 363 individuals were suspended and several monetary fines were recovered by the FINRA in over 73 cases during the period between 2008 and 2009. See further Morgan Lewis 2010 4-6 & 65-69 <http://www.morganlewis. com/lit_SECandYearlyReviewWP_Jan2010.pdf> (accessed 10-06-2013); see further the FINRA "2008 Year in Review and Annual Financial Report" (2008) 9 <http://www.finra.org> (accessed 02-03-2014).
[86] Palmiter *Securities Regulation* 34-35.
[87] This multi-functional regulatory approach has to date resulted in far greater market abuse enforcement in the USA.

regulatory organisations like the CFTC, the NASD, the NYSE and the FINRA may impose their own civil or administrative penalties against any person who violates the federal securities laws by engaging in market abuse and other illegal activities.[88] This allows the USA's market abuse regime to bring multiple enforcement actions against the offenders in all its financial markets.[89]

In South Africa, apart from the FSB and its committees, other regulatory bodies like the JSE may also enforce the market abuse ban. Accordingly, like the SEC,[90] the FSB may exercise supervisory authority over all the regulatory bodies that deal with market abuse in South Africa.[91] Thus, as stated before,[92] the FSB has the prerogative to make market abuse rules that govern the enforcement of market abuse laws in South Africa.[93] Apart from the FSB and the JSE, there are no self-regulatory organisations that are specifically responsible for enforcing market abuse laws in South Africa.[94] In relation to this, there is no specific provision in the Financial Markets Act which empowers other self-regulatory organisations to enforce the market abuse ban in South Africa.[95] While this approach is good in that it minimises bureaucracy, balkanisation, conflict of interests and confusion that may be associated with many regulatory bodies and self-regulatory organisations, it has not been fully utilised to obtain more settlements and prosecutions of market abuse cases in South Africa to date.[96]

4 3 Concluding Remarks

It was noted that both the USA and the South African market abuse regimes maintain similar enforcement goals and missions.[97] In spite of this, they adopt and implement very different approaches to achieve their enforcement

---

[88] See related comments above; also see Coffee 2007 *University of Pennsylvania Law Review* 230-311.

[89] In relation to this, the CFTC has to date managed to impose a variety of sanctions on the perpetrators of commodities-based market abuse practices in the USA. See the CFTC "About the Commodity Futures Trading Commission" (2006) <http://www.cftc.gov/cftcabout.htm> (accessed 07-10-2013); Also see the SEC "SEC, 2006 Performance and Accountability" (2006) *Report* 8 <http://www.sec.gov/about/secpar/secpar2006.pdf> (accessed 21-02-2014) & the SEC "SEC, 2005 Performance and Accountability" (2005) *Report* 7 <http://www.sec.gov/about/secpar/secpar2005.pdf> (accessed 21-02-2014).

[90] See paragraph 4 2 1 & other related remarks above.

[91] See related remarks in paragraph 4 2 1 above.

[92] See related remarks in paragraph 4 2 1 above.

[93] S 84(2)(f) of the Financial Markets Act. This implies that other regulatory bodies like the DMA do not have express statutory authority to make their own independent market abuse rules regarding the enforcement of market abuse laws in South Africa.

[94] The Financial Markets Act mainly empowers only the FSB to police the regulation and enforcement of market abuse ban in South Africa. See s 84.

[95] See relevant provisions in Chapter X entitled Market Abuse of the Financial Markets Act.

[96] See related remarks in paragraphs 4 2 1 & 4 2 2 above.

[97] See paragraphs 4 2 1; 4 2 2 & 4 2 3 above.

goals and/or targets. Put differently, the USA's anti-market abuse enforcement framework employs the multi-functional regulatory approach which offers competition among the regulatory authorities at a federal level,[98] but nevertheless resulting in far greater and effective enforcement. Moreover, the USA's anti-market abuse enforcement framework provides the much-needed resources, competent personnel in the courts and the SEC as well as better technological surveillance mechanisms to detect illicit trading practices.[99]

On the contrary, notwithstanding the fact that the South African market abuse legislation was relatively influenced by the corresponding legislation in the USA, it sometimes lacks a rigorous practical enforcement approach and infrastructure to combat market abuse activities.[100] Consequently, the DPP should introduce more specialised courts or tribunals that are staffed with judges and other persons with the relevant expertise to hear and/or prosecute market abuse cases in South Africa timeously and effectively. Furthermore, the Protection of Funds Act and/or the Financial Markets Act should be reviewed to enact provisions that expressly empower the EC to make its own market abuse rules to enhance the combating of market abuse practices in South Africa. Lastly, notwithstanding the potentially negative effects of bureaucracy, balkanisation and conflict of interests that may be associated with many regulatory bodies, it is submitted that more self-regulatory organisations should be statutorily empowered to impose their own penalties and/or take any other appropriate action against market abuse offenders in South Africa.

---

[98] See paragraph 4 2 3 read with paragraphs 4 2 1 & 4 2 2 above.

[99] This enhanced and contributed significantly to the success achieved by the USA in the enforcement of the market abuse laws as indicated by a considerable number of cases that were reported and successfully settled or prosecuted to date. See further *SEC v Texas Gulf Sulphur Company* 833; *Dirks v SEC* 646-655; *United States v O'Hagan* 2199; *United States v Falcone* 91 489 & *SEC v Yun* 1263; *SEC v One or more purchasers of call options for the Common Stock of CNS INC* (2006) US District Court 3004875 WL (EDPa) & Dolgopolov "Insider Trading and the Bid-Ask Spread: A Critical Evaluation of Adverse Selection in Market Making" 2004 *Capital University Law Review* 83 84.

[100] See paragraph 4 2 2 read with paragraphs 4 2 1 & 4 2 3 above.

References

Books

Ashe TM & Counsell L *Insider Trading: The Tangled Web* (Fourmat Publishing London 1990)

Avgouleas E *The Mechanics and Regulation of Market Abuse: A Legal and Economic Analysis* (Oxford University Press Oxford 2005)

Bainbridge SM *Corporation Law and Economics* (Foundation Press New York 2002)

Beuthin RC and Luiz SM *Beuthin's Basic Company Law* 3rd ed (Butterworths Durban 2000)

Hazen TL *The Law of Securities Regulation: Handbook Series Student Edition* (West Publishing Company St Paul, MN 1985)

Hazen TL *Federal Securities Law* 2nd ed (Federal Judicial Center United States of America 2003)

Lyon GJ & Du Plessis JJ *The Law of Insider Trading in Australia* (The Federation Press Sydney 2005)

Palmiter AR *Securities Regulation: Examples and Explanations* 3rd ed (Aspen Publishers New York 2005)

Swan EJ *Market Abuse Regulation* 1st ed (Oxford University Press United States of America 2006)

Journal articles

Bhattacharya U & Daouk H "The World Price of Insider Trading" 2002 *Journal of Finance* 75-108

Botha D "Control of Insider Trading in South Africa: A Comparative Analysis" 1991 *SA Merc LJ* 1-18

Botha D "Increased Maximum Fine for Insider Trading: A Realistic and Effective Deterrent?" 1990 *SALJ* 504-508

Brummer C "Disruptive Technology and Securities Regulation" 2015 *Fordham Law Review* 977-1052

Carlton DW & Fischel DR "The Regulation of Insider Trading" 1983 *Stanford Law Review* 857-895

Cassim R "An Analysis of Market Manipulation under the Securities Services Act 36 of 2004 (Part 1)" 2008 *SA Merc LJ* 33-60

Cassim R "An Analysis of Market Manipulation under the Securities Services Act 36 of 2004 (Part 2)" 2008 *SA Merc LJ* 177-199

Clifford Chance "Overview of United States and United Kingdom Derivative and Commodity Market Enforcement Regimes" 2016 *Clifford Chance Markets Publication Series* 1-226

Coffee JC "Law and the Market: The Impact of Enforcement" 2007 *University of Pennsylvania Law Review* 229-311

Dolgopolov S "Insider Trading and the Bid-Ask Spread: A Critical Evaluation of Adverse Selection in Market Making" 2004 *Capital University Law Review* 83-180

Dooley MP "Enforcement of Insider Trading Restrictions" 1980 *Virginia Law Review* 1-83

Friedman HM "The Insider Trading and Securities Fraud Enforcement Act of 1988" 1990 *North Carolina Law Review* 465-494

Gilson RJ & Kraakman RH "The Mechanisms of Market Efficiency" 1984 *VA.L.REV* 549-644

Henning JJ & Du Toit S "The Regulation of False Trading, Market Manipulation and Insider Trading" 2000 *Journal for Juridical Science* 155-165

Horwich A "The Origin, Application, Validity and Potential Misuse of Rule 10b5-1" 2007 *The Bus. Lawyer* 913-954

Jooste R "A Critique of the Insider Trading Provisions of the 2004 Securities Services Act" 2006 *SALJ* 437-460

Kaswell SJ "An Insider's View of the Insider Trading and Securities Fraud Enforcement Act" 1989 *Bus.Law* 145-180

Knepper ZT "Examining the Merits of Dual Regulation for Single-Stock Futures: How the Divergent Insider Trading Regimes for Federal Futures and Securities Markets Demonstrate the Necessity for (and Virtual Inevitability of) Dual CFTC-SEC Regulation for Single-Stock Futures" 2004 *Pierce Law Review* 33-47

Langevoort DC & Gulati GM "The Muddled Duty to Disclose under Rule 10b-5" 2004 *Vand L Rev* 1639-1680

Lastra RM "The Governance Structure for Financial Regulation and Supervision in Europe" 2003 *Colum J Eur L* 49-68

Luiz SM "Insider Trading Regulation – If at First You Don't Succeed..." 1999 *SA Merc LJ* 136-151

Luiz SM "Market Abuse and the Enforcement Committee" 2011 *SA Merc LJ* 151-172

Markham JW "'Front-Running'-Insider Trading under the Commodity Exchange Act" 1988 *Cath. U.Review* 69-127

Mossos E "Sarbanes-Oxley goes to Europe: A Comparative Analysis of United States and European Union Corporate Reforms after Enron" 2004 *Currents International Trade Law Journal* 9-22

Nelemans M "Redefining Trade-Based Market Manipulation" 2008 *Valparaiso University Law Review* 1169-1220

Osode PC "The New South African Insider Trading Act: Sound Law Reform or Legislative Overkill?" 2000 *Journal of African Law* 239-263

Osode PC "The Regulation of Insider Trading in South Africa: A Public Choice Perspective" 1999 *African Journal of International and Comparative Law* 688-708

Pearce BD "Broadening Actual Damages in the Context of the Commodities Exchange Act" 2007 *Journal of Law and Policy* 449-483

Pearson TC "When Hedge Funds Betray A Creditor Committee's Fiduciary Role: New Twists on Insider Trading in the International Financial Markets" 2009 *Review of Banking & Financial Law* 165-220

Ryan L "Rule14e-3's Disclose or Abstain Rule and Its Validity under Section 14(e)" 1991 *U. Cin. Law Review* 449-465

Steinberg MI "Insider Trading Regulation–A Comparative Perspective" 2003 *The International Lawyer* 153-171

Tomasic R "Insider Trading in the USA and United Kingdom" 1991 *Australian Studies in Law, Crime and Justice Series* 31-39

Van Deventer G "New Watchdog for Insider Trading" 1999 *FSB Bulletin* 2-3

Van Deventer G "Harnassing Administrative Law in Encouraging Compliance" 2009 *FSB Bulletin* 3-4

Case law

South Africa

Pather and Another v Financial Services Board and Others (57617/10) [2014] 3 All SA 208 (GP)

Pretorius and Another v Natal South Sea Investment Trust 1965 3 SA 410 (W)

Zietsman v Director of Market Abuse 2016 1 SA 218 (GP)

United States of America

Ashmore v CGI Group Inc. (2015) 138 F. Supp. 3d 329 (SDNY)

BP America Inc. (2016) 156 FERC 61,031

Cady, Roberts and Company [1961-1964 Transfer Binder] CCH Fed Sec L Rep 76. 803

Carpenters Pension Trust Fund of St. Louis v Barclays PLC, (2014) 750 F.3d 227 (2d Cir)

Chiarella v United States (1980) 445 US 222

Commodity Futures Trading Comm'n v Moncada (2014) No. 12-cv-8791 (SDNY)

Dirks v SEC (1983) 463 US 646

FMC Corp v Boesky (1988) 852 F2d 981 (7th Cir)

FMC Corp v Boesky (1987) 673 F2d 272 (ND I11)

In re Enron Corporation Securities Derivative and "ERISA"Litigation Plaintiffs v Enron Corp Oregon Corporation Defendants (2006) WL 2795321 (SD Tex)

In re World Com Inc Sec. Litig (2005) 388 F Supp 2d 319 (SDNY)

Santa Fe Industries Inc v Green (1977) 430 US 462

SEC v Anthony Fareri & others (2009) 09 Civ 80360 (SDFla)

SEC v Arthur J Cutillo & others (2009) 09 Civ 9208 (SDNY)

SEC v Boesky (1986) 86 Civ 8767

SEC v Galleon Management & others (2009) 09 Civ 8811(SDNY)

SEC v Levine (1986) 86 Civ 3726 (SDNY) (RO)

SEC v One or more purchasers of call options for the Common Stock of CNS INC (2006) US District Court 3004875 WL (EDPa)

SEC v Texas Gulf Sulphur Company (1968) 401 F2d 833 (2d Cir)

SEC v WorldCom Inc (2003) 02 Civ 4963(JSR)

SEC v Yun (2003) 327 F3d 1263 (11th Cir)

The Trane Company v O'Connor Securities (1983) 561 F Supp 301 (SDNY)
United States v Brown (1933) 5 F Supp 81 (SDNY)
United States v Chestman (1991) 947 F2d 551 (2d Cir)
United States v Falcone [2001 Transfer Binder] 91 489 Fed Sec L Rep CCH (2d Cir)
United States v O'Hagan (1997) 117 (SCt) 2199
US v Martha Stewart and Peter Bacanovic (2006) 433 F3d 273
US v Milken (1990) 759 F Supp 109 (SDNY)
US v Mulheren (1991) 938 F2d 364 (2nd Cir)
US v O`Hagan (1997) 521 US 642

Legislation

South Africa

Companies Act 61 of 1973
Companies Act 71 of 2008
Consumer Protection Act 68 of 2008
Financial Markets Act 19 of 2012
Financial Institutions (Protection of Funds) Act 28 of 2001 as amended
Financial Sector Regulation Act 9 of 2017

United States of America

Commodity Exchange Act of 1936 7 USC 1 *et seq.* (1994)
Commodities Futures Modernization Act 2000 Public Law 106-554, 114 Stat.2763A-365
Commodity Futures Trading Commission Act of 1974 Public Law 93-64, 88 Stat 1398
Derivatives Market Manipulation Prevention Act of 2009
Dodd-Frank Wall Street Reform and Consumer Protection Act of 2010, Public Law 111-203, 124 Stat.1376 (12 USC; s 5301 *et seq.*)
Insider Trading and Securities Fraud Enforcement Act of 1988 Public Law 100-704, 102 Stat 4677
Insider Trading Sanctions Act of 1984 Public Law 98-376, 98 Stat.1264 (1984)
International Securities Enforcement Cooperation Act of 1990
Investment Advisors Act of 1940
Investment Company Act of 1940
Public Company Accounting Reform and Investor Protection Act of 2002 Public Law 107-204, 116 Stat 745 (15; 28 USC)
Public Utility Holding Company Act of 1935
Racketeer Influenced and Corrupt Organization Act of 1970
Securities Act of 1933 Public Law 22 48 Stat 74 15 USC77a-77mm (1994)
Securities Act of 1933, Public Law 22 48 Stat.74 15 USC 77a-77mm *et seq.* (2000)

Securities Act of 1933 15 USC 77q(a) (2006) as amended by PL-111-229 (approved 11-08-2010)

Securities Exchange Act of 1934 Public Law 73-291, 48 Stat 881 15 USC 78a-78II

Securities Exchange Act of 1934 15 USC 78i(a)(2)-(5) (2006) as amended by PL-111-257 (approved 05-10-2010)

Securities Exchange Act Release Number 43154 [2000 Transfer Binder] Fed Sec L Rep CCH 86.319

Trust Indenture Act of 1939

Commissions, committees and reports

South Africa

Financial Services Board *Annual Report* 2011

Financial Services Board *Annual Report* 2013

United States of America

The Commodity Futures Trading Commission & the United States Securities and Exchange Commission "A Joint Report of the SEC and the CFTC on Harmonization of Regulation" *Report* 16 October 2009

Thesis and dissertations

Chitimira H *A Comparative Analysis of the Enforcement of Market Abuse Provisions* (LLD-thesis Nelson Mandela Metropolitan University 2012)

Chitimira H *The Regulation of Insider Trading in South Africa: A Roadmap for an Effective, Competitive and Adequate Regulatory Statutory Framework* (LLM-dissertation University of Fort Hare 2008)

Conference papers, media releases and other relevant material

Fons RJ & Rowe TA "The SEC Speaks: Aggressive Enforcement to Intensify in 2011" *Morrison & Foerster Client Alert* 09 February 2011

Morrison & Foerster "Insider Trading" 2010 *Year End Review* 1

SEC "SEC Files Fraud Charges in Bitcoin and Office Space Investment Schemes" *Press Release 2017-123* 30 June 2017

SEC "Law Firm Partner and Neighbor Charged in $1 Million Insider Trading Scheme" *Press Release 2017-100* 11 May 2017

SEC "SEC Freezes Brokerage Accounts Behind Alleged Insider Trading" *Press Release 2017-80* 14 April 2017

SEC "Investment Bank VP Charged With Insider Trading" *Press Release 2017-83* 24 April 2017

SEC "SEC Announces Charges in Hamilton Ticket Resale Ponzi Scheme" *Press Release 2017-37* 27 January 2017

SEC "Brokerage Firm Charged With Gatekeeper Failures Related to Pump-and-Dump Scheme" *Press Release 2017-33* 25 January 2017

SEC "Morgan Stanley, Citigroup Charged With Misleading Investors About Forex Trading Program" *Press Release 2017-30* 24 January 2017

SEC "SEC Charges Fake Filer With Manipulating Fitbit Stock" *Press Release 2017-107* 19 May 2017

SEC "SEC Charges Brokerage Firm With Failing to Comply With Anti-Money Laundering Laws" *Press Release 2017-112* 5 June 2017

SEC "Overseas Traders Paying Back All Profits Plus Penalties in Insider Trading Case" *Press Release 2017-70* 24 March 2017

Newspaper reports

Brown J "Gold Fields Zooms 11% on Bid Talk" *Business Report* (2007-04-12)

Brown J "FSB may Probe Bloomberg Story on Gold Fields" *Business Report* (2007-04-13)

Chanetsa B "Insider Trading is Notoriously Hard to Prosecute" *Business Report* (2004-04-26)

Internet sources

Commodity Futures Trading Commission "About the Commodity Futures Trading Commission" (2006) <http://www.cftc.gov/cftcabout.htm> (accessed 07-10-2013)

Department of Justice "US Department of Justice, Fact Sheet: Corporate Fraud Task Force" (2006) <http://www.usdoj.gov.opa/pr/2006/August/06_odag_525.html> (accessed 12-02-2014)

Financial Industry Regulatory Authority "2008 Year in Review and Annual Financial Report" (2008) <http://www.finra.org> (accessed 02-03-2014)

Financial Services Board "Enforcement Committee Actions" *Media Release* (28-06-2011) <http://www.fsb.co.za/ftp://ftp.fsb.co.za/public/documents/AReport2011.pdf> (accessed 22-11-2013)

Financial Services Board "List of Current Investigations of the Directorate of Market Abuse" *Media Release* (28-06-2011) <http://www.fsb.co.za/ftp://ftp.fsb.co.za/public/documents/AReport2011.pdf> (accessed 22-11-2013)

Karpoff JM, Lee DS & Martin GS "The Legal Penalties for Financial Misrepresentation" (2007) <http://www.ssrn.com/abstract=933333> (accessed 28-09-2013)

Morgan Lewis "2009 Year in Review: SEC and SRO Selected Enforcement Cases and Developments Regarding Broker-Dealers" 2010 <http://www.morganlewis.com/lit_SECandYearlyReviewWP_Jan2010.pdf> (accessed 10-06-2013)

Myburgh A & Davis B "The Impact of South Africa's Insider Trading Regime: A Report for the Financial Services Board" (25-03-2004) <http://www.genesis-analytics.com/public/FSBReport.pdf> (accessed 09-02-2013)

United States Securities and Exchange Commission "SEC, 2006 Performance and Accountability" (2006) *Report 8* <http://www.sec.gov/about/secpar/secpar2006.pdf> (accessed 21-02-2014)

United States Securities and Exchange Commission "SEC, 2005 Performance and Accountability" (2005) *Report 7* <http://www.sec.gov/about/secpar/secpar2005.pdf> (accessed 21-02-2014)

Van Deventer G "Anti-Market Abuse Legislation in South Africa" (10-06-2008) <http://www.fsb.co.za/public/marketabuse/FSBReport.pdf> (accessed 05-05-2013)

Chapter 5

The Establishment of Anti-Market Abuse Preventative Measures in the United States of America and South Africa

5 1 Introduction

A number of anti-market abuse preventative enforcement approaches and measures are employed in the United States of America (USA). Put differently, the USA has to date successfully developed and adopted several distinct enforcement approaches and preventative measures to combat market abuse[1] activities in all its capital and financial markets.[2] For instance, apart from relying on civil, criminal and administrative penalties, the USA anti-market abuse enforcement framework also employs a co-ordinated (joint) enforcement effort between the courts, self-regulatory organisations and the United States Securities and Exchange Commission (SEC) at a federal level.[3] Furthermore, other preventative measures such as private actions, public censure, bounty rewards and whistle-blower immunity are utilised to discourage and curb market abuse activities in the USA.[4] In light of this, the chapter examines whether the integration of some of these USA's anti-market abuse enforcement approaches and preventative measures will improve the

---

* This chapter is influenced in part, by an article that was initially published in the *Mediterranean Journal of Social Sciences*. The work was done with legal permission from the editors, see Chitimira "Aspects of the Establishment and Enforcement of Anti-Market Abuse Preventative Measures in the United States of America" 2014(5)(7) *Mediterranean Journal of Social Sciences* 253-262.

[1] Market abuse is a "generic term" that refers to insider trading and market manipulation in this chapter.

[2] See generally Steinberg "Insider Trading Regulation–A Comparative Perspective" 2003 *The International Lawyer* 153 169-171.

[3] Steinberg 2003 *The International Lawyer* 169-171.

[4] SEC "Whistleblower Award of More Than Half-Million Dollars for Company Insider" *Press Release 2017-90* 2 May 2017; Steinberg 2003 *The International Lawyer* 169-171. For further related comparative analysis in other countries, see Bhattacharya & Daouk "The World Price of Insider Trading" 2002 *Journal of Finance* 75 75-108; Lyon & Du Plessis *The Law of Insider Trading in Australia* (2005) 159-168; Avgouleas *The Mechanics and Regulation of Market Abuse: A Legal and Economic Analysis* (2005) 75-502; Botha "Control of Insider Trading in South Africa: A Comparative Analysis" 1991 *SA Merc LJ* 1 1-18; Botha "Increased Maximum Fine for Insider Trading: A Realistic and Effective Deterrent?" 1990 *SALJ* 504 504-508; Chitimira *The Regulation of Insider Trading in South Africa: A Roadmap for an Effective, Competitive and Adequate Regulatory Statutory Framework* (Unpublished LLM dissertation, University of Fort Hare) 2008, 41–72.

enforcement of the market abuse prohibition in South Africa.[5] Accordingly, selected preventative measures and enforcement approaches that are adopted in the USA will be discussed and, where appropriate, contrasted with similar measures and/or enforcement methods in South Africa so as to identify and recommend possible enforcement approaches that could be incorporated in the South African anti-market enforcement framework. Therefore, the co-operation between the SEC, the Department of Justice (DOJ) and the courts is discussed first. Thereafter, the co-operation between the SEC and other selected self-regulatory organisations is analysed. Lastly, the adoption and establishment of a good enforcement ethics culture in the USA will be examined.

---

[5] Chitimira "Unpacking Selected Key Elements of the Insider Trading and Market Manipulation Offences in South Africa" 2016 *Journal of Corporate and Commercial Law and Practice* 24 24-41; Chitimira "Overview of the Market Abuse Regulation under the Financial Markets Act 19 of 2012" 2014 *Obiter* 254 254-271; see further Loubser "Insider Trading and other Market Abuses (Including the Effective Management of Price–sensitive Information)" in the *Insider Trading Booklet* final draft, (2006) 18-20; 24-27 <http://www.jse.co.za/public/insider/JSEbooklet.pdf> (accessed 03-03-2014); the Johannesburg Stock Exchange Limited (JSE) "Insider Trading and other Market Abuses (Including the Effective Management of Price–sensitive Information)" in the *Insider Trading Booklet,* (2013) 1-26 <http://www.jse.co.za/Libraries/JSE_Regulatory_Environment_Insider_Trading/InsiderTrading_Bo oklet.sflb.ashx> (accessed 03-03-2014); Chitimira "A Historical Overview of the Regulation of Market Abuse in South Africa" 2014 *PER Journal* 937 938-965; Chitimira "The Regulation of Market Manipulation in Australia: A Historical Comparative Perspective" 2015 *PER Journal* 112 112-134; Chitimira *A Comparative Analysis of the Enforcement of Market Abuse Provisions* (Unpublished LLD thesis, Nelson Mandela Metropolitan University) 2012, 230-257; Van Deventer "Anti-Market Abuse Legislation in South Africa" (10-06-2008) 1-5 <http://www.fsb. co.za/public/marketabuse/FSBReport.pdf> (accessed 05-05-2013); Myburgh & Davis "The Impact of South Africa's Insider Trading Regime: A Report for the Financial Services Board" (25-03-2004) 8-33 <http://www.genesis-analytics.com/ public/ FSBReport.pdf> (accessed 09-02-2013); Chanetsa "Insider Trading is Notoriously Hard to Prosecute" (2004-04-26) *Business Report* page number unknown; *Pretorius and Another v Natal South Sea Investment Trust* 1965 3 SA 410 (W), were the courts failed to convict the suspected insider trading offenders; Blincoe "Datatec Directors Pay Up on Insider Trading Charges" (2001) <http://www.theregister.co.uk/2001/05/23/datatec_directors _pay_up/> (accessed 03-03-2014), where two Datatec directors, Jens Montanana and Robin Rindel were reportedly fined about R1 million each for insider trading by the Financial Services Board (FSB); Barron "Greg Draws a Blank in Belfort Parallel" (2014) <http://www.timeslive.co.za/Feeds/2014/02/02/greg-draws-a-blank-in-belfort-parallel> (accessed 03-03-2014), where Greg Blank was reportedly sentenced to eight years imprisonment for stock market-related fraud and front running in 1992; Osode "The New South African Insider Trading Act: Sound Law Reform or Legislative Overkill?" 2000 *Journal of African Law* 239 239-263; Jooste "A Critique of the Insider Trading Provisions of the 2004 Securities Services Act" 2006 *SALJ* 437 441–460; Van Deventer "New Watchdog for Insider Trading" 1999 *FSB Bulletin* 2 3; Beuthin & Luiz *Beuthin's Basic Company Law* (2000) 235–238; Luiz "Market Abuse and the Enforcement Committee" 2011 *SA Merc LJ* 151-172; Luiz "Insider Trading Regulation – If at First You Don't Succeed…" 1999 *SA Merc LJ* 136 136-151; Henning & Du Toit "The Regulation of False Trading, Market Manipulation and Insider Trading" 2000 *Journal for Juridical Science* 155 155-165 & Osode "The Regulation of Insider Trading in South Africa: A Public Choice Perspective" 1999 *African Journal of International and Comparative Law* 688 688-708.

5 2 Co-operation between Enforcement Authorities and the Adoption of Adequate Preventative Measures

5 2 1 Co-operation between the SEC, the DOJ and the Courts

The enforcement of the anti-market abuse prohibition has always been a co-operative and collaborative effort of the SEC and enforcement authorities in the USA. In other words, the success and effectiveness of the USA's market abuse regime has been attributed to a number of factors including, *inter alia*, the excellent co-operative enforcement effort of the SEC, DOJ and the courts. The SEC and the DOJ are mainly responsible for the civil and criminal enforcement of the market abuse prohibition respectively.[6] The DOJ may prosecute all criminal cases of market abuse referred to it by the SEC. This *prima facie* indicates that there is some co-operation between the SEC and the DOJ. The competent courts in the USA have, in most instances and on the advice of the SEC, successfully instituted criminal proceedings against the persons accused of committing market abuse offences.[7]

The DOJ revised its rules of engagement for pursuing suspected securities law offenders in 2003 and its focus was now mainly on improving the skills and expertise of prosecutors and other officials of the courts, especially, with regard to the combating of corporate crimes such as market abuse. Furthermore, the DOJ revised its co-operation-credit policies to enhance co-operation with the SEC and to guide its members of staff on how to investigate, charge or prosecute securities law violations and market abuse cases referred to it by the SEC.[8] The SEC further released its enforcement manual in 2008[9] which, *inter alia*, seeks to increase the investigations and prosecutions of market abuse cases by both the DOJ and the SEC. This eventually improved the sharing of information between the SEC and the DOJ as well as the parallel enforcement of the market abuse prohibition in the USA.[10]

---

[6] The DOJ and/or the relevant courts are further required to prosecute any criminal cases involving market abuse in private litigation.

[7] See generally related remarks in paragraph 5 1 above; Steinberg 2003 *The International Lawyer* 169-171.

[8] Prior to this, the SEC released the so-called Seaboard Report in 2001 in order to, *inter alia*, improve the disclosure of information regarding the results of any investigation carried by itself or by the Department of Justice. Saikin "SEC, DOJ Clarify Cooperation" <http://www.executivelegaladvisor.com/docs/SEC-DOJ-Clarify-Cooperation.htm> (accessed 28-02-2014).

[9] This is commonly referred to as "the Red Book".

[10] Nevertheless, this co-operative relationship does not allow either the SEC or the DOJ to circumvent the enforcement actions employed by other regulatory bodies like the Commodity Futures Trading Commission (CFTC). Clifford Chance "Overview of United States and United Kingdom Derivative and Commodity Market Enforcement Regimes" 2016 *Clifford Chance Markets Publication Series* 1 8-117.

Moreover, the SEC co-operatively enforces the anti-market abuse laws with the CFTC. The CFTC Division of Enforcement (DOE) is mainly empowered to investigate any market abuse-related practices in respect of the commodities and derivatives markets in the USA. On the other hand, the SEC enforces the federal anti-market abuse laws in respect of the securities and regulated financial markets in the USA. Thus, both the SEC and the CFTC are consistently and co-operatively enforcing the federal anti-market abuse criminal and civil laws in the USA. Precisely, the SEC has continued to co-operatively engage several other federal and state anti-market abuse law enforcement authorities such as the CFTC, the DOJ, the Federal Energy Regulatory Commission (FERC), the Federal Trade Commission (FTC), the New York Attorney General and the Manhattan District Attorney, for the purposes of conducting joint market abuse and investigations in USA.[11] In this regard, the CFTC successfully obtained over 300 requests for assistance and related responses from more than 70 different regulators in terms of its International Organisation of Securities Commission (IOSCO) Multilateral Memorandum of Understanding Concerning Consultation and Cooperation and the Exchange of Information and other information-sharing arrangements during the period between 2014 and 2015.[12]

Although the DOJ has the exclusive authority over the criminal enforcement of the federal securities laws, it often acts with the guidance and assistance from the SEC. In relation to this, the SEC's staff members are sometimes assigned to the DOJ or the courts to facilitate and help in the preparation of market abuse or other corporate criminal cases for trial.[13] On the other hand, the co-operation between the CFTC, the SEC and the DOJ is usually guided and executed in accordance with the Enron Task Force, the Financial Fraud Enforcement Task Force and the Corporate Fraud Task Force which were formed in 2002.[14] The DOJ also relies on the Mutual Legal Assistance Treaty (MLAT)[15] to conduct cross-border market abuse investigations. Precisely, the DOJ's Criminal Division, through its anti-market abuse and/or fraud section, investigates and prosecutes market manipulation, schemes to defraud other persons and related market abuse cases in the USA.[16]

---

[11] Clifford Chance 2016 *Clifford Chance Markets Publication Series* 102-104.

[12] Clifford Chance 2016 *Clifford Chance Markets Publication Series* 103; CFTC "President's Budget and Performance Plan Fiscal Year 2014" *CFTC Press Release* 2014 26; 56.

[13] This clearly shows that the SEC and the DOJ have a good co-operative relationship towards the curbing and prevention of all possible federal securities law violations in the USA. As a result the USA has been fairly successful in investigating and prosecuting several securities law violations and market abuse cases to date.

[14] Clifford Chance 2016 *Clifford Chance Markets Publication Series* 141; 157-158.

[15]18 USC (1984), see s 3292(a); also see Clifford Chance 2016 *Clifford Chance Markets Publication Series* 161.

[16] Clifford Chance 2016 *Clifford Chance Markets Publication Series* 150-153.

Notably, in South Africa, the FSB[17] and the Director of Public Prosecutions (DPP) are also responsible for the civil and criminal enforcement of the market abuse prohibition respectively. Like the position in the USA,[18] the DPP may prosecute criminal cases of market abuse that are referred to it by the FSB in South Africa.[19] However, in contrast to the position in the USA,[20] there is apparently little or minimal co-operation between the FSB and the DPP in South Africa. Put differently, the co-operative enforcement relationship between the FSB and the DPP has not been fully developed and utilised to increase and improve the criminal prosecution of market abuse cases in South Africa.[21]

5 2 2 Co-operation between the SEC and other Self-Regulatory Organisations

The SEC has entered into several co-operative relationships with similar enforcement bodies both at a local and international level in a bid to curb illicit trading practices in the USA's securities and financial markets.[22] The SEC supervises the regulation and enforcement of securities laws by the self-regulatory organisations in the USA.[23] The SEC has authority to approve, amend or revoke any rule or enforcement action imposed by the self-regulatory organisations.[24] This could indicate that the SEC and the self-regulatory organisations have some co-operative relationship which focuses mainly on the enforcement of the federal securities laws to combat market abuse and other related illicit activities.[25]

As indicated above, the SEC and the CFTC have both entered into a co-operative agreement with the futures and securities self-regulatory organisations regarding the joint in-field examinations and sharing of relevant information in a bid to improve the efficiency and effectiveness of securities law enforcement in the USA.[26] This agreement provides, on a voluntary basis, the

---

[17] S 84 read with s 82 of the Financial Markets Act 19 of 2012 (Financial Markets Act).

[18] See related comments above.

[19] S 84(10) of the Financial Markets Act; see further Chitimira "Overview of Selected Role-Players in the Detection and Enforcement of Market Abuse Cases and Appeals in South Africa" 2014 *Speculum Juris* 108 119-121.

[20] See related comments above.

[21] See FSB *Annual Report* 2011 4 99-101; the FSB *Annual Report* 2013 3 128-130; Chanetsa (2004-04-26) *Business Report* page number unknown; see further *Pretorius and Another v Natal South Sea Investment Trust* 417; Blincoe (2001) <http://www.theregister.co.uk/2001/05/23/datatec_directors_pay_up/> (accessed 03-03-2014) & Barron (2014) <http://www.timeslive.co.za/Feeds/2014/02/02/greg-draws-a-blank-in-belfort-parallel> (accessed 03-03-2014).

[22] Hopt & Wymeersch (eds) *European Insider Dealing–Law and Practice* (1991) 340-361.

[23] Chitimira *A Comparative Analysis of the Enforcement of Market Abuse Provisions* 230-257.

[24] Chitimira *A Comparative Analysis of the Enforcement of Market Abuse Provisions* 230-257.

[25] Chitimira *A Comparative Analysis of the Enforcement of Market Abuse Provisions* 230-257.

[26] Chitimira *A Comparative Analysis of the Enforcement of Market Abuse Provisions* 230-257.

opportunity for the SEC and the self-regulatory organisations to review each other's work papers and to share and exchange certain work papers or final investigation reports on any suspected market abuse and/or securities law violations. Likewise, the SEC and the CFTC have both proposed to operate a Joint Advisory Committee, a Joint Agency Enforcement Task Force, a Joint Information Technology Task Force and a joint cross-agency training programme for their staff members.[27] This is aimed at increasing the sharing of relevant information and/or market surveillance data to enhance enforcement and market oversight by developing solutions to emerging and ongoing regulatory risks in the futures and securities markets.[28]

Furthermore, the SEC has forged a co-operation agreement with the Intermarket Financial Surveillance Group (IFSG)[29] to enhance and expand co-operation among all the self-regulatory organisations and the SEC in order to combat market abuse in both securities and futures markets. This co-operative agreement has to date increased the financial surveillance and investigation of illicit trading activities by the SEC, self-regulatory organisations and other regulatory agencies in the US and abroad.

The SEC is a member of the IOSCO and has further adopted and signed international co-operative agreements (Memoranda of Understanding) with regulators and self-regulatory organisations in various foreign countries to discourage and combat illegal cross-border securities violations.[30] The SEC has also entered into approximately 20 bilateral enforcement Memoranda of Understanding with countries in other jurisdictions to enhance its ability to gather the relevant foreign-based information necessary to any ongoing investigation or prosecution regarding securities law violations.[31] Although

---

[27] The CFTC & the SEC "A Joint Report of the SEC and the CFTC on Harmonization of Regulation" *Report* 16 October 2009 10-11 & 14-15.

[28] The CFTC & the SEC *Report* 16 October 2009 10-11 & 14-15.

[29] The IFSG was formed in 1987 as an independent body comprising the self-regulatory organisations of the USA's securities and commodities exchanges.

[30] The countries include the United Kingdom (UK), Japan, Italy, Brazil, Switzerland, Netherlands, France, Mexico and Canada. See Hopt & Wymeersch *European Insider Dealing* 354.

[31] These bilateral Memoranda of Understanding (MOUs) are largely used by the SEC to share bank or audit work papers, Internet service provider information, brokerage records, beneficial ownership records and other relevant information regarding the investigation and enforcement of illicit securities law violations. See s 24(d) read with subsection (f) of the Securities Exchange Act of 1934 15 USC 78i(a)(2)-(5) (2006) as amended by PL-111-257 (approved 05-10-2010) (Securities Exchange Act), which allows the SEC to keep confidential any information it obtains from similar foreign regulatory bodies or self-regulatory organisations. Furthermore, the IOSCO Multilateral MOU permits the SEC to share with other regulatory bodies elsewhere specific information relating to an ongoing civil, administrative or criminal investigation of cross-border market abuse cases. This implies that the SEC may rely on other foreign regulatory bodies to investigate any suspected cross-border securities law contraventions and to assist it where necessary with information which could be used in a criminal prosecution. See Hopt & Wymeersch *European Insider Dealing* 351.

these MOUs are non-binding statements of intent between like-minded regulators, the SEC has fairly managed to utilise them to track and combat market abuse practices which are perpetrated in other countries.[32] In relation to this, it is submitted that the new European Union (EU)'s market abuse regime is also applicable to the USA issuers that have successfully applied to have their securities and/or financial instruments traded on any EU trading platforms such as multilateral trading facilities (MTFs) and organised trading facilities (OTFs). This suggests that such issuers whose securities and financial instruments are traded on the relevant EU regulated markets must comply with requirements and/or provisions of the new Market Abuse Regulation[33] and the Criminal Sanctions for Market Abuse Directive[34] which repealed and replaced the EU Directive on Insider Dealing and Market Manipulation (EU Market Abuse Directive)[35] in 2016. Be that as it may, it remains to be seen whether the SEC and other enforcement authorities will effectively and consistently ensure that the aforesaid cross-border issuers comply with the provisions of both the EU Market Abuse Regulation and the Criminal Sanctions Market Abuse Directive to combat cross-border market abuse practices in the USA and the EU.[36]

Like the USA position,[37] the FSB also polices the general enforcement of securities laws by other regulatory bodies such as the JSE and the Takeover

---

[32] See for example *SEC v Levine* (1986) 86 Civ 3726 (SDNY) (RO), where the SEC managed to track Levine's insider trading activities involving securities of about 54 companies and other illicit trading in securities relating to secret accounts and in the names of Panamanian corporations located in the Bahamian branch of Bank Leu International Limited. The SEC was, through the help of other foreign regulators, able to detect and identify Levine as the beneficial owner of these accounts and he was consequently charged with insider trading. See further *SEC v Kerherve* (1988) No 88 Civ 0227 (SDNY); Hopt & Wymeersch *European Insider Dealing* 348-351.

[33] Regulation (EU) No. 596/2014 of the European Parliament and of the Council of 16 April 2014 on market abuse (market abuse regulation) and repealing Directive 2003/6 of the European Parliament and of the Council and Commission Directives 200/124/EC, 2003/125/EC and 2004/72/EC, [2014] OJ L 173/1 (EU Market Abuse Regulation). This Regulation came into effect on 3 July 2016.

[34] Directive 2014/57/EU of the European Parliament and of the Council of 16 April 2014 on criminal sanctions for market abuse, [2014] OJ L 173/179 (Criminal Sanctions Market Abuse Directive). See also, Articles 1 to 10 of the new Criminal Sanctions Market Abuse Directive. This Directive came into effect on 3 July 2016. The UK and Denmark have opted not to be regulated by the new Criminal Sanctions Market Abuse Directive while Ireland has opted to be regulated by the same Directive in accordance with the provisions of the consolidated versions of the Treaty on European Union (TEU) and the Treaty on the Functioning of the European Union (TFEU), see Protocol 21 on the position of the UK and Ireland in Respect of the Area of Freedom, Security and Justice, [2012] OJ C 202/295.

[35] See the relevant provisions of Directive 2003/6/EC of the European Parliament and Council of 28 January 2003 on insider dealing and market manipulation (market abuse), [2003] OJ L 96/16 (EU Market Abuse Directive).

[36] Skadden "The New EU Market Abuse Regulation: Impact on US Issuers" *Skadden Press Release* 13 October 2016 1 1-10

[37] See related comments above.

Regulation Panel (TRP)[38] in South Africa. This *prima facie* suggests that the FSB has some co-operation relationship with other local regulatory bodies regarding the enforcement of such laws in South Africa. Although the degree or extent of the effectiveness of such co-operation relationship is unclear, the FSB has to date managed to obtain some settlements and to investigate market abuse cases referred to it by other self-regulatory organisations like the JSE.[39] However, unlike the position in the USA,[40] it is uncertain whether the FSB has entered into any binding co-operation agreements with specific local self-regulatory organisations like the TRP to combat market abuse practices in the South African financial markets.[41]

The FSB has reportedly entered into co-operation agreements with the SEC and the Financial Services Authority (FSA) which is now replaced by the Financial Conduct Authority (FCA), of the USA and the UK respectively[42] for the purposes of curbing cross-border market abuse activities. While this is a positive attempt to combat and reduce all potential cross-border market abuse practices as much as possible, relatively minimal success has been achieved in relation to the utilisation of such co-operation agreements in South Africa to date.[43] Thus, it remains uncertain whether such co-operation agreements have been fully implemented to improve the detection, investigation and prosecution of all possible unscrupulous trading practices in the relevant financial markets in South Africa and elsewhere.[44] One can, therefore, ascribe this inconsistent enforcement of cross-border market abuse laws to the low level of co-operation between the FSB and similar bodies in

---

[38] Ss 196; 201 & 202 of the Companies Act 71 of 2008 (Companies Act 2008).

[39] See the FSB *Annual Report* 2011 99-101; the FSB *Annual Report* 2013 128-130; Blincoe (2001) <http://www.theregister.co.uk/2001/05/23/datatec_directors_pay_up/> (accessed 03-03-2014) & Barron (2014) <http://www.timeslive.co.za/Feeds/2014/ 02/02/greg-draws-a-blank-in-belfort-parallel> (accessed 03-03-2014); Chitimira & Lawack "Overview of the Role-Players in the Investigation, Prevention and Enforcement of Market Abuse Provisions in South Africa" 2013 *Obiter Journal* 200 210-217.

[40] See related comments above.

[41] There are no self-regulatory organisations such as those in the USA that are specifically and statutorily empowered to supplement the FSB's efforts to enforce and combat commodities-based market abuse activities in South Africa and elsewhere. See the relevant provisions under Chapter X of the Financial Markets Act.

[42] Loubser (2006) 24-27 <http://www.jse.co.za/public/insider/JSEbooklet.pdf> (accessed 03-03-2014); see further related comments and discussion by the JSE (2013) 24-26 <http://www.jse.co.za/Libraries/JSE_Regulatory_Environment_Insider_Trading/InsiderTrading_Booklet.sflb.ashx> (accessed 03-03-2014).

[43] See the FSB *Annual Report* 2011 99-101 & the FSB *Annual Report* 2013 128-130 which, *inter alia*, reveals that relatively few market abuse cases were successfully investigated, settled and/or prosecuted by the relevant enforcement authorities in South Africa to date.

[44] See the FSB *Annual Report* 2011 99-101 & the FSB *Annual Report* 2013 128-130 which shows that relatively few cross-border market abuse cases were successfully investigated, settled and/or prosecuted by the relevant enforcement authorities in South Africa to date.

other jurisdictions.[45] Nonetheless, this flaw could be corrected if the Financial Markets Act's new provision which now empowers the FSB to assist foreign regulators with investigations pertaining to any cross-border market abuse cases is consistently enforced.[46]

5 2 3 Adoption and Establishment of a Good Enforcement Ethics Culture

Like several other countries, the USA has made numerous efforts to develop a strong anti-market abuse culture among the relevant persons in all its securities and financial markets. Various methods like the use of civil, criminal and administrative sanctions have been employed to discourage market abuse practices in the USA.[47]

Apart from relying on appropriate sanctions as earlier stated, the USA employs other methods like incentives and bounty rewards to encourage all persons to report any suspected illicit trading practices to the SEC or other relevant enforcement agencies.[48] Furthermore, in the wake of the Enron scandal, the USA introduced more incentives and whistle-blower immunity provisions to enable all persons with information regarding securities market manipulation, insider trading or other market abuse practices to register such information with the SEC without any fear of reprisals or victimisation.[49]

The USA also tightened and improved its corporate governance laws through the Sarbanes-Oxley Act[50] to discourage and avoid a recurrence of the Enron, World Com and Arthur Andersen cases.[51] The Sarbanes-Oxley Act, for instance, prohibits a public company to give a personal loan directly or indirectly to a director or an executive officer of that company in order to

---

[45] See related comments by Chitimira *A Comparative Analysis of the Enforcement of Market Abuse Provisions* 421-496; 230-257.

[46] S 84(2)(b).

[47] See related comments in paragraph 5 1 read with paragraphs 5 2 1 & 5 2 2 above.

[48] The SEC may pay bounty rewards of up to 30% of the civil compensatory penalties recovered to all *bona-fide* informants. See s 21F of the Securities Exchange Act; also see Palmiter *Securities Regulation: Examples and Explanations* (2005) 370.

[49] S 21F of the Securities Exchange Act; s 922 of the Dodd-Frank Wall Street Reform and Consumer Protection Act of 2010, Public Law 111-203, 124 Stat.1376 (12 USC; s 5301 *et seq.*) (Dodd-Frank Act) & ss 806 & 406 of the the Public Company Accounting Reform and Investor Protection Act of 2002 Public Law 107-204, 116 Stat 745 (as codified in scattered sections of 15; 28 USC) (Sarbanes-Oxley Act) which requires all issuers of securities and companies to disclose their code of ethics to detect reporting violations and to ensure compliance and fairness in the USA's securities markets. Also see Mossos "Sarbanes-Oxley goes to Europe: A Comparative Analysis of United States and European Union Corporate Reforms after Enron" 2004 *Currents International Trade Law Journal* 9 9-11.

[50] This Act requires all companies registered with the SEC to comply with its anti-market abuse provisions. See s 406(c) of the Sarbanes-Oxley Act.

[51] Mossos 2004 *Currents International Trade Law Journal* 9-11; Palmiter *Securities Regulation* 390-392.

discourage fraud and insider trading.[52] In addition, this Act provides some guidelines on the supervision of the relationship between issuers and auditors to prevent market abuse practices.[53] Moreover, the Sarbanes-Oxley Act introduced the Public Company Accounting Oversight Board to supervise the activities of the accounting profession in order to combat fraud and other market abuse practices.

Moreover, the USA's market abuse regime is based on the so-called multi-functional regulatory model. This multi-functional regulatory model entails that the federal securities law enforcement and regulatory authority does not rest on the SEC alone.[54] Thus, apart from the SEC, other self-regulatory organisations also have the authority to make their own rules and to enforce the federal securities laws.[55] As a result, the USA has so far been able to investigate and prosecute a number of market abuse cases.[56]

In addition to the enforcement by the SEC, the DOJ or the self-regulatory organisations, the USA's market abuse regime allows the prejudiced persons to bring the so-called class actions and claim their damages directly from the offenders in private litigation. This parallel enforcement permits the imposition of multiple sanctions (civil, criminal or administrative penalties) on a certain defendant in a private litigation or in the SEC and/or the DOJ enforcement action.[57] It is worth noting that during the period between 2004 and 2005, the civil monetary penalties awarded in the SEC enforcement actions and private class actions of the affected persons ranged from about

[52] S 402(a) read with s 306(a) of the Sarbanes-Oxley Act.

[53] The Sarbanes-Oxley Act requires all the SEC filings to provide accurate and detailed financial information. See s 302 & ss 201 to s 209. The Sarbanes-Oxley Act further requires all companies to develop their own standards or measures (code of ethics) that are designed to deter all persons from engaging in illicit trading activities. See ss 406 & 407.

[54] It comprises other enforcement agencies like the CFTC, the DOJ, the Federal Reserve Board and other self-regulatory organisations. See related analysis in paragraph 5 2 2 above.

[55] This has been so crucial to the effectiveness of the US's anti-market abuse laws in that the SEC as well as other regulatory bodies may take any appropriate enforcement action against the market abuse offenders.

[56] For instance, see *SEC v Texas Gulf Sulphur Company* (1968) 401 F2d 833 (2d Cir); *Dirks v SEC* (1983) 463 US 646 646-655; *Chiarella v United States* (1980) 445 US 222; *US v Martha Stewart and Peter Bacanovic* (2006) 433 F3d 273; *SEC v Galleon Management & others* (2009) 09 Civ 8811(SDNY); *SEC v Arthur J Cutillo & others* (2009) 09 Civ 9208 (SDNY) & *SEC v Anthony Fareri & others* (2009) 09 Civ 80360 (SDFla).

[57] See *SEC v Palmisiano* (1998) 135 F3d 860 (2d Cir) the court held that the offender was guilty of defrauding clients in a false investment scheme and sentenced him to fifteen years in jail and to pay $3, 8 million restitution to the actual prejudiced persons (in private litigation) plus $700 000 criminal fines. The same offender was also liable to disgorge profits of $9, 2 million plus interest and to pay a $500 000 civil penalty to the SEC. See further Palmiter *Securities Regulation* 440-441; 459-461.

$5, 3 billion to $11, 5 billion.[58] In many instances, the SEC's enforcement actions were accompanied by a private class action. For example, in the World Com scandal, a parallel private settlement was approximately $6, 2 billion. Furthermore, in 2005 alone, private class actions for market abuse violations produced settlements between $3, 5 billion and $9, 7 billion.[59]

A considerable number of methods are also used to prevent market abuse practices in South Africa. In other words, South Africa has made some significant efforts to promote and build a good anti-market abuse culture among all the relevant persons in both regulated and unregulated financial markets. As in the USA,[60] South Africa relies on civil, criminal, and administrative sanctions to deter and discourage unscrupulous persons from engaging in market abuse activities.[61] Nevertheless, unlike the position in the USA,[62] the Financial Markets Act's market abuse civil sanctions are only limited to cases involving insider trading.[63] Furthermore, apart from the workshops, seminars, presentations and the JSE's Insider Trading Booklet, no other measures were employed by the FSB or other enforcement agencies to increase awareness and prevent market abuse activity in the South African financial markets.[64] Moreover, the South African legislature did not employ other methods like incentives, bounty rewards and whistle-blower immunity to encourage informants to voluntarily report all suspected market abuse activities to the FSB or other relevant enforcement authorities.[65] It is submitted in line with the position in the USA,[66] that the Financial Markets Act should be amended to provide specific market abuse whistle-blower immunity provisions[67] for the purposes of encouraging all persons to report market abuse activities to the FSB and/or other relevant enforcement authorities in South Africa.

---

[58] Coffee "Law and the Market: The Impact of Enforcement" 2007 *University of Pennsylvania Law Review* 229 230-311; Pearce "Broadening Actual Damages in the Context of the Commodities Exchange Act" 2007 *Journal of Law and Policy* 449 449-483.

[59] Coffee 2007 *University of Pennsylvania Law Review* 230-311.

[60] See related comments above & in paragraphs 5 1; 5 2 1 & 5 2 2 above.

[61] See related comments above & in paragraphs 5 1; 5 2 1 & 5 2 2 above.

[62] See related comments above & in paragraphs 5 1; 5 2 1 & 5 2 2 above.

[63] S 82 read with ss 78; 80; 81 & 84.

[64] See related comments by Chitimira *A Comparative Analysis of the Enforcement of Market Abuse Provisions* 421-496.

[65] See related comments by Chitimira *A Comparative Analysis of the Enforcement of Market Abuse Provisions* 421-496.

[66] See related comments above & in paragraphs 5 1; 5 2 1 & 5 2 2 above.

[67] Notably, although s 159 of the Companies Act 2008; the Protected Disclosures Act 26 of 2000; s 9 of the South African constitution & the Promotion of Equality and Prevention of Unfair Discrimination Act 4 of 2000 can be employed to protect shareholders, directors and other employees from occupational reprisals, there are no specific provisions in the Financial Markets Act that can be used to encourage and/or protect market abuse whistle-blowers from such reprisals.

Moreover, in contrast to the USA's multi-functional regulatory model,[68] South Africa gives the FSB the main responsibility of enforcing the market abuse provisions.[69] In addition, other self-regulatory bodies like the JSE may only refer any suspected market abuse activities to the FSB for further investigations.[70] Furthermore, there is no express statutory private right of action for the affected persons to claim their damages directly from the offenders in South Africa.[71]

5 3 Concluding Remarks

As highlighted in this chapter, the impropriety of market abuse in the USA is generally accepted by the public, judiciary, market participants and all the relevant stakeholders in that country both at a State and federal level.[72] This is supported, in part, by the fact that the regulation and enforcement of the market abuse prohibition is a co-operative (joint) effort involving the SEC, private litigants, self-regulatory organisations, the CFTC and the DOJ at a federal level[73] as well as the relevant financial or corporation departments at the states level.

On the contrary, the most important characteristic of the regulatory and enforcement framework in the USA, namely a co-ordinated (joint) effort between the courts, self-regulatory organisations and the SEC[74] to combat market abuse and other illicit practices is relatively minimal or absent in South Africa probably due to the differences in relation to the financial markets sizes

[68] See related comments above.

[69] Although other regulatory bodies like the JSE, the Directorate of Market Abuse (DMA), the DPP, the Appeal Board (AB), the Enforcement Committee (EC) and the TRP are also involved in the enforcement of the securities and market abuse laws, there are no regulatory bodies or self-regulatory organisations other than the FSB that are expressly and statutorily empowered to make their own rules for the purposes of enforcing or combating market abuse practices in South Africa. See the relevant provisions under Chapter X of the Financial Markets Act.

[70] Accordingly, the FSB may investigate such matters and/or refer criminal matters to the DPP for prosecution or to the EC for further administrative action.

[71] See the relevant provisions under Chapter X of the Financial Markets Act.

[72] Steinberg 2003 *The International Lawyer* 169-171.

[73] In other words, the prevalent attitudes in the USA favour a rigorous enforcement of the market abuse prohibition. See paragraphs 5 2 1; 5 2 2; & 5 2 3 above; *SEC v Sargent* (2000) 229 F 3d 68-75 (1st Cir) which display the determination of the judiciary in enforcing insider trading provisions by upholding convictions based on circumstantial evidence. S 32(a) of the Securities Exchange Act; also see Bergmans *Inside Information and Securities Trading: A Legal and Economic Analysis of the Foundations of Liability in the US and the European Community* (1991) 41-60.

[74] This is the so-called multi-functional regulatory approach; also see paragraphs 5 2 1; 5 2 2; & 5 2 3 above.

and enforcement approaches.[75] Thus, unlike the position in the USA,[76] the South African market abuse regime relies mainly on the FSB to police and enforce the market abuse ban.[77] Nevertheless, this method has not been consistently employed to obtain more settlements and prosecutions in cases involving market abuse in South Africa to date.[78] Given this current *status quo*, it is submitted that the FSB should enter into specific binding co-operation agreements with more local self-regulatory organisations such as the JSE and the TRP to enhance the combating of market abuse practices in the South African financial markets. It is further submitted that the Financial Markets Act should be amended to enact a provision that expressly empowers the FSB to cooperate with other local regulatory bodies such as the JSE and the TRP in order to improve the enforcement of the market abuse prohibition in South Africa. In line with this, it is recommended that the provisions of the Financial Markets Act which now empowers the FSB to assist foreign regulators with investigations pertaining to any cross-border market abuse cases should be consistently employed to prevent and curb cross-border market abuse practices in South Africa.[79]

It is also recommended that the Financial Markets Act should be amended to explicitly provide a statutory private right of action for the aggrieved or prejudiced persons to claim their market abuse damages directly from the offenders. Moreover, the Financial Markets Act should be amended to introduce a specific commodities-based anti-market abuse enforcement commission or a regulatory body like the CFTC,[80] to deal effectively and exclusively with the commodities-based market manipulation violations in South Africa.

Additionally, the FSB should be statutorily mandated to assist the DPP and the relevant courts with the necessary information regarding ongoing market abuse cases in South Africa, by assigning certain persons with the relevant expertise to assist the DPP and/or the relevant courts in the prosecution of such cases in South Africa. It is also suggested that the Financial Markets Act should be reviewed to enact provisions that mandate companies and all the relevant persons to have anti-market abuse codes of conduct and to appoint

---

[75] See further related analysis by Chitimira *A Comparative Analysis of the Enforcement of Market Abuse Provisions* 421-496; the FSB *Annual Report* 2011 99-101; the FSB *Annual Report* 2013 128-130 which shows that very few successful prosecutions or civil claims have been obtained to date, especially, in the courts & related remarks in paragraphs 5 2 1; 5 2 2; & 5 2 3 above.

[76] See related comments above & in paragraph 5 2 3 above.

[77] See related comments above & in paragraph 5 2 3 above.

[78] See related comments in paragraph 5 2 1 read with paragraphs 5 2 2 & 5 2 3 above.

[79] See related comments in paragraph 5 2 2 above.

[80] See related remarks in paragraph 5 2 2 above.

anti-market abuse compliance officers so as to prevent market abuse activities in South Africa. The legislature should also consider enacting specific provisions which empower the FSB and the JSE to jointly form, fund and operate a Joint Market Abuse Advisory Committee that would be tasked with considering and developing solutions to emerging and ongoing market abuse issues of common interest involving commodity and commodity derivatives and futures or securities traded in both the regulated and over the counter markets in South Africa. In other words, the afore-mentioned Joint Market Abuse Advisory Committee should identify emerging regulatory risks, assess and quantify their implications for investors and other market participants, and recommend possible solutions to the FSB and the JSE.

Furthermore, it is suggested that the legislature should consider enacting specific provisions which empower the FSB, the TRP, the JSE and other relevant stakeholders to create a Joint Anti-Market Abuse Enforcement Task Force in order to harness synergies from shared market surveillance data, to improve market oversight, to enhance enforcement and to reduce duplicative regulatory burdens and/or balkanisation. The Joint Anti-Market Abuse Enforcement Task Force should prepare and offer training programmes for the employees of all the relevant enforcement authorities, develop practical market abuse investigation and enforcement measures, and timeously coordinate the sharing of relevant market abuse information. Moreover, the Joint Anti-Market Abuse Enforcement Task Force should oversee the general execution of the day-to-day duties by the employees of all the relevant enforcement agencies to enhance the enforcement of the market abuse ban in South Africa.

It is also submitted, as is the position in the USA,[81] that regulatory agencies such as the FSB and the JSE should establish a Joint Market Abuse Cross-Agency Training Programme for their employees to increase the enforcement of the market abuse provisions in South Africa. This could be achieved by developing a training programme to increase the consistent and/or regular sharing of relevant information and rotating of employees between the FSB and the JSE. This programme, could each year, give the employees of both the FSB and the JSE the opportunity to work at the other agency temporarily for a specified period of time to enhance greater collaboration and coordination between these two agencies.

Lastly, as is the position in the USA,[82] the FSB and the JSE should consider developing a Joint Market Abuse Information Technology Task Force to link

[81] See related remarks in paragraph 5 2 2 above.
[82] See related remarks in paragraph 5 2 2 above.

their relevant information pertaining to on-going market abuse investigations if they consider such information to be jointly useful and/or in the public interest. This could promote transparency and facilitate the use and understanding of such information by providing a comprehensive, consolidated database on persons and entities investigated by both the FSB and the JSE in order to combat market abuse activities in the South African regulated financial markets.

References

Books

Arshadi N & Eyssell TH *The Law and Finance of Corporate Insider Trading: Theory and Evidence* (Kluwer Academic Publishers Massachusetts 1993)

Ashe TM & Counsell L *Insider Trading: The Tangled Web* (Fourmat Publishing London 1990)

Avgouleas E *The Mechanics and Regulation of Market Abuse: A Legal and Economic Analysis* (Oxford University Press Oxford 2005)

Bainbridge SM *Corporation Law and Economics* (Foundation Press New York 2002)

Bergmans B *Inside Information and Securities Trading: A Legal and Economic Analysis of the Foundations of Liability in the US and the European Community* (Graham & Trotman London 1991)

Beuthin RC & Luiz SM *Beuthin's Basic Company Law* 3rd ed (Butterworths Durban 2000)

Hazen TL *The Law of Securities Regulation: Handbook Series Student Edition* (West Publishing Company St Paul, MN 1985)

Hazen TL *Federal Securities Law* 2nd ed (Federal Judicial Center United States of America 2003)

Hopt KJ & Wymeersch E (eds) *European Insider Dealing – Law and Practice* (Butterworths London 1991)

Lyon GJ & Du Plessis JJ *The Law of Insider Trading in Australia* (The Federation Press Sydney 2005)

Palmiter AR *Securities Regulation: Examples and Explanations* 3rd ed (Aspen Publishers New York 2005)

Swan EJ *Market Abuse Regulation* 1st ed (Oxford University Press United States of America 2006)

Journal articles

Bhattacharya U & Daouk H "The World Price of Insider Trading" 2002 *Journal of Finance* 75-108

Botha D "Control of Insider Trading in South Africa: A Comparative Analysis" 1991 *SA Merc LJ* 1-18

Botha D "Increased Maximum Fine for Insider Trading: A Realistic and Effective Deterrent?" 1990 *SALJ* 504-508

Carlton DW & Fischel DR "The Regulation of Insider Trading" 1983 *Stanford Law Review* 857-895

Cassim R "An Analysis of Market Manipulation under the Securities Services Act 36 of 2004 (Part 1)" 2008 *SA Merc LJ* 33-60

Cassim R "An Analysis of Market Manipulation under the Securities Services Act 36 of 2004 (Part 2)" 2008 *SA Merc LJ* 177-199

Chitimira H "Unpacking Selected Key Elements of the Insider Trading and Market Manipulation Offences in South Africa" 2016 *Journal of Corporate and Commercial Law and Practice* 24-41

Chitimira H "The Regulation of Market Manipulation in Australia: A Historical Comparative Perspective" 2015 *PER Journal* 112-134

Chitimira H "Overview of the Market Abuse Regulation under the Financial Markets Act 19 of 2012" 2014 *Obiter* 254-271

Chitimira H "A Historical Overview of the Regulation of Market Abuse in South Africa" 2014 *PER Journal* 937-965

Chitimira H "Overview of Selected Role-Players in the Detection and Enforcement of Market Abuse Cases and Appeals in South Africa" 2014 *Speculum Juris* 108-124

Chitimira H & Lawack VA "Overview of the Role-Players in the Investigation, Prevention and Enforcement of Market Abuse Provisions in South Africa" 2013 *Obiter Journal* 200-217

Clifford Chance "Overview of United States and United Kingdom Derivative and Commodity Market Enforcement Regimes" 2016 *Clifford Chance Markets Publication Series* 1-226

Coffee JC "Law and the Market: The Impact of Enforcement" 2007 *University of Pennsylvania Law Review* 229-311

Dolgopolov S "Insider Trading and the Bid-Ask Spread: A Critical Evaluation of Adverse Selection in Market Making" 2004 *Capital University Law Review* 83-180

Dooley MP "Enforcement of Insider Trading Restrictions" 1980 *Virginia Law Review* 1-83

Friedman HM "The Insider Trading and Securities Fraud Enforcement Act of 1988" 1990 *North Carolina Law Review* 465-494

Gilson RJ & Kraakman RH "The Mechanisms of Market Efficiency" 1984 *VA.L.REV* 549-644

Henning JJ & Du Toit S "The Regulation of False Trading, Market Manipulation and Insider Trading" 2000 *Journal for Juridical Science* 155-165

Horwich A "The Origin, Application, Validity and Potential Misuse of Rule 10b5-1" 2007 *The Bus. Lawyer* 913-954

Jooste R "A Critique of the Insider trading Provisions of the 2004 Securities Services Act" 2006 *SALJ* 437-460

Kaswell SJ "An Insider's View of the Insider Trading and Securities Fraud Enforcement Act" 1989 *Bus.Law* 145-180

Knepper ZT "Examining the Merits of Dual Regulation for Single-Stock Futures: How the Divergent Insider Trading Regimes for Federal Futures and Securities Markets Demonstrate the Necessity for (and Virtual Inevitability of) Dual CFTC-SEC Regulation for Single-Stock Futures" 2004 *Pierce Law Review* 33-47

Langevoort DC & Gulati GM "The Muddled Duty to Disclose under Rule 10b-5" 2004 *Vand L Rev* 1639-1680

Lastra RM "The Governance Structure for Financial Regulation and Supervision in Europe" 2003 *Colum J Eur L* 49-68

Luiz SM "Insider Trading Regulation – If at First You Don't Succeed..." 1999 *SA Merc LJ* 136-151

Luiz SM "Market Abuse and the Enforcement Committee" 2011 *SA Merc LJ* 151-172

Markham JW "'Front-Running'-Insider Trading under the Commodity Exchange Act" 1988 *Cath. U.Review* 69-127

Mossos E "Sarbanes-Oxley goes to Europe: A Comparative Analysis of United States and European Union Corporate Reforms after Enron" 2004 *Currents International Trade Law Journal* 9-22

Nelemans M "Redefining Trade-Based Market Manipulation" 2008 *Valparaiso University Law Review* 1169-1220

Osode PC "The New South African Insider Trading Act: Sound Law Reform or Legislative Overkill?" 2000 *Journal of African Law* 239-263

Osode PC "The Regulation of Insider Trading in South Africa: A Public Choice Perspective" 1999 *African Journal of International and Comparative Law* 688-708

Pearce BD "Broadening Actual Damages in the Context of the Commodities Exchange Act" 2007 *Journal of Law and Policy* 449-483

Pearson TC "When Hedge Funds Betray A Creditor Committee's Fiduciary Role: New Twists on Insider Trading in the International Financial Markets" 2009 *Review of Banking & Financial Law* 165-220

Ryan L "Rule14e-3's Disclose or Abstain Rule and Its Validity under Section 14(e)" 1991 *U. Cin. Law Review* 449-465

Steinberg MI "Insider Trading Regulation–A Comparative Perspective" 2003 *The International Lawyer* 153-171

Tomasic R "Insider Trading in the USA and United Kingdom" 1991 *Australian Studies in Law, Crime and Justice Series* 31-39

Van Deventer G "New Watchdog for Insider Trading" 1999 *FSB Bulletin* 2-3

Van Deventer G "Harnassing Administrative Law in Encouraging Compliance" 2009 *FSB Bulletin* 3-4

Case law

South Africa

Pretorius and Another v Natal South Sea Investment Trust 1965 3 SA 410 (W)

United States of America

Cady, Roberts and Company [1961-1964 Transfer Binder] CCH Fed Sec L Rep 76. 803

Chiarella v United States (1980) 445 US 222

Dirks v SEC (1983) 463 US 646

FMC Corp v Boesky (1988) 852 F2d 981 (7th Cir)

FMC Corp v Boesky (1987) 673 F2d 272 (ND I11)

In re Enron Corporation Securities Derivative and "ERISA"Litigation Plaintiffs v Enron Corp Oregon Corporation Defendants (2006) WL 2795321 (SD Tex)

In re World Com Inc Sec. Litig (2005) 388 F Supp 2d 319 (SDNY)

Santa Fe Industries Inc v Green (1977) 430 US 462

SEC v Anthony Fareri & others (2009) 09 Civ 80360 (SDFla)

SEC v Arthur J Cutillo & others (2009) 09 Civ 9208 (SDNY)
SEC v Boesky (1986) 86 Civ 8767
SEC v Galleon Management & others (2009) 09 Civ 8811(SDNY)
SEC v Kerherve (1988) No 88 Civ 0227 (SDNY)
SEC v Levine (1986) 86 Civ 3726 (SDNY) (RO)
SEC v One or more purchasers of call options for the Common Stock of CNS INC (2006) US District Court 3004875 WL (EDPa)
SEC v Palmisiano (1998) 135 F3d 860 (2d Cir)
SEC v Sargent (2000) 229 F 3d 68-75 (1st Cir)
SEC v Texas Gulf Sulphur Company (1968) 401 F2d 833 (2d Cir)
SEC v WorldCom Inc (2003) 02 Civ 4963(JSR)
SEC v Yun (2003) 327 F3d 1263 (11th Cir)
The Trane Company v O'Connor Securities (1983) 561 F Supp 301 (SDNY)
United States v Brown (1933) 5 F Supp 81 (SDNY)
United States v Chestman (1991) 947 F2d 551 (2d Cir)
United States v Falcone [2001 Transfer Binder] 91 489 Fed Sec L Rep CCH (2d Cir)
United States v O'Hagan (1997) 117 (SCt) 2199
US v Martha Stewart and Peter Bacanovic (2006) 433 F3d 273
US v Milken (1990) 759 F Supp 109 (SDNY)
US v Mulheren (1991) 938 F2d 364 (2nd Cir)
US v O`Hagan (1997) 521 US 642

Legislation

South Africa

Companies Act 71 of 2008
Consumer Protection Act 68 of 2008
Financial Markets Act 19 of 2012
Financial Institutions (Protection of Funds) Act 28 of 2001 as amended
Promotion of Equality and Prevention of Unfair Discrimination Act 4 of 2000
Protected Disclosures Act 26 of 2000

United States of America

Commodity Exchange Act of 1936 7 USC 1 *et seq.* (1994)
Commodities Futures Modernization Act 2000 Public Law 106-554, 114 Stat.2763A-365
Commodity Futures Trading Commission Act of 1974 Public Law 93-64, 88 Stat 1398
Derivatives Market Manipulation Prevention Act of 2009
Dodd-Frank Wall Street Reform and Consumer Protection Act of 2010, Public Law 111-203, 124 Stat.1376 (12 USC; s 5301 *et seq.*)

Insider Trading and Securities Fraud Enforcement Act of 1988 Public Law 100-704, 102 Stat 4677
Insider Trading Sanctions Act of 1984 Public Law 98-376, 98 Stat.1264 (1984)
International Securities Enforcement Cooperation Act of 1990
Investment Advisors Act of 1940
Investment Company Act of 1940
Public Company Accounting Reform and Investor Protection Act of 2002 Public Law 107-204, 116 Stat 745 (15; 28 USC)
Public Utility Holding Company Act of 1935
Racketeer Influenced and Corrupt Organization Act of 1970
Securities Act of 1933 Public Law 22 48 Stat 74 15 USC77a-77mm (1994)
Securities Act of 1933, Public Law 22 48 Stat.74 15 USC 77a-77mm *et seq.* (2000)
Securities Act of 1933 15 USC 77q(a) (2006) as amended by PL-111-229 (approved 11-08-2010)
Securities Exchange Act of 1934 Public Law 73-291, 48 Stat 881 15 USC 78a-78II
Securities Exchange Act of 1934 15 USC 78i(a)(2)-(5) (2006) as amended by PL-111-257 (approved 05-10-2010)
Securities Exchange Act Release Number 43154 [2000 Transfer Binder] Fed Sec L Rep CCH 86.319
Trust Indenture Act of 1939

European Union

European Union Directive on Insider Dealing and Market Manipulation 2003/6/EC of the European Parliament and Council of 28 January 2003 on insider dealing and market manipulation (market abuse), [2003] OJ L 96/16
Market Abuse Regulation (EU) No. 596/2014 of the European Parliament and of the Council of 16 April 2014 on market abuse (market abuse regulation) and repealing Directive 2003/6 of the European Parliament and of the Council and Commission Directives 200/124/EC, 2003/125/EC and 2004/72/EC, [2014] OJ L 173/1
Criminal Sanctions for Market Abuse Directive 2014/57/EU of the European Parliament and of the Council of 16 April 2014 on criminal sanctions for market abuse, [2014] OJ L 173/179

Commissions, committees and reports

South Africa

Financial Services Board *Annual Report* 2011
Financial Services Board *Annual Report* 2013

United States of America

The Commodity Futures Trading Commission & the United States Securities and Exchange Commission "A Joint Report of the SEC and the CFTC on Harmonization of Regulation" *Report* 16 October 2009

Thesis and dissertations

Chitimira H *A Comparative Analysis of the Enforcement of Market Abuse Provisions* (LLD-thesis Nelson Mandela Metropolitan University 2012)

Chitimira H *The Regulation of Insider Trading in South Africa: A Roadmap for an Effective, Competitive and Adequate Regulatory Statutory Framework* (LLM-dissertation University of Fort Hare 2008)

Conference papers, media releases and other relevant material

Fons RJ & Rowe TA "The SEC Speaks: Aggressive Enforcement to Intensify in 2011" *Morrison & Foerster Client Alert* 09 February 2011

Morrison & Foerster "Insider Trading" 2010 *Year End Review* 1

SEC "Whistleblower Award of More Than Half-Million Dollars for Company Insider" *Press Release 2017-90* 2 May 2017

Skadden "The New EU Market Abuse Regulation: Impact on US Issuers" *Skadden Press Release* 13 October 2016

Newspaper reports

Chanetsa B "Insider Trading is Notoriously Hard to Prosecute" *Business Report* (2004-04-26)

Internet sources

Barron C "Greg Draws a Blank in Belfort Parallel" (2014) <http://www.timeslive.co.za/Feeds/2014/02/02/greg-draws-a-blank-in-belfort-parallel> (accessed 03-03-2014)

Blincoe R "Datatec Directors Pay Up on Insider Trading Charges" (2001) <http://www.theregister.co.uk/2001/05/23/datatec_directors_pay_up/> (accessed 03-03-2014)

Commodity Futures Trading Commission "About the Commodity Futures Trading Commission" (2006) <http://www.cftc.gov/cftcabout.htm> (accessed 07-10-2013)

Department of Justice "US Department of Justice, Fact Sheet: Corporate Fraud Task Force" (2006) <http://www.usdoj.gov. opa/pr/2006/ August/06_odag_525.html> (accessed 12-02-2014)

Financial Industry Regulatory Authority "2008 Year in Review and Annual Financial Report" (2008) <http://www.finra.org> (accessed 02-03-2014)

Financial Services Board "Enforcement Committee Actions" *Media Release* (28-06-2011) <http://www.fsb.co.za/ftp://ftp.fsb.co.za/public/documents/AReport2011.pdf> (accessed 22-11-2013)

Financial Services Board "List of Current Investigations of the Directorate of Market Abuse" *Media Release* (28-06-2011) <http://www.fsb.co.za/ftp://ftp.fsb.co.za/public/documents/AReport2011.pdf> (accessed 22-11-2013)

Johannesburg Stock Exchange Limited "Insider Trading and other Market Abuses (Including the Effective Management of Price–sensitive Information)" in the *Insider Trading Booklet,* (2013) <http://www.jse.co.za/Libraries/JSE_Regulatory_Environment_Insider_Trading/InsiderTrading_Booklet.sflb.ashx> (accessed 03-03-2014)

Karpoff JM, Lee DS & Martin GS "The Legal Penalties for Financial Misrepresentation" (2007) <http://www.ssrn.com/abstract=933333> (accessed 28-09-2013)

Loubser R "Insider Trading and other Market Abuses (Including the Effective Management of Price–sensitive Information)" in the *Insider Trading Booklet* final draft, (2006) <http://www.jse.co.za/public/insider/JSEbooklet.pdf> (accessed 03-03-2014)

Morgan Lewis "2009 Year in Review: SEC and SRO Selected Enforcement Cases and Developments Regarding Broker-Dealers" (2010) <http://www.morganlewis.com/lit_SECandYearlyReviewWP_Jan2010.pdf> (accessed 10-06-2013)

Myburgh A & Davis B "The Impact of South Africa's Insider Trading Regime: A Report for the Financial Services Board" (25-03-2004) <http://www.genesis-analytics.com/public/FSBReport.pdf> (accessed 09-02-2013)

Saikin G "SEC, DOJ Clarify Cooperation" <http://www.executivelegaladvisor.com/docs/SEC-DOJ-Clarify-Cooperation.htm> (accessed 28-02-2014)

United States Securities and Exchange Commission "SEC, 2006 Performance and Accountability" (2006) *Report 8* <http://www.sec.gov/about/secpar/secpar2006.pdf> (accessed 21-02-2014)

United States Securities and Exchange Commission "SEC, 2005 Performance and Accountability" (2005) *Report 7* <http://www.sec.gov/about/secpar/secpar2005.pdf> (accessed 21-02-2014)

Van Deventer G "Anti-Market Abuse Legislation in South Africa" (10-06-2008) <http://www.fsb.co.za/public/marketabuse/FSBReport.pdf> (accessed 05-05-2013)

Chapter 6

The Combating of Market Abuse in the United Kingdom: A Historical Comparative Analysis

6 1 Introduction

There is currently no definition that adequately addresses all aspects of market abuse in the United Kingdom (UK) as well as in other several jurisdictions. Nonetheless, the term "market abuse" refers to both insider trading and market manipulation in this chapter. Accordingly, the UK's market abuse regime has a separate and specific statute that deals with insider trading[1] and another statute which broadly deals with market manipulation and other related market abuse activities.[2] In light this, it must be noted that the Financial Services Act 2012[3] amended the Financial Services and Markets Act and introduced a new regulatory framework that comprises the Financial Policy Committee (FPC), the Prudential Regulation Authority (PRA) and the Financial Conduct Authority (FCA) in the UK on 1 April 2013. These regulatory bodies took over most of the responsibilities that were initially vested in the Financial Services Authority (FSA). This new UK financial services regulatory framework statutorily empowers the Bank of England to have macro-prudential responsibility to oversee the financial system and the prudential supervision of the relevant financial services institutions in the UK.[4]

The market abuse legislation in the UK was carefully formulated to incorporate some of the provisions of the now repealed 2003 European Union (EU)

---

* This chapter is influenced in part, by an article that was initially published in the *Mediterranean Journal of Social Sciences* and this was done with legal permission from the editors of this *Journal*, see Chitimira "A Historical Overview of Market Abuse Prohibition in the United Kingdom" 2014(5)(20) *Mediterranean Journal of Social Sciences* 49-61.

[1] The Criminal Justice Act 1993 (c 36) (Criminal Justice Act).

[2] See the Financial Services and Markets Act 2000 (c 8) (Financial Services and Markets Act). Also see Avgouleas *The Mechanics and Regulation of Market Abuse: A Legal and Economic Analysis* (2005) 307.

[3] (c 21) (Financial Services Act 2012).

[4] Thus, the Financial Services Act 2012 further amended the Bank of England Act 1998 (c 11) as amended by the Bank of England and Financial Services Act 2016 (c 14) and the Banking Act 2009 (c 1), see Part 3 to Part 9 of the Financial Services Act 2012.

Directive[5] on market abuse.[6] For instance, the UK enacted the Financial Services and Markets Act[7] and the Market Abuse Regulations 2005[8] to implement the provisions of the EU Market Abuse Directive. However, the EU Market Abuse Directive was recently repealed and replaced by the EU Market Abuse Regulation[9] and the Criminal Sanctions for Market Abuse Directive[10] which were adopted in 2014 by the EU in a bid to improve the enforcement of the market abuse laws in the EU financial markets. Both the EU Market Abuse Regulation and the Criminal Sanctions Market Abuse Directive came into effect on 3 July 2016. Consequently, preceding the Brexit outcome, the Market Abuse Regulations 2005 and the Financial Services and Markets Act 2000's civil market abuse prohibition[11] were repealed by the Market Abuse Regulations 2016[12] to ensure compliance and compatibility with the provisions of both the EU Market Abuse Regulation and the Criminal Sanctions Market Abuse Directive.[13] In this regard, it must be noted that the EU Market Abuse Regulation is directly applicable in all the EU Member States. Thus, in contrast to the Criminal Sanctions Market Abuse Directive, the EU Market Abuse Regulation does not require any transposition into domestic law in order to implement its provisions in the UK and/or other EU Member States. Despite this, it remains to be seen whether the UK will continue to comply with these EU market abuse laws in light of its decision to withdraw from the EU after

---

[5] See the Directive of the European Parliament and Council of 28 January 2003 on insider dealing and market manipulation (market abuse) 2003/6/EC [2003] OJ L96/16 (EU Market Abuse Directive).

[6] Barnes *Stock Market Efficiency, Insider Dealing and Market Abuse* (2009) 125.

[7] S 118.

[8] Financial Services and Markets: The Prospectus Regulations, [2005] SI 2005/381 (Market Abuse Regulations 2005), which amended the Financial Services and Markets Act 2000 (Prescribed Markets and Qualifying Investments) Order 2001 SI 2001/1996 (Market Abuse Regulations 2001).

[9] Regulation (EU) No. 596/2014 of the European Parliament and of the Council of 16 April 2014 on market abuse (market abuse regulation) and repealing Directive 2003/6 of the European Parliament and of the Council and Commission Directives 200/124/EC, 2003/125/EC and 2004/72/EC, [2014] OJL 173/1 (EU Market Abuse Regulation).

[10] Directive 2014/57/EU of the European Parliament and of the Council of 16 April 2014 on criminal sanctions for market abuse, [2014] OJL 173/179 (Criminal Sanctions Market Abuse Directive). See also articles 1 to 10 of the Criminal Sanctions Market Abuse Directive. The UK and Denmark have opted not to be regulated by the Criminal Sanctions Market Abuse Directive while Ireland has opted to be regulated by the same Directive in accordance with the provisions of the consolidated versions of the Treaty on European Union (TEU) and the Treaty on the Functioning of the European Union (TFEU), see Protocol 21 on the position of the UK and Ireland in Respect of the Area of Freedom, Security and Justice [2012] OJC 202/295.

[11] Thus, Parts 6 and 8 of the Financial Services and Markets Act 2000 were repealed.

[12] Market Abuse Regulations 2016, SI 2016/680 (Market Abuse Regulations 2016).

[13] Morgan Lewis "UK Market Abuse Regime Extends its Reach: Implications for Market Participants" *Morgan Lewis* (2016) <https://www.morganlewis.com/ pubs/uk-market-abuse-regime-extends-its-reach-implications-for-market-participants> (accessed 12-07-2017).

the British EU (Brexit) referendum was conducted.[14] Despite this obscurity, the UK's broad and extensive regulatory approach has led several countries in other jurisdictions,[15] including South Africa,[16] to follow some of its anti-market abuse enforcement approaches, especially, with regard to the prohibition on insider trading.[17] Consequently, this chapter undertakes a comparative analysis of the market abuse prohibition in the UK and South Africa to explore their similarities and differences where applicable. To this end, a general historical overview of the insider trading legislation will be discussed first, followed by a similar discussion on the prohibition of market manipulation practices. Lastly, the available penalties will be discussed and thereafter, possible recommendations and/or concluding remarks will be provided.

---

[14] This referendum was held on 23 June 2016 to enable all British citizens to vote and decide whether to stay or leave the EU. The majority of British citizens in that referendum voted to leave the EU. Consequently, the UK must formally notify the European Council of its decision to leave the EU at least two years before the actual exit. This suggests that the UK remains an EU Member State which must currently comply with the relevant EU legislation. For related discussion see SIA Partners (Banking and Insurance) "Brexit and the Impact on the UK's Regulatory Framework" (2016) 1-4 <http://en.finance.sia-partners.com/brexit-and-impact-uks-regulatory-framework> (accessed 12-07-2017).

[15] See Bhattacharya & Daouk "The World Price of Insider Trading" 2002 *Journal of Finance* 75 75-108; Lyon & Du Plessis *The Law of Insider Trading in Australia* (2005) 159-168 & Avgouleas *The Mechanics and Regulation of Market Abuse* 75-502, for further analysis on the regulation and enforcement of the market abuse ban in other countries.

[16] Generally see ss 78; 80; 81 & 82 of the Financial Markets Act 19 of 2012 (Financial Markets Act). See further Van Deventer "Anti-Market Abuse Legislation in South Africa" (10-06-2008) 1-5 <http://www.fsb.co.za/public/marketabuse/FSBReport.pdf> (accessed 05-05-2013); Myburgh & Davis "The Impact of South Africa's Insider Trading Regime: A Report for the Financial Services Board" (25-03-2004) 8-33 <http://www.genesis-analytics.com/public/FSBReport.pdf> (accessed 09-02-2013); Chitimira *A Comparative Analysis of the Enforcement of Market Abuse Provisions* (Unpublished LLD thesis, Nelson Mandela Metropolitan University) 2012, 305-353; Botha "Control of Insider Trading in South Africa: A Comparative Analysis" 1991 *SA Merc LJ* 1 1-18; Botha "Increased Maximum Fine for Insider Trading: A Realistic and Effective Deterrent?" 1990 *SALJ* 504 504-508; Chitimira *The Regulation of Insider Trading in South Africa: A Roadmap for an Effective, Competitive and Adequate Regulatory Statutory Framework* (Unpublished LLM dissertation, University of Fort Hare) 2008, 41–72; Osode "The new South African Insider Trading Act: Sound Law Reform or Legislative Overkill?" 2000 *Journal of African Law* 239 239-263; Jooste "A Critique of the Insider Trading Provisions of the 2004 Securities Services Act" 2006 *SALJ* 437 441–460; Van Deventer "New Watchdog for Insider Trading" 1999 *FSB Bulletin* 2 3 & Luiz "Insider Trading Regulation – If at First You Don't Succeed…" 1999 *SA Merc LJ* 136 136-151.

[17] Other countries that were also influenced by the UK's insider trading legislation include Germany, Italy, Canada, Mexico and France. See further Steinberg "Insider Trading Regulation–A Comparative Perspective" 2003 *The International Lawyer* 153 154-171.

6 2 Historical Overview of Insider Trading Prohibition

It should be noted the UK's insider trading regime has a relatively short history.[18] Until 1980, insider trading was not statutorily prohibited in the UK.[19] Prior to this, two legislative attempts to outlaw insider trading in the early 1970s were unsuccessfully made.[20] This was further worsened by the fact that the common law failed to provide clear opportunities for the prejudiced persons to seek their redress in the civil courts.[21]

Consequently, the legislature enacted the Companies Act 1980.[22] However, this Act made insider trading a criminal offence only in certain specified circumstances.[23] Moreover, the Companies Act 1980 provided some requirements for directors, members of their families and substantial shareholders to report any dealings in shares of their companies to discourage the misuse of non-public inside information.[24]

The provisions of the Companies Act 1980 were later revised and consolidated into the Companies Act 1985,[25] in another bid to enhance the prohibition of insider trading in the UK. These provisions banning insider trading were further revised and re-branded as the Company Securities (Insider Dealing) Act 1985.[26] The Insider Dealing Act prohibited individuals (insiders)[27] who had access to material non-public inside information by virtue of their position within a company from dealing in the securities of the company while having such information. Furthermore, these insiders were prohibited from making a selective disclosure of non-public inside information to others

---

18 Avgouleas *The Mechanics and Regulation of Market Abuse* 308. Notably, in this sub-heading, the principal focus is on the provisions of the insider trading legislation in the UK that deal with the enforcement. Thereafter a comparative analysis with similar developments in South Africa will be carried out.

19 Barnes *Stock Market Efficiency, Insider Dealing* 125.

20 For instance in 1973, the Conservative government published a Companies Bill that would have prohibited insider trading, but it collapsed when the said government was defeated in the February 1974 general election. A similar Bill was proposed by the Labour government in 1978 and it suffered the same fate when the Labour government lost the May 1979 general election.

21 Put differently, the use of inside information without some affirmative obligation to disclose it did not give rise to civil liability for insider trading. See further Rider, Alexander, Linklater & Bazley *Market Abuse and Insider Dealing* (2009) 44.

22 (c 22) (Companies Act 1980).

23 Ss 68 to 73 of the Companies Act 1980. Also see generally Blair & Walker *Financial Services Law* (2006) 267.

24 Notwithstanding the fact that these disclosure and reporting duties were probably useful and justified in many respects, it is debatable whether such duties had the practical effect of prohibiting insider trading and other related illicit trading practices. See further Rider, Alexander, Linklater & Bazley *Market Abuse and Insider Dealing* 44.

25 (c 6) (Companies Act 1985).

26 (c 8) (Insider Dealing Act); also see Rider, Alexander, Linklater & Bazley *Market Abuse and Insider Dealing* 44.

27 Such insiders included directors, officers, employees and various kinds of agents of the company.

(tipping) and it also prohibited the tippees from dealing in securities on the basis of such information.[28] In addition, individuals with non-public information about a suggested takeover of a company were prohibited from dealing in that company's stock. However, the provisions of the Insider Dealing Act applied only to individuals who knowingly dealt in the affected securities while in possession of material non-public inside information.[29] Furthermore, the provisions of the Insider Dealing Act provided only criminal sanctions for insider trading violations. As a result, the scope and impact of this Act was somewhat restricted and narrow.[30]

Owing to a considerable uncertainty on the effectiveness of the provisions of the Insider Dealing Act, the legislature introduced the Financial Services Act 1986.[31] The provisions of the Financial Services Act were, *inter alia*, aimed at supplementing and strengthening the enforcement of the insider trading ban in the UK.[32] However, the provisions of this Act were still applicable only to individuals and offered no civil remedy for such individuals who were prejudiced by insider trading.

The provisions of the Insider Dealing Act (as amended by the Financial Services Act) were therefore, superseded by the Criminal Justice Act.[33] Thus, the provisions of the Criminal Justice Act were, among other things, targeted at removing the loopholes that were contained in its predecessors by incorporating some recommendations from the European Council Directive on insider trading[34] and extending the application of the prohibition on insider trading to a wider class of securities[35] and individuals.[36] Specifically, three classes of individuals (insiders) that are statutorily prohibited from committing insider trading include firstly, a person who has direct knowledge of non-public inside information (primary insider) by virtue of being a director, employee or

---

[28] See further Rider, Alexander, Linklater & Bazley *Market Abuse and Insider Dealing* 45.

[29] Thus, possible insider trading violations by juristic persons were not covered. Generally see s 10(b).

[30] In spite of the fact that the insider trading prohibition was effective since 1980, there were no convictions under the Insider Dealing Act until the late 1980s. See further Rider, Alexander, Linklater & Bazley *Market Abuse and Insider Dealing* 45.

[31] (c 60) (Financial Services Act).

[32] Ss 173 to 178 of the Financial Services Act. Also see further Rider, Alexander, Linklater & Bazley *Market Abuse and Insider Dealing* 44.

[33] The Criminal Justice Act came into force on 1 March 1994 together with two ancillary statutory instruments namely, the Insider Dealing (Securities and Regulated Markets) Order 1994 & the Traded Securities (Disclosure) Regulation 1994. See further Rider, Alexander, Linklater & Bazley *Market Abuse and Insider Dealing* 45.

[34] See Council Directive (89/592)/EEC, Article 1(2). This enabled the UK enforcement authorities to investigate all individuals who engage in insider trading activity in the UK and elsewhere in the EU. See further Rider, Alexander, Linklater & Bazley *Market Abuse and Insider Dealing* 48.

[35] See the definition of price-affected securities in Schedule 2 of the Criminal Justice Act.

[36] S 57 read with ss 52; 55(3)(b) & 56(2) of the Criminal Justice Act.

shareholder of an issuer of securities or by virtue of their employment or office.[37] Secondly, the Criminal Justice Act prohibits an individual (secondary insider) who obtains non-public inside information either directly or indirectly from a primary insider from committing insider trading offences.[38] Lastly, the Criminal Justice Act further discourages any secondary insider's tippees from indulging in insider trading.[39]

Additionally, the Criminal Justice Act prohibits individuals from engaging in approximately three forms of conduct that would amount to insider trading. Firstly, individuals are prohibited from dealing in price-affected securities on the basis of non-public material inside information.[40] Secondly, individuals are prohibited from encouraging (tipping) other persons to deal in price-affected securities on the basis of non-public material inside information.[41] Lastly, the Criminal Justice Act prohibits individuals from knowingly and improperly disclosing non-public material inside information to other persons.[42] No individual (insider) may be convicted of insider trading unless he knew that he was in possession of non-public inside information and dealt in the affected securities on the basis of such information.

Notwithstanding the fact that the Criminal Justice Act introduced a number of significant changes such as a wider definition of securities,[43] its provisions are still flawed in some respects. For instance, its prohibition may only give rise to criminal sanctions against individuals who practise insider trading. Put differently, the definition of "individual" only covers unincorporated partnerships or corporations comprising a collection of individuals.[44] This is arguably one of the main weaknesses of the insider trading ban contained in the Criminal Justice Act.[45] Moreover, individuals will only be liable for insider trading when they deal in affected securities on a regulated market or where such

---

[37] S 57(1)(a) & (2)(a).

[38] S 57(1)(b) & (2)(b).

[39] S 57. Also see generally Rider, Alexander, Linklater & Bazley *Market Abuse and Insider Dealing* 47.

[40] S 52(1).

[41] S 52(2)(a).

[42] S 52(2)(b). It is of interest to note that individuals could be liable for insider trading in terms of s 52 if the prosecuting authorities prove that such accused individuals are insiders as stipulated in s 57 and that they were in possession of non-public inside information as proscribed in s 56 of the Criminal Justice Act. See Part V of the Criminal Justice Act. See further Rider, Alexander, Linklater & Bazley *Market Abuse and Insider Dealing* 46-51.

[43] This definition of securities included shares, debentures and derivatives in companies as well as gilts and local authority stock in both local and foreign public bodies and their derivatives. See Schedule 2 of the Criminal Justice Act.

[44] This could suggest that other corporations and entities like public companies are exempted from insider trading liability. Rider, Alexander, Linklater & Bazley *Market Abuse and Insider Dealing* 46.

[45] See further Rider, Alexander, Linklater & Bazley *Market Abuse and Insider Dealing* 46.

dealing is conducted on the over the counter markets through a professional intermediary.[46]

Apart from the Criminal Justice Act, the insider trading practice is also indirectly prohibited in the Companies Act 2006.[47] For instance, the directors of a company are prohibited from accepting benefits from third parties[48] and dealing in such company's securities if they have a direct or indirect interest that contradicts the interests of the company, especially with regard to their use of privileged inside information to avoid possible conflicts of interests and/or insider trading.[49] Moreover, circumstances in which a company can deal in its own securities or capital to repurchase, cancel stock, or redeem preference shares are carefully regulated to prevent the abuse of non-public price-sensitive information through insider trading.[50]

6 2 1 Evaluation and Analysis of the Historical Overview of Insider TradingProhibition

In contrast to the developments of the regulation and enforcement of the insider trading ban in the UK,[51] the legislature in South Africa introduced a statutory prohibition on insider trading in 1973.[52] However, both South Africa and the UK's insider trading regulatory frameworks prohibit individuals from committing insider trading offences, especially, in relation to securities listed on regulated financial markets.[53] Moreover, both South Africa[54] and the UK's[55] insider trading regulatory frameworks prohibit primary insiders, secondary

---

[46] Face to face over the counter (OTC) transactions between non-professional intermediaries are excluded from insider trading liability under the Criminal Justice Act. Avgouleas *The Mechanics and Regulation of Market Abuse* 320 & Rider, Alexander, Linklater & Bazley *Market Abuse and Insider Dealing* 46.

[47] (c 46) (Companies Act 2006).

[48] S 176 of the Companies Act 2006.

[49] S 175 of the Companies Act 2006 & ss 177; 182; 187 read with s 178(2) of the same Act which imposes a duty on the directors to disclose their interests in proposed or ongoing transactions. See further Rider, Alexander, Linklater & Bazley *Market Abuse and Insider Dealing* 20.

[50] Also see generally Part 18 of the Companies Act 2006 & s 170(4) of the same Act which states that the general duties of directors shall be interpreted and applied in the same way as common law rules or equitable principles. This is probably aimed at affording equitable damages or redress to any persons prejudiced by insider trading. Rider, Alexander, Linklater & Bazley *Market Abuse and Insider Dealing* 12-13 &17-18.

[51] See paragraph 6 2 above.

[52] S 233 of the Companies Act 61 of 1973 (Companies Act).

[53] In other words, similar classes of individuals are discouraged from engaging in illicit insider trading activities in both South Africa and the UK.

[54] Ss 77; 78 & 82 of the Financial Markets Act.

[55] S 52 of the Criminal Justice Act.

insiders and their tippees from knowingly dealing directly or indirectly[56] in securities on the basis of non-public price-sensitive (material) inside information for their own benefit or for the benefit of others.[57]

In contrast to the UK position,[58] there is no express provision that discourages dealing in securities on unregulated over the counter markets through agents or professional intermediaries in South Africa.[59] This could be due to the fact that insider trading activities in the over the counter markets are probably very restricted since such transactions are mostly done on a face-to-face basis between persons who know each other quite well. Furthermore, although the words "through an agent" are used in some provisions that discourage insider trading under the Financial Markets Act,[60] this Act does not expressly provide a statutory definition for the term "agent".[61]

On the contrary, the term "professional intermediary" which is similar to the term "agent" is employed and fully defined in the UK.[62] Notably, the South African insider trading ban has an unlimited extra-territorial application. Thus, in contrast to the UK's insider trading regime which only applies to any dealing that takes place on a regulated market which operates in the UK or if the person dealing in the price-affected securities is a professional intermediary or relies on a professional intermediary to deal in such securities on a regulated financial market in the UK,[63] an insider who unlawfully deals in the South African securities listed on a foreign market can be prosecuted for insider trading in South Africa even if the territorial (nexus) link to South Africa does not exist.[64] Furthermore, unlike the position in the Criminal Justice Act,[65] insider trading is treated both as a civil and criminal offence in South Africa.[66] Nevertheless, no attempt has been made to statutorily define the

[56] Individuals (insiders) are therefore prohibited from encouraging or discouraging others to deal in the affected securities while in possession of non-public inside information or to improperly disclose non-public inside information relating to such securities.

[57] This could further indicate that similar conduct that may give rise to insider trading is prohibited in South Africa as well as in the UK.

[58] Ss 59 & 52(3) of the Criminal Justice Act.

[59] Ss 78 & 82 of the Financial Markets Act.

[60] S 78(1)(a); (2)(a) & (3)(a) read with s 82 of the Financial Markets Act.

[61] Although it can be argued that the ordinary meaning of the term "agent" is generally known to all the relevant persons, the Financial Markets Act did not provide an adequate and clear definition of this term for the purposes of improving the implementation of the insider trading prohibition in South Africa.

[62] S 59 of Criminal Justice Act.

[63] Ss 62 & 79(2) of the Criminal Justice Act which outlines the scope of the insider trading offence. See further Rider, Alexander, Linklater & Bazley *Market Abuse and Insider Dealing* (2009) 56-57 & Avgouleas *The Mechanics and Regulation of Market Abuse* 323-324.

[64] Jooste 2006 SALJ 453; also see the definition of "regulated market" in s 77 of the Financial Markets Act.

[65] See paragraph 6 2 above.

[66] Ss 78 & 82 of the Financial Markets Act.

concept of insider trading in both South Africa[67] and the UK.[68] Nevertheless, the FCA has successfully obtained some considerable convictions against the market abuse offenders in the recent past few years in relation to insider trading prosecutions that were instituted under the Criminal Justice Act.[69] Over and above, in South Africa, attempted insider trading is not expressly prohibited in the Financial Markets Act.

6 3 Historical Overview of Market Manipulation Prohibition

Despite the fact that market abuse also constitutes insider trading activity,[70] this sub-heading will mainly discuss market manipulation and other forms of market abuse that do not necessarily amount to insider trading.

Market manipulation and other related market abuse activities have been statutorily prohibited in the UK, probably since the early 1860s.[71] The initial attempt to prohibit market manipulation in the UK was made by the Larceny Act 1861. This Act criminalised fraudulent misrepresentations intended to create a false market.[72] The second attempt to regulate market manipulation in the UK was possibly introduced under the Prevention of Fraud (Investments) Act 1939.[73] However, this Act was repealed by the Prevention of Fraud (Investments) Act 1958.[74] The Prevention of Fraud (Investments) Act 1958 prohibited dishonest concealment of material non-public inside information relating to any securities for personal gain or the benefit of others.[75] However,

---

[67] Ss 77; 78 & 82 of the Financial Markets Act.

[68] See Part V of the Criminal Justice Act.

[69] For instance, two of the five offenders were recently convicted of insider trading and the longest custodial sentence for insider trading in the UK (four and half years) was imposed on each of the offenders. This was made possible through the FCA's insider trading investigation initiative which was known as the "Operation Tabernula" in 2016. Hitchins "Focusing on the Latest Trends, Risks and Developments in Financial Services Investigations" *Allen & Overy Investigations Insight* (17-10-2016) <http://www.aoinvestigationsinsight.com/further-drop-in-number-of-market-abuse-cases-concluded-by-the-fca/> (accessed 13-07-2017).

[70] In light of this, it is essential to note that about seven types of market abuse practices are statutorily prohibited in the UK. Barnes *Stock Market Efficiency, Insider Dealing* 132; Russen *Financial Services Authorisation, Supervision and Enforcement: A Litigator's Guide* (2006) 206-208.

[71] S 84 of the Larceny Act 1861 (24 and 25 Vict c 96). Also see Avgouleas *The Mechanics and Regulation of Market Abuse* 314.

[72] S 84 of the Larceny Act 1861; also see *R v Kylsant* [1932] 1 KB 442, where the court employed s 84 of the Larceny Act 1861 and convicted Lord Kylsant for misrepresentations made in his company's prospectus & see further related remarks in Avgouleas *The Mechanics and Regulation of Market Abuse* 314.

[73] (c 16); see s 12(1).

[74] (c 45); also see Avgouleas *The Mechanics and Regulation of Market Abuse* 314; Rider, Alexander, Linklater & Bazley *Market Abuse and Insider Dealing* 44.

[75] This was mainly aimed at discouraging market manipulation and other related market abuse practices. See further s 13 of the Prevention of Fraud (Investments) Act 1958.

its purported market abuse ban was extremely difficult to enforce, especially where the wrongful conduct was committed outside the UK.

Consequently, the legislature enacted a new market manipulation prohibition under the Financial Services Act.[76] A two-fold market manipulation prohibition was formulated under the Financial Services Act. Firstly, it prohibited the making of misleading statements or concealment of material non-public inside information relating to any securities.[77] Secondly, the Financial Services Act prohibited the perpetration of market manipulation through misleading conduct or practices.[78]

The market manipulation prohibition under the Financial Services Act was, however, flawed in some areas. For instance, it failed to obtain more convictions against the market manipulation offenders. This could have been triggered by its heavy reliance on the criminal sanctions alone to combat market manipulation or similar market abuse activities.[79]

In order to improve and align the UK's market abuse legislation with the international best standards, the legislature enacted the Financial Services and Markets Act.[80] The Financial Services and Markets Act came into effect on 1 December 2001. This Act defined and treated market manipulation and other market abuse practices both as criminal and civil offences. The initial civil provisions of the Financial Services and Markets Act discouraged three conducts, namely the misuse of information, the making or publishing of false or misleading impressions and market distortion or manipulation.[81] These provisions were extensively revised on 1 July 2005 after the adoption of the Treasury's Market Abuse[82] and Investment Recommendation (Media) Regulations[83]

---

[76] Also see generally Avgouleas *The Mechanics and Regulation of Market Abuse* 314; Rider, Alexander, Linklater & Bazley *Market Abuse and Insider Dealing* 44.

[77] S 47(1).

[78] S 47(2). Also see Avgouleas *The Mechanics and Regulation of Market Abuse* 314; Black & Nobles "Personal Pensions Misselling: The Causes and Lessons of Regulatory Failure" 1998 *MLR* 789; Rider "Policing the City-Combating Fraud and Other Abuses in the Corporate Securities Industry" 1988 *Current Legal Problems* 47 & Swan *Market Abuse Regulation* (2006) 5.

[79] Avgouleas *The Mechanics and Regulation of Market Abuse* 308.

[80] Avgouleas *The Mechanics and Regulation of Market Abuse* 307.

[81] See the original s 118(2)(a) to (c). Also see Russen *Financial Services Authorisation, Supervision* 185.

[82] See the Financial Services and Markets Act 2000 (Market Abuse) Regulations 2005 SI 2005/381. Also see the Financial Services Authority's *Market Abuse Directive Instrument* 2005, 17 March 2005 & the Financial Services Authority's *Market Abuse Directive Disclosure Rules Instrument* 2005, 17 March 2005.

[83] 2005 SI 2005/382.

to implement the EU Market Abuse Directive[84] and its so-called Level 2 Implementing Measures.[85]

The new civil provisions under the Financial Services and Markets Act provided a broader and comprehensive definition of various conducts that could amount to market manipulation and other related market abuse practices.[86] These provisions also retained civil offences for engaging in conduct that will give rise to the misuse of material inside information[87] and creation of a false or misleading impression or distortion of the financial markets.[88] The new civil offence under the Financial Services and Markets Act was now applicable to both natural and juristic persons.[89] Moreover, this civil offence need only be proved on the balance of probabilities. It is not necessary to prove intention on the part of the alleged offenders; negligent action or inaction may be sufficient for such offenders to incur liability.[90]

As indicated earlier, there are seven types of market abuse practices in the UK and these practices will each now be briefly discussed. Firstly, insider dealing[91] is expressly outlawed in the Financial Services and Markets Act. Consequently, any person or insider who deals or attempts to deal in qualifying and related investments on the basis of non-public price-sensitive inside

---

[84] Avgouleas *The Mechanics and Regulation of Market Abuse* 307 & Russen *Financial Services Authorisation, Supervision* 206.

[85] Also see Commission Directive 2003/124/EC of 22 December 2003 implementing Directive 2003/6/EC of 28 January 2003 on the definition and public disclosure of inside information and the definition of market manipulation [2003] OJ L339/70; Commission Directive 2003/125/EC of 22 December 2003 on the fair presentation of investment recommendations and the disclosure of conflicts of interest [2003] OJ L339/073. Also see Avgouleas *The Mechanics and Regulation of Market Abuse* 259-260 & 307, for further related analysis.

[86] S 118(1) to (8); also see the initial Part VIII of the Financial Services and Markets Act.

[87] S 118(2) to (4) of the Financial Services and Markets Act.

[88] See s 118(5) to (8) of the Financial Services and Markets Act. These civil offences are enforced parallel to the criminal offences contained in the Criminal Justice Act.

[89] See s 150 read with ss 90; 380; 382; 118(1); 118B & 118C of the Financial Services and Markets Act. Additionally see Avgouleas *The Mechanics and Regulation of Market Abuse* 391-446 for related analysis.

[90] It is only primarily important to establish whether the alleged market abuse conduct occurred in relation to any qualifying investments on a prescribed market before imposing any liability on the alleged offenders. Prescribed markets include but are not limited to markets listed under the rules of the UK recognised investment exchange such as the London Stock Exchange, the International Petroleum Exchange, the London Metal Exchange, EDX London, Euronext-LIFFE and Virt-x. Qualifying investments include financial instruments like options, bonds and other forms of securities debt, derivatives on commodities, company shares (and securities equivalent to company shares), money market instruments, financial futures contracts, forward interest rate agreements, interest rate, equity swaps and other securities giving right to acquire shares or bonds. See s 118(1)(a) & (b) of the Financial Services and Markets Act; also see Russen *Financial Services Authorisation, Supervision* 206-208; Barnes *Stock Market Efficiency, Insider Dealing* 129-132 & Rider, Alexander, Linklater & Bazley *Market Abuse and Insider Dealing* 74-75.

[91] This conduct is also criminally prohibited under the Criminal Justice Act. See paragraph 6 2 above.

information relating to the investments in question will incur civil liability under the Financial Services and Markets Act.[92] Secondly, improper disclosure is also prohibited in the Financial Services and Markets Act. Accordingly, the disclosure of non-public price-sensitive information by an insider or any individual to another person in instances other than for the proper performance of his employment, profession or duties will give rise to a civil offence on the part of that individual under the Financial Services and Markets Act.[93] Thirdly, any misuse of information is discouraged under the Financial Services and Markets Act. Therefore, conduct based on information that is not generally available but that would affect the decision of the investors to deal or not to deal in certain qualifying investments could amount to market manipulation or other market abuse offences.[94] Such conduct must also be based on information which a "regular user"[95] of the market or the person in the position of the alleged offender would consider relevant in determining the terms on which to deal before civil liability can be imputed against any accused persons.[96]

Fourthly, manipulating transactions are further prohibited in the Financial Services and Markets Act. As a result, any behaviour or dealing that gives a false or misleading impression of the supply of or demand for one or more investments to raise the price of the investments in question to abnormal or artificial levels amounts to a civil offence of market manipulation.[97] Such behaviour also includes the making of false or misleading transactions so as to give a false impression of the volume of trade in the affected securities.[98] Manipulating transactions further includes price positioning. This usually occurs when a person enters small orders into an electronic trading system at

---

[92] S 118(2). Also see further Barnes *Stock Market Efficiency, Insider Dealing* 132-133 & Rider, Alexander, Linklater & Bazley *Market Abuse and Insider Dealing* 72-73 & 78.

[93] S 118(3). In other words, the disclosure of inside information by a director of a company to another person in mere social context or selective briefing of market participants like financial analysts by directors or other persons with managerial positions will suffice for such persons to incur liability for improper disclosure of inside information.

[94] S 118(4).

[95] S 130A read with ss 118A & 118C of the Financial Services and Markets Act.

[96] Factors that are considered when determining whether the information in question is relevant to a "regular user" includes the extent to which the information is reliable (including how close the person or offender involved is to the tipper or the person who is the original source); whether such information is not already generally available to market participants and whether the information is fresh and different from information which is generally available or that would lead to a disclosure to be made in the future. Also see Barnes *Stock Market Efficiency, Insider Dealing* 134 & Rider, Alexander, Linklater & Bazley *Market Abuse and Insider Dealing* 78-80 & Avgouleas *The Mechanics and Regulation of Market Abuse* 344-345.

[97] S 118(5).

[98] For example, wash trades; buying qualifying investments at the close of the market to mislead investors who act at closing prices; buying and selling a specific security by persons among themselves to create an illusion (painting the tape) of high volumes of trading.

prices which are higher than the previous bid or lower than the previous offer, in order to move the price of the qualifying investments in question.[99] Fifthly, manipulating devices are also prohibited under the Financial Services and Markets Act. Accordingly, any persons who trade or place orders to trade through employing fictitious devices or any other form of deception or contrivance will incur civil liability for market manipulation.[100] Examples of conduct that involve the use of manipulative devices include "flipping" or disclosing conflicting statements about certain qualifying investments through the Internet and engaging in transactions that are aimed at concealing the ownership of a qualifying investment to avoid compliance with the disclosure requirements.

Sixthly, illicit dissemination of information is prohibited in the Financial Services and Markets Act. Put differently, an insider or any person who knowingly gives information that conveys or is likely to convey a false or misleading impression about an investment or the issuer of an investment will be liable for market manipulation.[101] Lastly, distortion and misleading behaviour is also outlawed in the Financial Services and Markets Act. Thus, any conduct that gives a false or misleading impression of either the demand for or the supply of investments and behaviour that distorts or is likely to distort the market in such investments leads to civil liability on the part of the offenders.[102]

A separate civil prohibition against persons who encourage or require others to engage in market manipulation or other market abuse activities is also prescribed in the Financial Services and Markets Act.[103] The requirement or encouragement offence is committed where, by taking or refraining from taking any action,[104] a person in question has required or encouraged others to indulge in market manipulation or other related market abuse activities. This may indicate that the Financial Services and Markets Act has a broader market abuse civil prohibition than its predecessors. Nevertheless, most of these civil provisions were significantly amended by the Financial Services Act 2012.

---

[99] Other examples of price positioning involve the so-called abusive squeezes, where a person has a position (directly or indirectly) in an investment under which quantities of qualifying investment or related investment are deliverable.

[100] S 118(6).

[101] S 118(7); also see further Barnes *Stock Market Efficiency, Insider Dealing* 138 & Rider, Alexander, Linklater & Bazley *Market Abuse and Insider Dealing* 78.

[102] S 118(8); also see Russen *Financial Services Authorisation, Supervision* 206-207 & Avgouleas *The Mechanics and Regulation of Market Abuse* 332-358 for further related analysis.

[103] S 123; also see Rider, Alexander, Linklater & Bazley *Market Abuse and Insider Dealing* 78.

[104] Rider, Alexander, Linklater & Bazley *Market Abuse and Insider Dealing* 78; see the FSA's Code of Market Conduct 1.8.2.

Market manipulation is also treated as a criminal offence under the Financial Services and Markets Act.[105] Precisely, any person who makes misleading statements or who dishonestly conceals material facts relating to qualifying investments for the purpose of inducing or who is reckless as to whether they may induce other persons to enter or exercise or refrain from exercising any rights conferred by the relevant investments will be criminally liable for market manipulation.[106]

Additionally, engaging in misleading practices and conduct which creates a false or misleading impression in respect of the market or the value of any qualifying investments for the purposes of creating that impression and inducing other persons to acquire, dispose of, subscribe for, or underwrite such investments or to refrain from doing so is criminalised under the Financial Services and Markets Act.[107] This presupposes that misleading statements or omissions and other forms of market manipulation such as artificial transactions and trade-based manipulations are further prohibited and criminalised under the Financial Services and Markets Act.[108] Nevertheless, it must be noted that section 397 of the Financial Services and Markets Act was extensively amended by the Financial Services Act 2012 and its aspects relating to misleading statements were repealed and replaced by three new offences relating to: (a) misleading statements, (b) misleading impressions, and (c) misleading impressions relating to benchmarks.[109] In this regard, it must be noted that the FCA has to date, relatively managed to curb some market manipulation-related practices such as spoofing and layering in the UK financial markets.[110]

---

[105] S 397. This section replicates s 47(1) of the Financial Services Act.

[106] S 397(1) & (2). Also see Avgouleas *The Mechanics and Regulation of Market Abuse* 314-316.

[107] See s 397(3). While the prohibition under s 397(1) & (2) requires proof of dishonest or recklessness, liability in terms of s 397(3) may suffice even where mere misleading acts were executed by the accused persons. Also see Avgouleas *The Mechanics and Regulation of Market Abuse* 314-318.

[108] S 397(3); see further Avgouleas *The Mechanics and Regulation of Market Abuse* 318-320.

[109] Part 7 of the Financial Services Act 2012.

[110] Aitken "Market Abuse: Spoofing, Layering & the Complexity of Proving Intent" (12-04-2016) https://www.b-next.com/general/market-abuse-spoofing-layering-the-complexity-of-proving-intent/ (accessed 13-07-2017); *7722656 Canada Inc. (t/a Swift Trade Inc) v FSA* [2013] All ER (D) 266, where "layering" was defined as a practice that, *inter alia*, involves the fictitious electronic entering of relatively large orders of securities or financial instruments on a regulated market without a genuine intention that such orders will be executed in order not to attract counterparties (other investors) to deal on them while the orders, nevertheless, helps to move the price of the relevant securities and/or financial instruments due to the false price movements that were created by the initial false electronic orders. On the hand, in the context of market abuse, the term "spoofing" occurs when one intentionally places fictitious orders of securities or financial instruments on a regulated market to create a false impression in relation to the dealing, trading or supply and demand for such securities or financial instruments.

Market manipulation has further been indirectly made a criminal offence under the Fraud Act.[111] This Act introduced a new general offence fraud which discourages false representations, failure to disclose non-public material inside information and fraud by abuse of position.[112] Thus, although it is most likely that violations for market manipulation or other related activities may be prosecuted under the Financial Services and Markets Act or the Criminal Justice Act, such violations may also fall under the general offence of fraud as stipulated in the Fraud Act.[113]

6 3 1 Evaluation and Analysis of the Historical Overview of Market Manipulation Prohibition

Although market manipulation has been discouraged in the UK from as early as the 1860s,[114] it was only statutorily prohibited in South Africa in the late 1980s.[115] Prior to this, market manipulation was mainly prohibited by the common law in South Africa.[116] In contrast to the position in the UK where the concept of, and conduct amounting to market manipulation or other market abuse practices is statutorily defined,[117] this concept is not statutorily defined in the Financial Markets Act.[118]

Moreover, unlike the position in the UK where about seven types of market abuse are clearly enumerated and statutorily prohibited, only three forms of market abuse practices, namely, insider trading, prohibited trading practices (trade-based market manipulation) and the making or publication of false, misleading or deceptive promises, statements or forecasts (disclosure-based market manipulation) are statutorily discouraged in South Africa.[119]

---

[111] 2006 (c 35) (Fraud Act).

[112] A person may be regarded as having abused their position to commit market abuse even when their conduct consisted of an omission rather than an actual act. S 4 read with s 3.

[113] Barnes *Stock Market Efficiency, Insider Dealing* 128-129.

[114] See paragraph 6 3 above.

[115] Also see the relevant provisions of the now repealed statutes, the Stock Exchanges Control Act 1 of 1985, hereinafter referred to as the Stock Exchanges Control Act, see s 40 & the Financial Markets Control Act 55 of 1989, hereinafter referred to as the Financial Markets Control Act, see s 20 to s 23. Notably, s 1 of the Stock Exchanges Control Act prohibited the market manipulation of securities which included stocks, shares and debentures while the relevant provisions of the Financial Markets Control Act prohibited market manipulation of financial instruments, as defined in s 1 including futures contracts, option contracts and loan stock on a financial market. Cassim "An Analysis of Market Manipulation under the Securities Services Act 36 of 2004 (Part 1)" 2008 *SA Merc LJ* 33 34.

[116] Under common law, market manipulation is usually referred to as a crime of "rigging the market". Also see Cassim 2008 *SA Merc LJ* 34; 40-42.

[117] S 118 of the Financial Services and Markets Act.

[118] Ss 80 & 81 read with s 77. Also see further Cassim 2008 *SA Merc LJ* 34-35.

[119] Ss 78; 80; 81 & 82 of the Financial Markets Act.

Moreover, unlike the position under the Financial Markets Act,[120] the Financial Services and Markets Act treats insider trading,[121] market manipulation and other forms of market abuse practices on a more equal footing in the UK.[122] For instance, as discussed earlier,[123] market manipulation and other market abuse practices are all treated as civil or criminal offences under the Financial Services and Markets Act in the UK. This approach is desirable in that it has enabled the FSA, its successor (FCA) and other enforcement authorities to enforce the market abuse prohibition consistently in order to combat market manipulation and other related practices in the UK. In light of this and notwithstanding the fact that the market manipulation victims could utilise the relevant provisions of the Financial Institutions (Protection of Funds) Act[124] to recover their damages, it is submitted that the Financial Markets Act should be amended to enact provisions that extends the civil liability compensation orders to cases involving market manipulation[125] in order to improve and increase the enforcement of the market abuse prohibition in South Africa.[126]

Notably, behaviour would constitute market manipulation and/or other market abuse offences in terms of the Financial Services and Markets Act if it occurs in the UK or in relation to any qualifying investments which are mainly traded on a prescribed market in the UK[127] or the relevant EU member states. Thus, in order for the FCA to impose liability on the alleged offenders, there must be a territorial nexus with the relevant financial markets in the UK or elsewhere. This could imply that the UK's provisions on market manipulation and other market abuse practices have a restricted extra-territorial application.[128]

However, in South Africa, conduct may amount to market manipulation or insider trading if it was made in relation to securities listed on a regulated market (whether domestic or foreign) which is run in terms of the laws of the country in which the market conducts business as a market for dealing in

---

[120] This Act does not impose civil liability on persons who make or publish false, misleading or deceptive statements, promises and forecasts (disclosure-based market manipulation) or engage in prohibited trading practices (trade-based market manipulation). Ss 80 & 81 read with ss 78 & 82 of the Financial Markets Act.

[121] See further paragraph 6 2 above.

[122] S 118.

[123] See paragraph 6 3 above.

[124] 28 of 2001 as amended (Protection of Funds Act).

[125] Ss 80 & 81 of the Financial Markets Act.

[126] This approach could, if properly enforced, increase market abuse deterrence in South Africa without causing double jeopardy and/or over-criminalisation.

[127] S 118A(1)(a).

[128] See related remarks in paragraph 6 3 read with paragraphs 6 2 & 6 2 1 above.

securities listed on that market.[129] This implies, in contrast to the position in the UK,[130] that the South African market abuse prohibition is unlimitedly applicable to securities listed on any regulated foreign market and to both natural and juristic persons.[131] However, it remains to be seen whether the South African enforcement authorities will be able to mobilise and have sufficient resources necessary to implement and enforce the prohibition on market manipulation extra-territorially. Moreover, it is not expressly and statutorily provided how this so-called extra-territorial application will be utilised to protect the South African financial markets from non-resident persons who manipulate securities listed on a foreign market where such conduct has no effect on the related securities listed on the regulated financial markets in South Africa.[132]

As stated earlier, the UK amended its market abuse legislation in order to align it with the EU Market Abuse Directive[133] and subsequently with the EU Market Abuse Regulation and the Criminal Sanctions for Market Abuse Directive.[134] In light of this, the FSA was conferred more powers as a single administrative regulator to ensure that the prohibition on market manipulation and related practices is consistently complied with. The FSA, for instance, issued the Code of Market Conduct to guide all the relevant persons on conduct that amounts to market manipulation and related practices (including factors to be considered when determining whether such conduct amounts to market abuse) in the UK.[135] This Code of Market Conduct has, for instance, stipulated some factors to be considered when determining whether a person dealing in any qualifying investment has created a false or deceptive appearance of a trading activity in relation to a certain security or an artificial price or value of the qualifying investment and the extent to which the price, rate or option volatility movements for the affected investment are outside their normal daily, weekly or monthly range.[136] Notably, all the aforesaid powers and responsibilities are now vested in the FCA. Although such market conduct is also prohibited by the Financial Markets Act,[137] it is not quite clear whether

---

[129] S 77 of the Financial Markets Act, for the definition of "regulated market".

[130] S 118A(1)(a).

[131] Ss 77; 78; 80; 81& 82 of the Financial Markets Act. Also see generally Jooste 2006 *SALJ* 453; Cassim "Some Aspects of Insider Trading – Has the Securities Services Act, 36 of 2004 Gone too Far?" 2007 *SA Merc LJ* 44 66-67.

[132] See s 77 which defines the term "regulated market" read with ss 80 & 81 of the Financial Markets Act.

[133] See article 11 of the EU Market Abuse Directive. Also see further Cassim 2008 *SA Merc LJ* 38; paragraph 6 3 above.

[134] See paragraph 6 1 above.

[135] This Code of Market Conduct was revised on 1 July 2005 in accordance with s 119 of the Financial Services and Markets Act. The Code of Market Conduct is usually referred to as the "MAR".

[136] See MAR 1.6.10E.

[137] S 80(1)(a) read with s 81.

the Financial Services Board (FSB) has a similar Code or booklet containing the guidelines regarding the behaviour that amounts to market manipulation or related practices in South Africa.

In addition, market manipulation practices such as the creation of a false or deceptive appearance of trading activity in connection with a security,[138] dealing that will create an artificial practice[139] and placing orders to buy or sell listed securities in order to create an artificial price for a security or a false or deceptive appearance in trading activity in relation to that security[140] are merely stated and prohibited in the Financial Markets Act. Similarly, like the UK,[141] South Africa prohibits certain conduct that is deemed manipulative, improper, false or deceptive.[142] For example, the Financial Markets Act discourages practices such as: (a) wash sales,[143] (b) engaging in conduct that amounts to or creates matched orders,[144] (c) buying orders at successively higher prices and selling such orders at successively lower prices in order to improperly influence the market prices of certain securities,[145] (d) entering orders to buy securities (marking the close) at or near the close of the market to change or maintain the close price of a listed security,[146] (e) auctioning process,[147] (f) effecting a market corner,[148] and (g) maintaining an artificial price.[149] Notably, employing manipulating devices, schemes or artifices or manipulative act, practice or course of business to defraud other investors[150] is no longer expressly outlawed under the Financial Markets Act.[151] Furthermore, in contrast to the position in the UK, disclosure-based market manipulation and/or other related activities that are perpetrated through the Internet are not statutorily prohibited in the Financial Markets Act.[152] Moreover, the Financial Markets Act does not expressly provide practical

---

[138] S 80(1)(a)(i).
[139] S 80(1)(a)(ii).
[140] S 80(1)(b).
[141] See paragraph 6 3 above.
[142] S 80(3).
[143] S 80(3)(a).
[144] S 80(3)(b).
[145] S 80(3)(c).
[146] S 80(3)(d).
[147] S 80(3)(e).
[148] S 80(3)(f).
[149] S 80(3)(g).
[150] This conduct was previously outlawed in s 75(3)(h) of the Securities Services Act 36 of 2004 (Securities Services Act). The wording of this subsection is almost identical to s 118(6) of the Financial Services and Markets Act. Such related conduct was repealed from the Securities Services Act (see repealed ss 94(e); 97; 98; 99; 100 to 106 & s 111(1)(b)) when it was amended by the Financial Services General Laws Amendment Act 22 of 2008 (General Laws Amendment Act) which came into effect on 01 November 2008 and transposed into the Protection of Funds Act, see ss 6A to 6I.
[151] S 80.
[152] S 81 read with s 80.

guiding factors on how to determine whether certain practices may be deemed to be amounting to market manipulation.[153]

6 4 Available Penalties

Various sanctions and penalties such as civil, criminal and administrative penalties are employed to combat and discourage market abuse practices in the UK. However, it is important to note that the discussion under this sub-heading will mainly focus on penalties as prescribed in the Criminal Justice Act and the Financial Services and Markets Act.

Criminal penalties may be imposed on all persons who knowingly engage in market abuse practices in the UK. Thus, the contravention of the insider trading provisions contained in the Criminal Justice Act[154] and other market abuse provisions contained in the Financial Services and Markets Act will give rise to criminal penalties in the UK.[155] Criminal penalties for insider trading under the Criminal Justice Act may only be imposed on individuals.[156] However, the criminal penalties for insider trading under the Financial Services and Markets Act are now applicable to both natural and juristic persons.[157] Criminal penalties that may be imposed on individuals for insider trading or market manipulation include a fine or imprisonment for a term not exceeding six months, or both on summary conviction; or upon conviction on indictment, a fine or imprisonment for a term not exceeding seven years, or both.[158] For instance, Michael Coscia, a futures and high-frequency trader, was fined by the FCA for allegedly manipulating commodities futures prices and illegally obtaining profits of nearly $1.6m in 2016. The FCA also imposed a financial penalty on Michael Coscia for his alleged layering and contravention of section 118(5) of the Financial Services and Markets Act.[159] However, it must be noted that the FCA has relatively managed to institute more market abuse-related investigations without successfully concluding many of such cases to date. For instance, the FCA opened about 55 new investigations of market abuse cases in the UK as at 31 March 2016. Nonetheless, the FCA only managed to investigate and conclude one market abuse case during the

[153] S 80(3) read with subsections (4) & (5).

[154] See Part V read with ss 52 & 61 of the Criminal Justice Act.

[155] S 402 read with the repealed s 397 of the Financial Services and Markets Act; also see Part V of the Criminal Justice Act.

[156] See paragraph 6 2 read with paragraphs 6 2 1 & 6 3 above.

[157] S 402; see related remarks in paragraph 6 3 above.

[158] S 402 of the Financial Services and Markets Act; also see Avgouleas *The Mechanics and Regulation of Market Abuse* 323-324 & Rider, Alexander, Linklater & Bazley *Market Abuse and Insider Dealing* 93-94.

[159] Aitken (12-04-2016) <https://www.b-next.com/general/market-abuse-spoofing-layering-the-complexity-of-proving-intent/> (accessed 13-07-2017).

2014/2015 financial year.[160] In this regard, the FCA held that the low number of market abuse cases that were being successfully settled was influenced in part, by the fact that such cases are more complex, time-consuming, more sophisticated and very difficult to investigate.[161]

The perpetrators of market abuse in the UK may also be liable for civil penalties. Although these penalties apply to both juristic and natural persons under the Financial Services and Markets Act,[162] there are no civil penalties for insider trading under the Criminal Justice Act.[163] Civil penalties that may be imposed on the perpetrators (offenders) of market abuse under the Financial Services and Markets Act comprise unlimited monetary fines,[164] disgorgement of profits and/or the payment of compensation to the prejudiced persons.[165] A number of factors have to be considered when determining the appropriate amount of the fine to be imposed on the offenders. Such factors are provided for in the Financial Services and Markets Act as well as in the enforcement section of the FSA's Enforcement (Manual) Handbook[166] and this *status quo* is currently maintained by the FCA. The factors include the following: (a) the adverse effect of the behaviour on the market in question; (b) whether the person on whom the penalty is to be imposed is an individual or a juristic person; (c) the amount of profits accrued or loss avoided; (d) the degree to which the conduct in question was deliberate or reckless and (e) the conduct following the behaviour of the alleged offender in question.[167]

With regard to the last factor, the FCA may further consider the degree of co-operation that the accused person gave during the investigations of the wrongful conduct and whether any remedial steps were taken by that person from the time that behaviour was initially identified.[168] However, the FCA has somewhat struggled to obtain more settlements in market abuse-related cases in the UK in the past few years.[169]

---

[160] Hitchins (17-10-2016) <http://www.aoinvestigationsinsight.com/further-drop-in-number-of-market-abuse-cases-concluded-by-the-fca/> (accessed 13-07-2017).

[161] Hitchins (17-10-2016) <http://www.aoinvestigationsinsight.com/further-drop-in-number-of-market-abuse-cases-concluded-by-the-fca/> (accessed 13-07-2017).

[162] S 402; see similar comments in paragraph 6 3 above.

[163] See Part V; also see related remarks in paragraph 6 2 above.

[164] S 123(1).

[165] Also see further Avgouleas *The Mechanics and Regulation of Market Abuse* 375; Rider, Alexander, Linklater & Bazley *Market Abuse and Insider Dealing* 94.

[166] *Release 064* April 2007 (ENF).

[167] Ss 205; 206 & 210 of the Financial Services and Markets Act. See further ENF 14.7.4G & Avgouleas *The Mechanics and Regulation of Market Abuse* 374-377.

[168] See ENF 14.7.4.G(5). Also see Swan *Market Abuse Regulation* 113-123.

[169] Hitchins (17-10-2016) <http://www.aoinvestigationsinsight.com/further-drop-in-number-of-market-abuse-cases-concluded-by-the-fca/> (accessed 13-07-2017).

The courts may, at the request of the FCA, further impose monetary fines on a person who violates any market abuse provisions.[170] This usually follows after an application to the court by the FCA for an injunctive or restitution relief.[171] For instance, a financial advisor, Mark Samuel Taylor was fined £78,819 which was later reduced to £36,285 on the grounds of serious financial constraints on his part and banned from performing any function in relation to any regulated activity on the UK financial markets on 5 May 2016 after he committed insider trading and contravened section 118(2) of the Financial Services and Markets Act.[172]

In addition, a number of administrative penalties are used to curb market abuse in the UK.[173] For example, disciplinary sanctions such as variation of (withdrawal of authorisation) Part IV permission;[174] injunctions (including cease or desist orders) to take remedial steps, secure or freeze assets and to discourage a certain conduct.[175] These court injunctions can be imposed on any person who commits market abuse practices, regardless of whether such person is regulated by the FCA.[176] For instance, the FCA obtained a High Court judgment against Da Vinci Invest Ltd, Mineworld Ltd, Mr Szabolcs Banya, Mr Gyorgy Szabolcs Brad and Mr Tamas Pornye in respect of their various market abuse offences in August 2015. Four of these offenders were incorporated in Switzerland, Seychelles and Hungary and were found guilty of layering and other market manipulation-related offences involving about 186 UK-listed shares. Consequently, the FCA obtained a permanent court injunction and imposed financial penalties of over £7, 57 million against five of the aforesaid offenders in respect of their market abuse offences.[177] Nevertheless, proving intention of the offenders in respect of layering and/or spoofing has

---

[170] S 129 of the Financial Services and Markets Act.

[171] S 384 read with ss 381 & 383 of the Financial Services and Markets Act; also see Russen *Financial Services Authorisation, Supervision* 147-151.

[172] Anonymous "FCA Fines and Bans Financial Adviser for Committing Market Abuse" *Allen & Overy Investigations Insight* (10-06-2016) <http://www.allenovery.com/ publications/en-gb/Pages/FCA-fines-and-bans-financial-adviser-for-committing-market-abuse.aspx> (accessed 13-07-2017); also see s 6.5C of the FCA's Decision Procedure and Penalties Manual (DEPP).

[173] Swan *Market Abuse Regulation* 112.

[174] Ss 53 & 54 read with s 63 of the Financial Services and Markets Act; also see ENF 3, 4 & 5.

[175] Ss 380 & 381 of the Financial Services and Markets Act; also see ENF 6.1.1.G; ENF 6.2.1.G; ENF 6.6.1.G; ENF 6.3.2.G & ENF 6.3.7.G.

[176] ENF 6.1.1.G. A person who disobeys or fails to comply with an injunction may be held in contempt of court and could be liable to imprisonment, monetary fine or seizure of the assets. S 206 of the Financial Services and Markets Act; also see ENF 6.2.5.G & see further Swan *Market Abuse Regulation* 125.

[177] Aitken (12-04-2016) <https://www.b-next.com/general/market-abuse-spoofing-layering-the-complexity-of-proving-intent/> (accessed 13-07-2017).

been very difficult for both the courts as well as the FCA, especially, when conducting its market abuse investigations.[178]

Other administrative penalties that can be levied against market abuse offenders are public censure,[179] withdrawal of approval on former approved persons who are not fit to perform their initial authorised functions,[180] prohibition of individuals who engage in illicit trading activities from dealing or carrying out functions related to regulated activities[181] and imposing restitution and redress orders on any persons who commit market manipulation and/or other market abuse offences.[182] It should be borne in mind that these administrative penalties are applicable to all persons (natural and juristic persons), especially, under the Financial Services and Markets Act.[183]

The Financial Services and Markets Act further confers a private right of action to the FCA to apply to the courts for a restraining order or restitution order against any person who knowingly contravenes its relevant market abuse provisions.[184] Moreover, the FCA may also seek a court order against any alleged offenders to disgorge the profits gained or directly pay compensation to the persons affected by their market abuse activities.[185] Although a civil private right of action is available as indicated above to the persons who suffer losses due to other forms of market abuse, there is no such express private right of action for persons affected by market manipulation as contained in the Financial Services and Markets Act[186] and insider trading as contained in the Criminal Justice Act.[187]

6 4 1 Evaluation and Analysis of the Available Penalties

Both the UK[188] and South Africa use civil, criminal[189] and administrative penalties and/or remedies to combat market abuse practices in their respective

[178] Aitken (12-04-2016) <https://www.b-next.com/general/market-abuse-spoofing-layering-the-complexity-of-proving-intent/> (accessed 13-07-2017).

[179] S 205 of the Financial Services and Markets Act; also see ENF 12.

[180] S 59 read with ss 66 & 210 of the Financial Services and Markets Act; also see ENF 7.5.1.G.

[181] S 56(2) of the Financial Services and Markets Act. See generally ENF 8.1.2.G.

[182] Ss 382; 383 & 384 of the Financial Services and Markets Act. Also see ENF 9.1.2.G; ENF 9.4.2.G & ENF 9.5.1.G. See further Russen *Financial Services Authorisation, Supervision* 136-166.

[183] In this regard, it should be noted that administrative penalties under the Criminal Justice Act are possibly still limited to individuals (natural persons) alone.

[184] Ss 150; 380 & 382. The court orders for a private right of action do not however, apply to market abuse violations regarding the now repealed s 397 of the Financial Services and Markets Act.

[185] Rider, Alexander, Linklater & Bazley *Market Abuse and Insider Dealing* 94.

[186] See the repealed s 397 of the Financial Services and Markets Act and related sections under the Financial Services Act 2012; also see Rider, Alexander, Linklater & Bazley *Market Abuse and Insider Dealing* 94.

[187] Part V of the Criminal Justice Act.

[188] See paragraph 6 4 above.

financial markets. As is the position in the UK,[190] criminal and administrative penalties are used to discourage all forms of market abuse in South Africa.[191] On the other hand, civil penalties are employed only to curb insider trading under the Financial Markets Act.[192] In contrast to this position in South Africa, no civil penalties for insider trading are provided for under the Criminal Justice Act in the UK.[193] However, a number of civil penalties are now available to discourage and curb insider trading as well as other market abuse practices under the Financial Services and Markets Act and the Financial Services Act 2012.[194]

With regard to criminal penalties, South Africa rigidly imposes a maximum fine of R50 million, or imprisonment for a period not exceeding ten years, or both such fine and imprisonment against the offenders.[195] In contrast to this, unlimited monetary and other penalties may be imposed on the offenders by the FCA in the UK.[196]

As earlier discussed,[197] several factors are considered in order to determine appropriate civil monetary fines that will be imposed on the market abuse offenders in the UK. Likewise, almost similar factors are used to determine appropriate civil compensatory fines and administrative penalties in South Africa.[198] Moreover, like the UK,[199] and as already indicated above, South Africa imposes a variety of unlimited administrative penalties on persons who commit market abuse offences.[200] Additionally, like the FCA,[201] the FSB is now allowed to publish by notice on its official website or by means of other appropriate public media, any outcome, status or details of market abuse investigations (public censure) if such publication is in the public interest.[202]

---

[189] S 109(a) of the Financial Markets Act.

[190] See paragraph 6 4 above.

[191] Ss 78; 80; 81 & 82 of the Financial Markets Act.

[192] S 82.

[193] See paragraph 6 4 above.

[194] See paragraph 6 4 above.

[195] S 109(a) of the Financial Markets Act.

[196] S 123(1) of the Financial Services and Markets Act; also see Avgouleas *The Mechanics and Regulation of Market Abuse* 375.

[197] See paragraph 6 4 above.

[198] S 6D read ss 6A; 6B & 6C to 6I of the Protection of Funds Act. Read with ss 82 & 99 of the Financial Markets Act & see further Cassim "An Analysis of Market Manipulation under the Securities Services Act 36 of 2004 (Part 2)" 2008 *SA Merc LJ* 177 195.

[199] See paragraph 6 4 above.

[200] Ss 6A to 6I of the Protection of Funds Act; read with ss 82 & 99 of the Financial Markets Act & also see Cassim 2008 *SA Merc LJ* 195.

[201] Ss 123(3) & 124 of the Financial Services and Markets Act. Also see ENF 14.4.1.G.

[202] S 84(2)(e) of the Financial Markets Act.

6 5 Concluding Remarks

The failure to provide separate and distinct penalties for companies and individuals could have marred the successful enforcement of the market abuse prohibition in South Africa to date. Accordingly, it is recommended that the FSB should be expressly and statutorily authorised to impose separate and different penalties on individuals and juristic persons or companies that engage in market abuse activities in South Africa. Put differently, the FSB should be expressly and statutorily authorised to impose separate, different and unlimited monetary and other appropriate penalties, apart from those stipulated in the Financial Markets Act, on individuals and juristic persons or companies that engage in market abuse activities in South Africa. Moreover, the FSB, like the FCA,[203] should carefully and consistently utilise its statutory powers to publicise the names of the culprits who commit market abuse offences (public censure or name and shame approach) in South Africa.[204]

As is the position in the UK,[205] that the Financial Markets Act should be reviewed to enact provisions that give private rights of action to the affected persons for them to claim their damages directly from the market abuse offenders. In relation to this, it is submitted that the FSB should be statutorily required to provide its own Code of Market Abuse Conduct containing sufficient and adequate guidelines on factors that should be considered from time to time, in determining whether a trading practice and/or behaviour will give rise to or amounts to market abuse practices in order to increase the combating of such practices in South Africa.

It is further suggested that the Financial Markets Act should be amended to enact provisions that expressly and adequately define the concepts of "insider trading" and "market manipulation" in South Africa. Additionally, as is the position in the UK,[206] the Financial Markets Act should be amended to enact provisions that expressly discourage any market abuse activity or illicit dealing in securities on unregulated over the counter markets through agents or professional intermediaries and face-to-face transactions between non-professional intermediaries in South Africa. Lastly, the Financial Markets Act should also be reviewed to enact provisions that clearly enumerate sufficient guidelines or conditions under which the extra-territorial application of the market abuse ban will be employed to prevent cross-border market abuse activities consistently in South Africa and elsewhere.

---

[203] Generally see paragraphs 6 2; 6 3 & 6 4 above.
[204] See related remarks in paragraph 6 4 1 above.
[205] Generally see paragraph 6 4 above.
[206] See paragraph 6 2 above, for related remarks.

References

Books

Avgouleas E *The Mechanics and Regulation of Market Abuse: A Legal and Economic Analysis* (Oxford University Press Oxford 2005)

Barnes P *Stock Market Efficiency, Insider Dealing and Market Abuse* (Gower Publishing Limited Surrey England 2009)

Beuthin RC and Luiz SM *Beuthin's Basic Company Law* 3rd ed (Butterworths Durban 2000)

Blair MQC & Walker GA (eds) *Financial Services Law* 1st ed (Oxford University Press Oxford United Kingdom 2006)

Lyon GJ & Du Plessis JJ *The Law of Insider Trading in Australia* (The Federation Press Sydney 2005)

Rider B, Alexander K, Linklater L & Bazley S *Market Abuse and Insider Dealing* 2nd ed (Tottel Publishing Haywards Heath 2009)

Russen J *Financial Services Authorisation, Supervision, and Enforcement: A Litigator's Guide* (Oxford University Press New York 2006)

Swan EJ *Market Abuse Regulation* 1st ed (Oxford University Press United States of America 2006)

Journal articles

Bhattacharya U & Daouk H "The World Price of Insider Trading" 2002 *Journal of Finance* 75-108

Black J & Nobles R "Personal Pensions Misselling: The Causes and Lessons of Regulatory Failure" 1998 *MLR* 789-820

Botha D "Control of Insider Trading in South Africa: A Comparative Analysis" 1991 *SA Merc LJ* 1-18

Botha D "Increased Maximum Fine for Insider Trading: A Realistic and Effective Deterrent?" 1990 *SALJ* 504-508

Cassim R "An Analysis of Market Manipulation under the Securities Services Act 36 of 2004 (Part 1)" 2008 *SA Merc LJ* 33-60

Cassim R "An Analysis of Market Manipulation under the Securities Services Act 36 of 2004 (Part 2)" 2008 *SA Merc LJ* 177-199

Cassim R "Some Aspects of Insider Trading – Has the Securities Services Act, 36 of 2004 Gone too Far?" 2007 *SA Merc LJ* 44-70

Jooste R "A Critique of the Insider Trading Provisions of the 2004 Securities Services Act" 2006 *SALJ* 437-460

Luiz SM "Insider Trading Regulation – If at First You Don't Succeed..." 1999 *SA Merc LJ* 136-151

Osode PC "The New South African Insider Trading Act: Sound Law Reform or Legislative Overkill?" 2000 *Journal of African Law* 239-263

Rider BAK "Policing the City-Combating Fraud and Other Abuses in the Corporate Securities Industry" 1988 *Current Legal Problems* 47-68

Steinberg MI "Insider Trading Regulation–A Comparative Perspective" 2003 *The International Lawyer* 153-171
Van Deventer G "New Watchdog for Insider Trading" 1999 *FSB Bulletin* 2-3
Van Deventer G "Harnassing Administrative Law in Encouraging Compliance" 2009 *FSB Bulletin* 3-4

Case law

South Africa

Pretorius and Another v Natal South Sea Investment Trust 1965 3 SA 410 (W)

United Kingdom

R v Kylsant [1932] 1 KB 442
7722656 Canada Inc. (t/a Swift Trade Inc) v FSA [2013] All ER (D) 266

Legislation

South Africa

Companies Act 61 of 1973
Companies Act 71 of 2008
Consumer Protection Act 68 of 2008
Financial Institutions (Protection of Funds) Act 28 of 2001 as amended
Financial Markets Act 19 of 2012
Financial Markets Control Act 55 of 1989
Financial Services General Laws Amendment Act 22 of 2008
Securities Services Act 36 of 2004
Stock Exchanges Control Act 1 of 1985

United Kingdom

Bank of England Act 1998 (c 11) as amended
Bank of England and Financial Services Act 2016 (c 14)
Banking Act 2009 (c 1)
Companies Act 1980 (c 22)
Companies Act 1985 (c 6)
Companies Act 2006 (c 46)
Company Securities (Insider Dealing) Act 1985 (c 8)
Criminal Justice Act 1993 (c 36)
Financial Services and Markets Act 2000 (c 8)
Financial Services Act 1986 (c 60)
Financial Services Act 2012 (c 21)
Fraud Act 2006 (c 35)
Larceny Act 1861 (24 and 25 Vict c 96)

Prevention of Fraud (Investments) Act 1939 (c 16)
Prevention of Fraud (Investments) Act 1958 (c 45)

European Union

Commission Directive 2003/124/EC of 22 December 2003 implementing Directive 2003/6/EC of 28 January 2003 on the definition and public disclosure of inside information and the definition of market manipulation [2003] OJ L339/70

Commission Directive 2003/125/EC of 22 December 2003 on the fair presentation of investment recommendations and the disclosure of conflicts of interest [2003] OJ L339/073

Criminal Sanctions for Market Abuse Directive 2014/57/EU of the European Parliament and of the Council of 16 April 2014 on criminal sanctions for market abuse, [2014] OJ L 173/179

European Union Directive on Insider Dealing and Market Manipulation, the Directive of the European Parliament and Council of 28 January 2003 on insider dealing and market manipulation (market abuse) 2003/6/EC [2003] OJ L96/16

European Union Insider Dealing Directive, Council Directive 89/592/EEC of 13 November 1989 [1989] OJ 1989 L334/30

Financial Services and Markets: The Prospectus Regulations [2005] SI 2005/381

Financial Services and Markets Act 2000 (Prescribed Markets and Qualifying Investments) Order 2001 SI 2001/1996

Market Abuse Regulation (EU) No. 596/2014 of the European Parliament and of the Council of 16 April 2014 on market abuse (market abuse regulation) and repealing Directive 2003/6 of the European Parliament and of the Council and Commission Directives 200/124/EC, 2003/125/EC and 2004/72/EC, [2014] OJ L 173/1

Market Abuse Regulations 2016, SI 2016/680

Commissions, committees, statutory instruments and reports

South Africa

Financial Services Board *Annual Report* 2011

Financial Services Board *Annual Report* 2013

The King Task Group into Insider Trading Legislation *Minority Report on Insider Trading* 1997

The King Task Group into the Insider Trading Legislation *First Report* 15 May 1997

The King Task Group into the Insider Trading Legislation *Final Report* 21 October 1997

Van Wyk de Vries Commission of Inquiry into the *Companies Act* of 1973

United Kingdom

Financial Services and Markets Act 2000 (Market Abuse) Regulations 2005 SI 2005/381

Financial Services and Markets Act 2000 (Prescribed Markets and Qualifying Investments) Order 2001, SI 2001/1996 as amended by Regulation 10 of the Market Abuse Regulations 2005

Financial Services Authority Handbook (Code of Market Conduct) *FSA Release* 19 July 2001

Financial Services Authority's *Market Abuse Directive Disclosure Rules Instrument* 2005, 17 March 2005

Financial Services Authority's *Market Abuse Directive Instrument* 2005, 17 March 2005

Insider Dealing (Securities and Regulated Markets) Order 1994

Traded Securities (Disclosure) Regulation 1994

Thesis and dissertations

Chitimira H *A Comparative Analysis of the Enforcement of Market Abuse Provisions* (LLD-thesis Nelson Mandela Metropolitan University 2012)

Chitimira H *The Regulation of Insider Trading in South Africa: A Roadmap for an Effective, Competitive and Adequate Regulatory Statutory Framework* (LLM-dissertation University of Fort Hare 2008)

Internet sources

Aitken R "Market Abuse: Spoofing, Layering & the Complexity of Proving Intent" (12-04-2016) <https://www.b-next.com/general/market-abuse-spoofing-layering-the-complexity-of-proving-intent/> (accessed 13-07-2017)

Anonymous "FCA Fines and Bans Financial Adviser for Committing Market Abuse" *Allen & Overy Investigations Insight* (10-06-2016) <http://www. allenovery.com/publications/en-gb/Pages/FCA-fines-and-bans-financial-adviser-for-committing-market-abuse.aspx> (accessed 13-07-2017)

Financial Services Board "Enforcement Committee Actions" *Media Release* (28-06-2011) <http://www.fsb.co.za/ftp://ftp.fsb.co.za/public/documents/AReport2011.pdf> (accessed 22-11-2013)

Financial Services Board "List of Current Investigations of the Directorate of Market Abuse" *Media Release* (28-06-2011) <http://www.fsb.co.za/ftp://ftp.fsb.co.za/public/documents/AReport2011.pdf> (accessed 22-11-2013)

Hitchins "Focusing on the Latest Trends, Risks and Developments in Financial Services Investigations" *Allen & Overy Investigations Insight* (17-10-2016) <http://www.aoinvestigationsinsight.com/further-drop-in-number-of-market-abuse-cases-concluded-by-the-fca/> (accessed 13-07-2017).

Morgan Lewis "UK Market Abuse Regime Extends its Reach: Implications for Market Participants" *Morgan Lewis* (2016)

<https://www.morganlewis.com/pubs/uk-market-abuse-regime-extends-its-reach-implications-for-market-participants> (accessed 12-07-2017)

Myburgh A & Davis B "The Impact of South Africa's Insider Trading Regime: A Report for the Financial Services Board" (25-03-2004) <http://www.genesis-analytics.com/public/FSBReport.pdf> (accessed 09-02-2013)

SIA Partners (Banking and Insurance) "Brexit and the Impact on the UK's Regulatory Framework" (2016) <http://en.finance.sia-partners.com/brexit-and-impact-uks-regulatory-framework> (accessed 12-07-2017).

Van Deventer G "Anti-Market Abuse Legislation in South Africa" (10-06-2008) <http://www.fsb.co.za/public/marketabuse/FSBReport.pdf> (accessed 05-05-2013)

Chapter 7

Selected Aspects of the Implementation of Market Abuse Laws in the United Kingdom: Lessons for South Africa

7 1 Introduction

Several anti-market abuse regulatory and enforcement approaches are employed by the relevant authorities to curb the occurrence and effects of market abuse practices in the United Kingdom (UK). Thus, like several other countries, the UK has a regulatory and enforcement framework in place to combat insider trading,[1] as well as other forms of market manipulation[2] practices. Put differently, a robust and relatively effective anti-market abuse regulatory and enforcement framework is in place in the UK. In this regard, it must be noted that both insider trading and market manipulation practices are collectively treated as "market abuse" in this chapter. Consequently, and where appropriate, the relevant enforcement approaches of the UK's market abuse regime will be compared with similar approaches that are provided for in the South African anti-market abuse framework.[3] This is primarily done to,

---

* This chapter is influenced in part, by an article that was initially published in the *Mediterranean Journal of Social Sciences* and this was done with legal permission from the editors of this *Journal*, see Chitimira "Overview of the Enforcement of the Market Abuse Prohibition in the United Kingdom" 2014(5)(20) *Mediterranean Journal of Social Sciences* 272-283.

[1] See the relevant provisions of the Criminal Justice Act 1993 (c 36) (Criminal Justice Act).

[2] See the relevant provisions of the Financial Services and Markets Act 2000 (c 8) (Financial Services and Markets Act). Also see Avgouleas *The Mechanics and Regulation of Market Abuse: A Legal and Economic Analysis* (2005) 307. For further related analysis on the enforcement of the market abuse ban in other countries, see Bhattacharya & Daouk "The World Price of Insider Trading" 2002 *Journal of Finance* 75 75-108; Lyon & Du Plessis *The Law of Insider Trading in Australia* (2005) 159-168.

[3] For further related analysis, see ss 78; 80; 81 & 82 of the Financial Markets Act 19 of 2012 (Financial Markets Act); Chitimira *A Comparative Analysis of the Enforcement of Market Abuse Provisions* (Unpublished LLD thesis, Nelson Mandela Metropolitan University) 2012, 319-332. Also see Botha "Control of Insider Trading in South Africa: A Comparative Analysis" 1991 *SA Merc LJ* 1 1-18; Botha "Increased Maximum Fine for Insider Trading: A Realistic and Effective Deterrent?" 1990 *SALJ* 504 504-508; Chitimira *The Regulation of Insider Trading in South Africa: A Roadmap for an Effective, Competitive and Adequate Regulatory Statutory Framework* (Unpublished LLM dissertation, University of Fort Hare) 2008, 41–72; Loubser "Insider Trading and other Market Abuses (Including the Effective Management of Price–sensitive Information)" in the *Insider Trading Booklet* final draft, (2006) 18-20; 24-27 <http://www.jse.co.za/public/ insider/JSEbooklet.pdf> (accessed 03-03-2014); the Johannesburg Stock Exchange Limited (JSE) "Insider Trading and other Market Abuses (Including the Effective Management of Price–sensitive Information)" in the *Insider Trading Booklet*, (2013) 1-26

inter alia, isolate possible and applicable anti-market abuse enforcement approaches from the UK's market abuse regime[4] that could be adopted and/or integrated in the South African anti-market abuse enforcement framework. Accordingly, the role of the Financial Services Authority (FSA) and its successor, the Financial Conduct Authority (FCA) is analysed first. Secondly, a similar analysis will be carried out in respect of the courts. Thirdly, the role of the self-regulatory organisations will be discussed. Lastly, final concluding remarks will be provided.

7 2 Detection, Prosecution and Enforcement of the Market Abuse Prohibition

7 2 1 The Role of the FCA and its Predecessor, the FSA

The FSA was established as the main single body which administers an integrated regulatory system for all the financial services and markets in the UK.[5] This further suggests that the FSA had the main responsibility for administering and enforcing the prohibition on market abuse in the UK.[6] Notably, the

---

<http://www.jse.co.za/Libraries/JSE_Regulatory_Environment_Insider_Trading/InsiderTrading_Booklet.sflb.ashx> (accessed 03-03-2014); Van Deventer "Anti-Market Abuse Legislation in South Africa" (10-06-2008) 1-5 <http://www.fsb.co.za/public/marketabuse/FSBReport.pdf> (accessed 05-05-2013); Myburgh & Davis "The Impact of South Africa's Insider Trading Regime: A Report for the Financial Services Board" (25-03-2004) 8-33 <http://www.genesis-analytics.com/public/FSBReport.pdf> (accessed 09-02-2013); Chanetsa "Insider Trading is Notoriously Hard to Prosecute" (2004-04-26) *Business Report* page number unknown; *Pretorius and Another v Natal South Sea Investment Trust* 1965 3 SA 410 (W), were the courts failed to convict the suspected insider trading offenders; Blincoe "Datatec Directors Pay Up on Insider Trading Charges" (2001) <http://www.theregister.co.uk/2001/05/23/ datatec_directors_pay_up/> (accessed 03-03-2014), where two Datatec directors, Jens Montanana and Robin Rindel were reportedly fined about R1 million each for insider trading by the Financial Services Board (FSB); Barron "Greg Draws a Blank in Belfort Parallel" (2014) <http://www.timeslive.co.za/Feeds/2014/02/02/greg-draws-a-blank-in-belfort-parallel> (accessed 03-03-2014), where Greg Blank was reportedly sentenced to eight years imprisonment for stock market-related fraud and front running in 1992; Osode "The New South African Insider Trading Act: Sound Law Reform or Legislative Overkill?" 2000 *Journal of African Law* 239 239-263; Jooste "A Critique of the Insider Trading Provisions of the 2004 Securities Services Act" 2006 *SALJ* 437 441–460; Beuthin & Luiz *Beuthin's Basic Company Law* (2000) 235–238; Luiz "Market Abuse and the Enforcement Committee" 2011 *SA Merc LJ* 151 152-172; Luiz "Insider Trading Regulation – If at First You Don't Succeed…" 1999 *SA Merc LJ* 136 136-151 & Henning & Du Toit "The Regulation of False Trading, Market Manipulation and Insider Trading" 2000 *Journal for Juridical Science* 155 155-165, for historical analysis of the regulation and enforcement of the market abuse prohibition in South Africa.

[4] Barnes *Stock Market Efficiency, Insider Dealing and Market Abuse* (2009) 125.

[5] The FSA was introduced on 27 October 1997 as the main regulatory body which replaced all earlier and similar regulatory agencies in the UK. See Blair & Walker *Financial Services Law* (2006) 3.

[6] This is the so-called single regulator model which in this context entails that only one regulatory body (previously the FSA), currently the FCA, has the main authority to supervise the regulation and enforcement of the market abuse ban in the UK. It is, however, not the purpose of this sub-heading to discuss all the merits and demerits of this so-called single regulator model.

Financial Services Act 2012[7] amended the Financial Services and Markets Act and replaced the FSA with the FCA on 1 April 2013.

Although there are a number of other regulatory bodies, the FSA had the sole responsibility and powers to police the enforcement of the market abuse prohibition in the UK. These powers include to investigate or refer a matter to its Regulatory Decisions Committee (RDC);[8] impose unlimited monetary penalties; make a public statement that a person has engaged in market abuse, and to apply to the courts for an injunction to claim restitution or restrain continued market abuse.[9] The FSA could further make market abuse rules and determine the general policy and principles to govern the performance of particular functions in the relevant financial markets.[10] All these responsibilities are now vested in the FCA.

In order to enhance its enforcement, the FSA was divided into several divisions such as the Supervision, Markets and Enforcement Divisions.[11] The Supervision Division's sub-divisions within the FSA could make referrals to the Enforcement Division consist of major retail groups, retail firms, contact revenue and information management groups and the financial markets.[12] The FSA was further equipped with extensive interrogatory and investigatory powers which it may objectively exercise against any persons who violate the market abuse provisions.[13] It could, for example, by written notice require an authorised person to provide specific information and other specified documents relevant to an ongoing investigation.[14] Moreover, the FSA could appoint additional persons as investigators of certain market abuse cases.[15] The aforesaid interrogatory and investigatory powers are now bestowed upon the FCA.[16]

---

[7] (c 21) (Financial Services Act 2012).

[8] Ss 123(1) & 126 of the Financial Services and Markets Act.

[9] S 2(4) of the Financial Services and Markets Act which stipulated the general functions of the FSA; also see Part 2; 4; 5 read with Parts 6 & 7 of the Financial Services Act 2012, which provides related general functions of the FCA. Also see Barnes *Stock Market Efficiency, Insider Dealing* 138-139.

[10] Ss 138 to 158. For further analysis, check Blair & Walker *Financial Services Law* 14-17.

[11] Swan *Market Abuse Regulation* (2006) 88.

[12] Therefore, supervisors are responsible for isolating market abuse cases in order to submit them to the Enforcement Division or the Crown Prosecution Services (CPS) or the Director of Public Prosecutions (DPP) for further investigation and prosecution.

[13] Ss 165 to 169 & s 284 of the Financial Services and Markets Act.

[14] S 165(1); (2) & (3) of the Financial Services and Markets Act; also see further Avgouleas *The Mechanics and Regulation of Market Abuse* 368-370.

[15] Ss 97; 167; 168; 173 & 175 of the Financial Services and Markets Act; see further Rider, Alexander, Linklater & Bazley *Market Abuse and Insider Dealing* (2009) 189-190.

[16] Ss 118(5); 126 read with ss 174(2); 176 and other relevant provisions under Parts 8 & 11 of the Financial Services and Markets Act; Clifford Chance "Overview of United States and United Kingdom Derivative and Commodity Market Enforcement Regimes" 2016 *Clifford Chance Markets Publication Series* 1 194-199.

Before the FSA was replaced by the FCA, it could act as a quasi-judicial and quasi-legislative regulatory body. This quasi-judicial and quasi-legislative regulatory authority is now bestowed upon the FCA. Consequently, the FCA may seek judicial and quasi-judicial remedies from the High Courts, namely, issuer freezing orders or restitution orders against market abuse offenders, in order to stop a particular market abuse conduct. Moreover, the FCA's legislative role comprises, *inter alia*, powers to promulgate relevant rules regarding market abuse to guide all market participants in the UK.[17] In light of this, the FSA had a Code of Market Conduct which provides guidance regarding conduct that amounts to market abuse in the UK.[18] A similar Code of Market Conduct and an Enforcement Guide are now provided by the FCA.[19]

Furthermore, the Code of Market Conduct outlines in more detail the standards required of all participants in the UK's financial markets. It broadly defines three categories of conduct that amount to market abuse, namely misuse of information, dissemination of false or misleading information and market distortion. Misuse of information is defined to involve behaviour (action or inaction) that is based on information which is not generally available but which would be relevant to an investor's dealings in a particular investment and which is ordinarily disclosed to the market. Dissemination of false or misleading information is defined to involve behaviour that gives rise to or that is likely to give rise to false or misleading impression as to the supply or demand, price or value of an investment.[20] Distortion of the market is defined in the Code of Market Conduct to include conduct that interferes with the normal process of supply and demand and which manipulates the market price of an investment.[21]

Information gathering and relying on competent companies or skilled persons is another tool that is used by the FCA. This enables the FCA to gather information from both authorised persons and in certain instances, from non-regulated persons to prevent possible market abuse activity from occurring. Specifically, this is done by the use of skilled person's reports to identify

---

[17] S 119 read with s 122 of the Financial Services and Markets Act.

[18] See the FSA Handbook (Code of Market Conduct) released on 19 July 2001.

[19] See further the FCA's Code of Market Conduct *MAR Release 18* July 2017 & the FCA Enforcement Guide 01 April 2014.

[20] Both the FCA and its predecessor, the FSA, utilised the Internet bulletin boards to disclose relevant information relating to, inter alia, a number of qualifying investments. This is aimed at preventing market manipulation activities like the so-called pump and dump schemes which often prejudice innocent investors.

[21] For example, when a person purchases large amounts of a particular share at or near the end of the day to mislead other investors.

or track market abuse practices in the UK's financial markets.[22] In other words, the FCA is empowered to appoint skilled persons to collect and update it with the relevant market abuse-related information.[23] The FCA is also obliged to share relevant market abuse-related information with other regulatory bodies such as the Financial Policy Committee (FPC), the Prudential Regulation Authority (PRA), the Serious Fraud Office (SFO), the Serious Organised Crime Agency (SOCA), the National Crime Agency (NCA), the National Fraud Authority (NFA), the Economic Crime Agency (ECA) and the Financial Ombudsman Service (FOS).[24] The FCA and the PRA will have a joint responsibility to continue with the independent dispute resolution service in respect of the Financial Services Compensation Scheme (FSCS). Additionally, the FCA has the responsibility to operate the Financial Crime Information Network (Fin-Net).[25]

The FCA may impose disciplinary sanctions on persons who commit market abuse offences. Such disciplinary sanctions comprise injunctions to disgorge the profits gained or stop certain market abuse activity, issuing warning notices, cancelling or withdrawing of Part IV permission, and prohibiting certain individuals from carrying out their functions that relate to regulated activities.[26] These duties were previously imposed on the FSA prior to 1 April 2013.

With regard to detection, the FSA in conjunction with the London Stock Exchange (LSE) relied on the Stock Exchange Automated Quotation market marking system to detect all possible market abuse activities in the relevant financial markets.[27] This function is now executed by the FCA in conjunction with the LSE. Moreover, all listed UK equities and other investments listed on a subsidiary market known as the Alternative Investment Market could further rely on the Stock Exchange Alternative Trading System or Stock Exchange Automated Quotation or another trading system known as the Stock Exchange Alternative Trading System Plus to detect and curb market

---

[22] Thus, the FCA employs various people with the relevant expertise the purposes of executing its market abuse supervisory and regulatory mandate in the UK. Likewise, its predecessor (FSA) was manned by about 2500 to 3000 competent persons (staff). This could further imply that that the Enforcement Division and other Divisions of the FSA had competent and skilled persons. See generally Rider, Alexander, Linklater & Bazley *Market Abuse and Insider Dealing* 190-195 & Blair & Walker *Financial Services Law* 34-35.

[23] Ss 166 & 166A of the Financial Services and Markets Act.

[24] Ss 230A & 232A of the Financial Services and Markets Act; ss 24F; 24G & 24H of the Financial Services and Markets Act 2000 (Regulated Activities) Order 2001 & related provisions under the of the Financial Services and Markets Act 2000 (Regulated Activities) Amendment Order 2013. See further Anonymous "The Financial Conduct Authority: An Overview" 2013 *Allen & Overy Investigations Insight* 3 3-27.

[25] Anonymous 2013 *Allen & Overy Investigations Insight* 8.

[26] Rider, Alexander, Linklater & Bazley *Market Abuse and Insider Dealing* 203 & 225-229.

[27] Barnes *Stock Market Efficiency, Insider Dealing* 19.

abuse practices. Any market abuse activities that are detected will be reported to the FCA for further adjudication. The FCA is also obliged to co-operate with other regulatory authorities such as the FPC, the PRA, the Bank of England, the FOS, the FSCS and the Money Advice Service.[28] Accordingly, the FCA has reportedly entered into some co-operation Memoranda of Understanding (MOUs) with most of these institutions for the purposes of, *inter alia*, enhancing the combating of market abuse in the UK.[29]

In order to combat cross-border market abuse practices, the FSA concluded some co-operation with similar bodies in other jurisdictions. It has, for instance, signed various MOUs with other regulatory bodies like the United States Securities and Exchange Commission (SEC), the Commodity Futures Trading Commission (CFTC) and the International Organisation of Securities Commissions (IOSCO).[30] It is expected that the FCA will continue to abide by the stated MOUs in order increase the combating of cross-border market abuse practices in the UK and elsewhere. This could improve the extra-territorial application of the market abuse prohibition as well as the combating of cross-border market abuse practices in the UK.[31] Nevertheless, in light of the British European Union (EU) Brexit referendum outcome of 23 June 2016 (Brexit) where majority of the British citizens voted to leave the EU,[32] it is uncertain whether the FCA will continue to co-operate with other international regulatory authorities from the EU such as the European Systemic Risk Board (ESRB), the European Banking Authority (EBA), the

---

[28] Anonymous 2013 *Allen & Overy Investigations Insight* 33-36; see further ss 3D; 3E; 3I; 3Q; 9H; 9Q & 9Y of the Financial Services and Markets Act.

[29] Anonymous 2013 *Allen & Overy Investigations Insight* 33-36.

[30] In 2008, the FSA co-chaired the IOSCO task force on other unregulated entities and hedge funds in order to examine alternative regulatory approaches that mitigate the risk associated with their illicit market abuse practices. Generally see the CFTC & the FSA's *Memorandum of Understanding on Consultation, Cooperation and the Exchange of Information Related to Market Oversight* (2006) <http://www.fsa.gov.uk/pubs/ mou/cftc.pd> (accessed 27-01-2014) & see further the FSA "FSA Signs Regulatory Cooperation Agreement with the CFTC" (20-11-2006) http://www.fsa.gov.uk/ pages/Library/Communication/PR/2006/118.shtml> (accessed 27-01-2014). Also see the CFTC & the SEC "A Joint Report of the SEC and the CFTC on Harmonization of Regulation" *Report* 16 October 2009 81; also see Memoranda of Understanding (MOUs) which can be accessed at <http://www.hm-treasury.gov.uk/documents/financial_services/regulating_financial_services/fin_rfs_mou.cfm> (accessed 26-01-2014) & generally see the IOSCO Technical Committee Working Party 4 on *Principles for Memorandum of Understanding, XVI Annual Conference* 5 September 1991, which provides the model adopted by the FSA on several financial information sharing agreements (MOUs) that it has entered into with other regulatory bodies since 1992. Blair & Walker *Financial Services Law* 35-38.

[31] *7722656 Canada Inc. (t/a Swift Trade Inc) v FSA* [2013] All ER (D) 266; the FCA "Michael Coscia Final Notice" *FCA Final Notice* (03-07-2013) <http://www.fca.org.uk/your-fca/documents/final notices/2013/michael-coscia> (accessed 15-07-2017) & Clifford Chance 2016 *Clifford Chance Markets Publication Series* 178-179.

[32] SIA Partners (Banking and Insurance) "Brexit and the Impact on the UK's Regulatory Framework" (2016) 1-4 <http://en.finance.sia-partners.com/brexit-and-impact-uks-regulatory-framework> (accessed 12-07-2017).

European Insurance and Occupational Pensions Authority (EIOPA), the European Securities and Markets Authority (ESMA) and the Joint Committee of the European Supervisory Authorities.[33]

The FCA also plays a key role in the enforcement of the securities and market abuse provisions in the UK. For instance, notwithstanding the fact that the FCA is primarily responsible for the enforcement of the civil remedy for market abuse, it further oversees the enforcement of other securities laws in the UK.

Moreover, although a few criminal cases of market manipulation and insider trading have been successfully prosecuted since the inception of the UK's market abuse regime in 1986, relatively more prosecutions of such cases have been obtained, especially, after 2001 when the FSA took over from the Department of Trade and Industry (DTI).[34] For instance, about five criminal cases of market abuse were successfully prosecuted by the FSA.[35] Notably, the number of successfully prosecuted market abuse cases increased in the recent past years. Additionally, in the *Rigby* and *Bailey* scandal, Carl Rigby and Gareth Bailey were convicted for making a reckless statement, promise or forecast which was deceptive and misleading and sentenced to eighteen months imprisonment each.[36] They were further convicted of contravening the disclosure provisions of the Financial Services and Markets Act[37] and sentenced to a two-year jail term each. In the *Hipwel* and *Bhoyrul* scandal, Hipwell was jailed for six months; Shepherd was also jailed for three months while Bhoyrul was sentenced to 180 hours of community service for market abuse and conspiracy to commit market abuse on 17 December 2005.[38] Related responsibilities are now vested in the FCA. In this regard, it is important to note that the FCA has limited prosecutorial powers in respect of

[33] Anonymous 2013 *Allen & Overy Investigations Insight* 37-40.

[34] The DTI was previously responsible for enforcing the insider trading prohibition in the UK. It was generally believed that the DTI failed to obtain more convictions in criminal cases involving insider trading in the UK. Precisely, about 15 cases involving 19 individuals were prosecuted for insider trading during the period between 1984 & 1996 in the UK. However, no convictions were obtained in all these 15 cases. Barnes *Stock Market Efficiency, Insider Dealing* 161.

[35] See generally Barnes *Stock Market Efficiency, Insider Dealing* 161.

[36] Barnes *Stock Market Efficiency, Insider Dealing* 161.

[37] See the repealed s 397(1) and related provisions under the Financial Services Act 2012 ; also see Barnes *Stock Market Efficiency, Insider Dealing* 161.

[38] Hipwell, Bhoyrul & Shepherd allegedly conspired between August 1999 & February 2000 to buy shares in 44 companies that they later tipped in their column over the Internet. As a result, Hipwell made £41 000, Anil Bhoyrul £15 000 & Terry Shepherd gained about £17 000. Barnes *Stock Market Efficiency, Insider Dealing* 162-164.

market abuse criminal offences where such offences fall within the scope of other specific criminal offences.[39]

In contrast to the few successful prosecutions achieved in the criminal cases of market abuse by the FSA,[40] relatively more settlements in civil cases involving market abuse, especially, after enactment of the enactment of the Financial Services and Markets Act[41] and the Financial Services Act 2012 were obtained by both the FSA and the FCA respectively. For instance, about twelve cases of market abuse offences which were committed during the period between April 2004 and March 2007 were successfully settled with the FSA.[42] Moreover, about five cases which constituted a breach of the FSA's Listing Rules were settled with the FSA during the same period.[43] The number of successfully settled market abuse cases has relatively increased with the introduction of the FCA in 2013.

The FSA had, in the wake of the early 1980s market abuse scandals such as the *Guinness-Distillers*[44] and the *Blue Arrow* cases,[45] subsequently introduced stricter measures to curb and prevent the recurrence of similar scandals in all the prescribed markets in the UK.[46] For example, after a bogus take-over scheme for the shares of Distillers company, the chairman and chief executive officer of Guinness company, Ernest Saunders, financiers and the share support group members namely, Gerald Ronson, Sir Jack Lyons and stockbroker Antony Parnes were all convicted of conspiracy, theft and issuing false, misleading or deceptive accounting statements.[47] Sir Jack Lyons was stripped of his knighthood, Saunders was sentenced to ten years in jail (he, however, served five months of this sentence but it was later halved on appeal due to his pre-senile dementia medical condition) and Gerald Ronson was fined for five million pounds plus a one-year jail term. Antony Parnes was sentenced to

[39] *R v Rollins* [2010] UKSC 39; *FCA v Hannam* [2014] UKUT 0233; *FCA v David John Hobbs* [2013] EWCA Civ 918; *FCA v Da Vinci Invest Limited* [2015] EWHC 2401 (Ch) & Clifford Chance 2016 *Clifford Chance Markets Publication Series* 188.

[40] Rider, Alexander, Linklater & Bazley *Market Abuse and Insider Dealing* 94.

[41] See Barnes *Stock Market Efficiency, Insider Dealing* 174 & Rider, Alexander, Linklater & Bazley *Market Abuse and Insider Dealing* 95.

[42] Eight of these cases involved insider trading; one case constituted improper disclosure of non-public material information; two involved the unlawful dissemination and one constituted distortion and misleading behaviour. Barnes *Stock Market Efficiency, Insider Dealing* 174.

[43] Barnes *Stock Market Efficiency, Insider Dealing* 174.

[44] See related discussion in paragraph 7 2 2 below; also see Rider, Alexander, Linklater & Bazley *Market Abuse and Insider Dealing* 93-94.

[45] Directors and some members of the County NatWest and National Westminster Bank's merchant banking subsidiary were convicted of misleading the market by disguising the failure of their Blue Arrow rights issue in February 1992. However, their convictions were set aside on appeal in August in 1992.

[46] Generally see Barnes *Stock Market Efficiency, Insider Dealing* 148-152.

[47] Barnes *Stock Market Efficiency, Insider Dealing* 148-152.

two and half years imprisonment, but this sentence, however, was later reduced to 21 months on appeal in 1991.[48] Consequently, the FSA imposed penalties and other appropriate administrative actions against any individuals or companies involved in market abuse activity. For example, in *ABN Amro Equities UK* case, on 23 April 2003 this company was fined £900 000 for market manipulation. In the same case, Michael Ackers was also fined £70 000 for violation of Principle 3 of the FSA's Listing Requirements which requires companies and the individuals concerned to maintain good corporate standards so as to combat market abuse conduct.[49] In *Shell Transport and Trading and Royal Dutch/Shell Group of companies,*[50] a £17 000 000 fine was imposed on the directors as well as other persons who issued false or misleading information to the financial markets contrary to the Listing Rules and the relevant provisions of the Financial Services and Markets Act. Likewise, several market abuse cases have been successfully investigated by the FCA to date, especially, in 2016.[51]

Disciplinary action for a public censure was invoked by the FSA in *Marconi plc* case.[52] In this case, the FSA issued a public statement to the effect that *Marconi plc* had failed to speedily release price-sensitive information regarding a change in its performance expectation to the relevant financial market.[53] In another case, the FSA found Roberto Casoni (a former equities analyst) guilty for failing to observe the required proper standards of market conduct contrary to its general principles for approved persons.[54] Such disciplinary actions and measures are now imposed on the market abuse offenders by the FCA.

---

[48] Barnes *Stock Market Efficiency, Insider Dealing* 148-152.

[49] Barnes *Stock Market Efficiency, Insider Dealing* 164-166.

[50] See the FSA *Final Notice* 2004-08-24; also see Rider, Alexander, Linklater & Bazley *Market Abuse and Insider Dealing* 215.

[51] Hitchins "Focusing on the Latest Trends, Risks and Developments in Financial Services Investigations" *Allen & Overy Investigations Insight* (17-10-2016) <http://www.aoinvestigationsinsight.com/further-drop-in-number-of-market-abuse-cases-concluded-by-the-fca/> (accessed 13-07-2017).

[52] Generally see *Barnes Stock Market Efficiency, Insider Dealing* 164-165; also see other similar cases such as the *Financial Services Authority v (1) Sean Fradley (t/a Top Bet Placement Services) (2) Gary Woodward* [2004] EWHC 3008 (Ch), where the FSA successfully obtained injunctions against the market abuse offenders & *Philip Jabre v Financial Services Authority* (2006) 36 fin 06/2006, where the FSA successfully charged the accused persons for engaging in conduct that give rise to market abuse. Also see Rider, Alexander, Linklater & Bazley *Market Abuse and Insider Dealing* 76-77; 206.

[53] In so doing it was stated that *Marconi plc* company had contravened Rule 9.2(c) of the FSA's Listing Rules.

[54] Additionally see the General Principle 3 of the FSA's Listing Requirements. Also see other civil cases that were successfully settled with the FSA's in table seven of Barnes *Stock Market Efficiency, Insider Dealing* 164-165 & Rider, Alexander, Linklater & Bazley *Market Abuse and Insider Dealing* 206-209.

On the other hand, like the FCA in the UK,[55] the FSB bears the sole responsibility and function to oversee the enforcement of the securities and market abuse provisions in South Africa.[56] However, unlike the UK former position, where the Bank of England's regulatory mandate did not include banks because they were regulated by the FSA,[57] the South African Reserve Bank (not the FSB) oversees the regulation of banks in South Africa. In this regard, the FSA's regulatory powers were broader than those of the FSB.[58] Nonetheless, the Financial Services Act 2012 now empowers the Bank of England to have a macro-prudential responsibility to oversee the prudential supervision of the relevant financial services institutions in the UK.[59] Thus, the Bank of England (and not the FCA), is now responsible for the supervision of financial institutions in the UK. Nevertheless, like the FCA,[60] the FSB administers and enforces the civil market abuse provisions in South Africa.[61] Be that as it may, it is not very clear whether the FSB is also adjudicated by sufficient and competent persons to enhance its cross-border market abuse enforcement efforts in South Africa and elsewhere.[62] Nonetheless, like the FCA,[63] the FSB has quasi-legislative (rule-making) powers.[64] While this is a commendable achievement and must be welcomed as such, it is not quite certain whether the FSB has to date been able to make any such rules or to issue its own adequate Code of Market Abuse Conduct to guide all the relevant market participants on conduct that amounts to market abuse in South Africa. Unlike the FCA's Code of Market Conduct which supplemented and defined market abuse conduct in the UK,[65] such conduct is merely outlined, mainly in Chapter X of the Financial Markets Act.[66] In addition, the FSB may only commence its investigations when it has received some tip-offs regarding any suspected market abuse activity from the Johannesburg Stock Exchange Limited (JSE).[67] As indicated earlier,[68] this is not the position in the

---

[55] See earlier related remarks above.

[56] S 84 of the Financial Markets Act.

[57] See earlier related remarks above.

[58] S 84 of the Financial Markets Act.

[59] See Part 3 to Part 9 of the Financial Services Act 2012.

[60] See related remarks above.

[61] S 84 read with s 82 of the Financial Markets Act.

[62] See further related remarks by Chitimira & Lawack "Overview of the Role-Players in the Investigation, Prevention and Enforcement of Market Abuse Provisions in South Africa" 2013 *Obiter* 200 200-217; Chitimira "Overview of Selected Role-Players in the Detection and Enforcement of Market Abuse Cases and Appeals in South Africa" 2014 *Speculum Juris* 108 108-124.

[63] See related remarks above.

[64] S 84(2)(f) of the Financial Markets Act.

[65] See related remarks above.

[66] However, the FSB has to date issued several booklets and bulletins with general information regarding the regulation of market abuse practices in South Africa.

[67] See related remarks by Chitimira & Lawack 2013 *Obiter* 200-217; Chitimira 2014 *Speculum Juris* 108-124.

UK where the FCA is authorised to appoint other additional skilled persons to provide it with reports or relevant information relating to any suspected market abuse violations. Nevertheless, like the FCA,[69] the FSB may impose disciplinary, administrative and civil sanctions like orders for compensatory and punitive damages as well as desist or cease orders on market abuse offenders.[70]

Notably, in order to enhance compliance and the general enforcement of market abuse prohibition in South Africa, the FSB has also purportedly entered into co-operation agreements with other international regulatory bodies like the FCA, the SEC and the IOSCO.[71] However, it remains to be seen whether these co-operation agreements will be fully exploited by the FSB to combat cross-border market abuse activities in South Africa.

7 2 2 The Role of the Courts

The courts have a crucial role in the enforcement of the market abuse laws in the UK. Accordingly, the relevant courts and the DTI have played an important role in the enforcement of securities and market abuse laws in the UK.[72] Put differently, the DTI[73] and the courts initially had the main prerogative to prosecute all criminal cases involving market abuse in the UK. Thus, in spite of the fact that the FCA may now itself prosecute market abuse cases, it used to refer such criminal cases to the DTI and the courts for further investigations and/or prosecution.[74] In most instances, the DTI could prosecute securities violations that relate to general corporate matters, for example, the disqualification of directors. On the other hand, the courts may hear and prosecute any market abuse cases referred to them by the FCA.

The CPS is the public prosecuting body in England and Wales. On the other hand, the DPP and the Crown Office are the bodies responsible for prosecuting market abuse cases in Northern Ireland and Scotland respectively. The courts have the power to investigate, prosecute and impose appropriate penalties on market abuse offenders. For example, the courts may impose civil, criminal and administrative sanctions on any person who

---

[68] See related remarks above.

[69] See related remarks above.

[70] Generally see s 82 read with s 84 of the Financial Markets Act.

[71] See generally related remarks by Chitimira & Lawack 2013 *Obiter* 200-217.

[72] Blair & Walker *Financial Services Law* 299-300.

[73] It is reported that the DTI's market abuse prosecutorial powers are now vested in the Department for Business Enterprise and Regulatory Reform (DBERR). Herbert Smith "UK Market Abuse Update" 2009 *Financial Regulation Briefing* 1 2-3; see the DBERR's market abuse prosecutions on <http://www.fsa.gov.uk/pages/Library/Communication/PR/2009/002.shtml> (accessed 28-01-2014).

[74] S 402(1)(a) of the Financial Services and Markets Act.

indulges in market abuse activities.[75] The courts may, on application of the FCA or any prejudiced person, further grant orders for judicial and quasi-judicial remedies such as injunction for restitution, freezing assets, declaratory relief, prohibitory and mandatory injunction relief as well as desist or seize orders against market abuse offenders.[76] Undoubtedly, this has, in a way, further enhanced the FCA's imposition of administrative sanctions against the market abuse offenders in the UK.[77] Additionally, the courts (including the Equity and Chancery Courts) may further award financial orders and damages to compensate all the persons affected by market abuse.[78]

Despite the fact that some weaknesses and irregularities still exist in the criminal enforcement of the market abuse prohibition, the courts have to date successfully prosecuted a considerable number of cases involving market abuse in the UK. For example, cases like the *Chase Manhattan Equities v Goodman*[79] have been adequately prosecuted. In this case Knox J held that any transaction or dealing based on the misuse of inside information was against public policy, unenforceable and consequently resulted in criminal liability on the part of the offenders.[80] Moreover, in the *Scott v Brown*[81] case, the Court of Appeal held that an agreement to stabilise the price of shares while a number of certain shares were brought into the financial market was illegal and unenforceable. This decision was, *inter alia*, probably intended at preventing market abuse practices like insider trading and market manipulation. In the *Financial Services Authority v Fitt*[82] the High Court used

---

[75] S 381 of the Financial Services and Markets Act; also see s 148 of the Powers of Criminal Courts (Sentencing) Act 2000 (c 6), which empowers courts to impose restitution orders against all the convicted persons.

[76] For further clarity check ss 129; 380; 381; 382 & 383 read with s 348 of the Financial Services and Markets Act. Also see Russen *Financial Services Authorisation, Supervision, and Enforcement: A Litigator's Guide* (2006) 146-166.

[77] Significantly high penalties have further been, in many cases, successfully levied against individuals or companies that commit market abuse offences. See Rider, Alexander, Linklater & Bazley *Market Abuse and Insider Dealing* 226-230.

[78] This clearly suggest that the courts have a discretion to award equitable remedies like specific performance or rescission of Part IV permission against any person who violates market abuse provisions. S 50 of the Supreme Court Act 1981 (c 54). Also see *Seager v Copydex (No 2)* [1969] 1 WLR 809, where damages for misuse of price-sensitive (confidential) information were granted against the perpetrators of securities and market abuse violations; see further Rider, Alexander, Linklater & Bazley *Market Abuse and Insider Dealing* 38-39.

[79] [1991] BCLC 897.

[80] Also see related cases such as *R v Rigby, Bailey* & Rowley (2005) FSA/PN/106/2005 2005-10-07; *R v Ghosh* [1982] QB 1053; *SIB v Pantell SA (No 2)* [1993] BCLC 146 (CA); *R v Rollins* 39; *FCA v Hannam* 0233; *FCA v David John Hobbs* 918; *FCA v Da Vinci Invest Limited* 2401. Generally see s 62(2) of the Criminal Justice Act; see further Rider, Alexander, Linklater & Bazley *Market Abuse and Insider Dealing* 38-39.

[81] [1892] QB 724.

[82] [2004] EWHC 1669 Ch.

its discretion to impose a freezing order against the persons accused of market abuse.[83]

In a nutshell, the successful prosecution of the *Guinness-Distillers, Blue Arrow, Geoffrey Collier* and the *Smith, Spearman and Payne* scandals is clear evidence of the competence of the relevant courts to enforce the market abuse prohibition in the UK. For instance, in the *Smith, Spearman and Payne* case the defendants were found guilty of conspiracy to commit insider trading in January 2004 after Payne, who was a proofreader at a company of commercial printers, passed non-public information that he had seen at that company to the other defendants, involving drafts of the prospectus and offer documents prior to the announcement on the LSE. Eventually, about 27 takeover and merger transactions were made and all the defendants made almost £336 000 profit. The Court of Appeal sentenced Smith and Catherine Spearman to 18 months imprisonment terms each. Payne was sentenced to 21 months in jail while Richard Spearman was imprisoned for 30 months.

Likewise, in the *Financial Services Authority v Martin and* Anor,[84] Alton J gave an injunctive relief against the defendants to cancel all the transactions that contravened some market abuse provisions. In some instances, the defendants were also ordered to compensate the affected investors directly for their incurred losses.

As indicated above, one can conclude that the effectiveness of the UK's market abuse regime is attributed to the competence of the relevant courts in enforcing and prosecuting market abuse cases. Accordingly, in spite of the inconsistent and relatively few successful criminal prosecutions recorded in market abuse cases by the courts during the DTI era, a notable increase in the number of successful prosecutions of such cases has been achieved since the FSA succeeded the DTI in 2001.[85] In other words, although the DBERR and the FCA are empowered to prosecute market abuse cases, the relevant courts have to date consistently utilised their main prerogative to hear and prosecute all criminal cases involving market abuse violations in the UK.

---

[83] This injunction or freezing order was generally awarded in accordance with s 381(3) & (4) of the Financial Services and Markets Act.

[84] [2005] 1 BCLC 495; also see *R v Caldwell* [1982] AC 341, where the court charged the accused for disseminating false and misleading information & *Bell v Lever Brothers Ltd* [1932] AC 161, where the defendant was sued for engaging in market manipulation practices that influenced the price of the affected securities.

[85] See *El Ajovu v Dollar Holdings* [1993] 1 BCLC 760; *Chaston v SWP Group Ltd* [2003] 4 Current Law 78 & the *R v Rigby, Bailey & Rowley* FSA/PN/106/2005 2005-10-07 scandal which was criminally prosecuted on 18 August 2005; also see Rider, Alexander, Linklater & Bazley *Market Abuse and Insider Dealing* 94.

In contrast to the position in the UK,[86] it appears that apart from the FSB and the Enforcement Commitee (EC), only the High Courts or Regional Courts have the jurisdiction to hear market abuse cases under the Financial Markets Act.[87] Nevertheless, the high evidentiary burden employed in criminal cases of market abuse remains probably the main contributory factor of the paucity of convictions obtained in such cases in both the UK and South Africa. In line with this, it remains to be seen whether the Financial Markets Act's market abuse provisions will enhance the combating and prosecution of market abuse cases in South Africa. Additionally, unlike the position in the UK,[88] it is not quite certain whether the relevant courts in South Africa may also rely on any skilled persons from the FSB itself or on persons who are assigned to them by the FSB to adjudicate in market abuse cases. Furthermore, the absence of sufficient persons with the relevant expertise to adjudicate in matters involving market abuse remains a significant challenge for the relevant courts in South Africa.[89]

7 2 3 The Role of Other Self-Regulatory Organisations

Although the FCA was established as the main agency solely responsible for the enforcement of market abuse laws in the UK,[90] several self-regulatory organisations (SROs) have also made a significant contribution to the supervision and regulation of the securities and financial services industry in the UK to date.[91]

During the 1970s and the early 1980s, the SROs such as the Bank of England, the Personal Investment Authority, the Investment Management Regulatory Organisation, the Securities and Investments Board (SIB) and the Securities and Futures Authority (SFA) played a leading role in the prevention, investigation and prosecution of securities and market abuse cases in the UK.[92] Nevertheless, serious systemic flaws were still evident in the regulation of the financial services industry in the UK. Therefore, in an attempt to rectify these flaws and to make the enforcement of the securities and market abuse laws more effective, most of the responsibilities of the Bank of England, the SIB and the SFA were transferred to the FSA in 1997. Notably, as stated earlier,[93] these responsibilities were recently re-vested in the Bank of England in terms of the Financial Services Act 2012 after 1 April 2013.

---

[86] See related comments above.
[87] S 84 read with ss 77; 78; 80; 81 & 82; also see Chitimira 2014 *Speculum Juris* 108-124.
[88] See related comments in paragraph 7 2 1 above.
[89] See related analysis by Chitimira 2014 *Speculum Juris* 108-124.
[90] See paragraph 7 2 1 above.
[91] Avgouleas *The Mechanics and Regulation of Market Abuse* 308-310.
[92] Avgouleas *The Mechanics and Regulation of Market Abuse* 309.
[93] See related comments in paragraph 7 2 1 above.

A number of regulatory institutions and organisations like the LSE, the London International Financial Futures and Options Exchange Administration and Management (LIFFOEAM), the SFO, the Financial Services and Markets Tribunal (FSMT), the FOS, the FSCS, the DBERR, the RDC, and the Treasury are currently involved in the regulation and enforcement of market abuse in the UK.

The LSE is the main securities exchange in the UK which oversees the public trading of listed qualifying investments in the relevant financial markets to minimise and curb market abuse activities. This is done by adopting relevant rules and guidelines that restrict and discourage market abuse practices. The LSE further employs sophisticated and computerised surveillance systems to detect all possible market abuse activity. Where such activity is detected, a publication is made to the relevant financial markets and the FCA through the so-called Suspicious Transaction Reports to inform all the investors and possible investors.[94]

One of the Recognised Investment Exchange which plays a pivotal role in the regulation of market abuse is the LIFFOEAM. The LIFFOEAM has the mandate to investigate, operate and employ necessary measures that detect and discourage market abuse activities. For instance, it has powers to take disciplinary action like issuing private warnings to any person accused of serious misconduct or contravening market abuse provisions.[95]

The SFO was established under the Criminal Justice Act 1987[96]and was granted wide investigatory and prosecutorial powers in respect of serious and complex corporate frauds. Consequently, since its introduction, the SFO has investigated and prosecuted several cases involving insider trading and market manipulation.[97] The SFO is further allowed to extract any information or documents necessary for an ongoing investigation from any accused persons. In addition, the SFO has the power to indict persons accused of fraud and/or market abuse offences and refer such matters to the CPS or the DPP for prosecution.[98]

For the purposes of obtaining more settlements in cases involving securities violations, the FOS was introduced under the auspices of the Financial Services and Markets Act.[99] The FOS was formally launched in December 2001

[94] Barnes *Stock Market Efficiency, Insider Dealing* 199.

[95] *Swan Market Abuse Regulation* 89.

[96] (c 38); see s 1 of the Criminal Justice Act 1987.

[97] Avgouleas *The Mechanics and Regulation of Market Abuse* 383-387.

[98] S 401(2) of the *Financial Services and Markets Act*; also see Avgouleas *The Mechanics and Regulation of Market Abuse* 384; Kiernan "The Regulatory Bodies Fraud: Its Enforcement in the Twenty-First Century" 2003 *The Company Lawyer* 293 294-299

[99] S 225; also see Blair & Walker *Financial Services Law* 166-183.

with the main aim of providing an independent alternative method of redress to all the affected persons or investors. Thus, the FOS is not a regulatory body *per se*; its main role is to resolve individual disputes between consumers (investors) and other market participants like financial services organisations.[100] The FOS deals with all kinds of financial disputes involving securities violations. This could imply that the FOS may also deal with disputes involving market abuse violations. Moreover, the FOS administers the FSCS in instances where it has either compulsory or voluntary jurisdiction.[101] The FSCS provides compensation to all eligible and successful complainants who were prejudiced by any securities violations.[102]

The FSMT is an independent regulatory body established to provide a platform for any person aggrieved by the decisions of the FCA to appeal.[103] Consequently, the FSMT may hear any references or appeal against the FCA regarding its disciplinary decisions, cancellation of Part IV permission, imposed penalties, prohibition orders and its verdicts or final decisions on matters relating to market abuse.[104] This is probably targeted at maintaining the stability and integrity in the UK's financial markets. However, it should be noted that the appeal against any FCA's decision must be made within 28 days of the date on which the decision notice or supervisory notice was issued.[105] The FSMT may, if satisfied, conduct a *de novo* review of matters referred to it by authorised persons or by any other aggrieved persons. For purposes of providing appropriate redress to the affected persons, the FSMT is obliged to derive its rules or course of action in accordance with the provisions of the Financial Services and Markets Act.[106] The FSMT may, for example, take decisions like re-hearing a matter, reviewing, dismissing an appeal or setting aside its own decision.[107] Additionally, the FSMT may determine and give directions regarding the appropriate action to be followed by the FCA.[108] The

---

[100] In contrast to the regulatory powers of the FSA which are usually invoked to seek redress on a more broad scale, the FOS is responsible for resolving disputes on an individual basis.

[101] Ss 226 & 227 of the Financial Services and Markets Act; also see Blair & Walker *Financial Services Law* 169-170.

[102] Russen *Financial Services Authorisation, Supervision* 340-346.

[103] S 132 read with s 133 of the Financial Services and Markets Act. The FSMT is administered by the Tribunal Service, an executive organ of the Ministry of Justice in the UK. Avgouleas *The Mechanics and Regulation of Market Abuse* 382-383.

[104] S 127(4) read with s 133 of the Financial Services and Markets Act.

[105] S 133(1) of the Financial Services and Markets Act.

[106] Ss 133; 127 & 388 of the Financial Services and Markets Act.

[107] A person aggrieved by a decision of the FSMT is free to apply to a Court of Appeal for permission to appeal within fourteen days. See Rules 23 & 24(5) of the FSMT.

[108] S 133(4); (5) & (7) of the Financial Services and Markets Act.

FSMT may further give recommendations to the FCA regarding its rules and regulating procedures.[109]

The Treasury has also played a crucial role in the general regulation of the securities and financial services industry in the UK. It is responsible for the overall institutional structure of the securities and financial services regulation and/or relevant legislation. Consequently, the Treasury may take action in instances where serious securities law violations are reported to it. The Treasury can further appoint or remove members of the executive governing body and the non-executive committee of the FCA. Moreover, the Treasury can appoint an independent person to conduct a review and/or a separate independent inquiry into the efficiency or effectiveness of certain functions of the FCA[110] and the specific circumstances regarding securities, market abuse or any other violations where such action is considered to be in the public interest.[111]

Another regulatory body which deserves some consideration is the RDC. The RDC was established as a committee of the FCA which exercises certain regulatory powers on behalf of the FCA.[112] In spite of the fact that the chairman of the RDC is appointed by the FCA and that it is accountable for its decisions to the FCA, the RDC may conduct its own independent investigations and make its own decisions regarding market abuse violations.[113] According to the Decision Making Manual of the FCA, the RDC is a separate regulatory body outside the FCA's management structure.[114] In short, the RDC is also responsible for the enforcement, authorisation and supervision of the securities and market abuse laws in the UK.[115]

As indicated above, it is quite clear that SROs like the LSE, the LIFFOEAM, the SFO, the FSMT, the FOS and the RDC currently play an equally important role in preventing and curbing market abuse practices in the UK. These SROs may also take their own appropriate action regarding any market abuse violations. For example, the LSE has in most instances offered some relevant information to the FCA regarding its market abuse prosecutions.[116] This

---

[109] See s 133(8) of the Financial Services and Markets Act; see further Rules 20 & 21 of the FSMT. Also see generally Russen *Financial Services Authorisation, Supervision* 312-315.

[110] Ss 12 & 13 of the Financial Services and Markets Act.

[111] Blair & Walker *Financial Services Law* 25-27.

[112] See Rider, Alexander, Linklater & Bazley *Market Abuse and Insider Dealing* 209-210 & Russen *Financial Services Authorisation, Supervision* 296-298. Also see s 395(2) of the Financial Services and Markets Act.

[113] Rider, Alexander, Linklater & Bazley *Market Abuse and Insider Dealing* 210.

[114] See Chapter 4.2 of the Decision Making Manual which was inserted by the Enforcement (Settlement and Other Procedures) Instrument in October 2005.

[115] See further Blair & Walker *Financial Services Law* 146-148; Swan *Market Abuse Regulation* 106-107.

[116] See related comments in paragraph 7 2 1 above.

culminated in the speedy settlement and prosecution of market abuse cases by the FCA.[117] In addition, the FCA co-operates quite well with other international regulatory bodies like the IOSCO in order to combat cross-border market abuse practices in the prescribed financial markets in the UK.[118]

Additionally, in contrast with the position in the UK regarding the role of SROs,[119] it appears as if the importance of the role of such organisations has to some extent been overlooked in South Africa.[120] This may be reflected, in part, by the fact that only a few SROs, namely, the JSE, the EC, the Directorate of Market Abuse (DMA) and the Takeover Regulation Panel (TRP), are either directly or indirectly involved in the enforcement of the securities and market abuse laws in South Africa.[121] Nevertheless, apart from the FSB, there are no other SROs that are statutorily, specifically and mainly responsible for enforcing market abuse laws in South Africa.[122] As a result, not many SROs have been actively involved in the enforcement of the market abuse prohibition to supplement the efforts of the FSB in South Africa to date.[123] South Africa seems to have blindly adopted some of the enforcement methods that are employed in the UK by empowering the FSB as the only main regulatory board that oversees the enforcement of its market abuse ban. In relation to this, it is suggested that South Africa should consider practically implementing only the relevant principles of the UK's single regulator model because it is economical and less complex. This could increase the number of settlements and convictions in market abuse cases in South Africa. Additionally, it is not certain whether other SROs in South Africa have the same or similar statutory leverage available to the FSB to make their own decisions, rules and appropriate regulations in relation to market abuse offences.[124] However, it is important to note that the DMA and the EC have

---

[117] See further related comments in paragraph 7 2 1 above.

[118] See similar comments above.

[119] See similar comments above.

[120] See related remarks by Chitimira & Lawack 2013 *Obiter* 200-217; Chitimira 2014 *Speculum Juris* 108-124.

[121] See related remarks on the role of each of these SROs by Chitimira & Lawack 2013 *Obiter* 200-217; Chitimira 2014 *Speculum Juris* 108-124.

[122] See Chapter X of the Financial Markets Act & related remarks by Chitimira & Lawack 2013 *Obiter* 200-217; Chitimira 2014 *Speculum Juris* 108-124.

[123] See similar analysis by Chitimira & Lawack 2013 *Obiter* 200-217; Chitimira 2014 *Speculum Juris* 108-124.

[124] See Chapter X of the Financial Markets Act & related remarks by Chitimira & Lawack 2013 *Obiter* 200-217; Chitimira 2014 *Speculum Juris* 108-124.

functions[125] almost similar to those of their UK counterparts, the RDC and the FSMT respectively.[126]

7 3 Concluding Remarks

As already pointed out,[127] the UK employs an extensive regulatory approach which statutorily authorises only one regulator (FCA) to oversee the enforcement of its securities and market abuse laws. Therefore, other the SROs may only exercise certain functions on behalf of the FCA in order to complement its enforcement efforts.[128] The rationale for this single regulator model was, *inter alia*, to establish a more coherent and proportionate approach in relation to the regulation and enforcement of financial services, securities and market abuse laws as well as a level playing field for all investors and other relevant market participants in the UK.[129] Thus, as pointed out earlier,[130] the FCA has fairly managed to formulate high-level objectives and measures, especially, in relation to the enforcement of market abuse laws in order to obtain more settlements and prosecutions in market abuse cases.[131]

On the contrary, it was noted that South Africa has so far not been able to enforce its market abuse prohibition successfully and consistently in order to increase the combating of market abuse practices in its financial markets.[132] The reason for this disparity could be that, unlike South Africa, the UK has devoted significantly more resources towards the enforcement of its securities and market abuse laws.[133] Consequently, it is suggested that the Financial Markets Act[134] should be reviewed to enact provisions that specifically empower the FSB to appoint other additional skilled persons, apart from its own employees, to provide it with reports or relevant information relating to any suspected market abuse violations in South Africa. Moreover, South Africa should not have blindly adopted some of the enforcement methods that are employed in the UK without proper measures in place to ensure that such methods will be practically compatible and consistently enforced to combat market abuse activities in the South African financial markets.[135] Accordingly,

---

[125] Ss 85 & 99 of the Financial Markets Act; ss 6A to 6I of the Financial Institutions (Protection of Funds) Act 28 of 2001 as amended (Protection of Funds Act) & related remarks by Chitimira & Lawack 2013 *Obiter* 200-217; Chitimira 2014 *Speculum Juris* 108-124.

[126] See related remarks above.

[127] See paragraph 7 2 1 above.

[128] See paragraphs 7 2 3 above.

[129] See generally Blair & Walker *Financial Services Law* 53-55.

[130] See paragraph 7 2 1 above.

[131] See paragraph 7 2 1 above.

[132] See related comparative analysis in paragraphs 7 2 1; 7 2 2 & 7 2 3 above.

[133] See paragraph 7 2 1 above.

[134] See related comments in paragraph 7 2 1 above.

[135] See related analysis in paragraph 7 2 3 above.

South Africa should consider practically implementing only the relevant principles of the UK's single regulator model because it is economical and less complex.[136] Additionally, notwithstanding the possible constitutional-related conflicts and/or possible negative effects of double jeopardy, the Financial Markets Act should be amended to enact provisions that expressly empower other SROs in South Africa, apart from the FSB, to impose their own penalties or take any other appropriate action against any persons who indulge in market abuse activities in South Africa to increase deterrence.

It is also suggested, notwithstanding the challenges involving the availability of adequate resources, that more specialised market abuse courts manned by sufficient persons with the relevant expertise to adjudicate in matters involving market abuse should be established in all the provinces of South Africa to increase awareness and/or the combating of market abuse practices in the South African financial markets. The FSB should be statutorily required to support the DPP and the relevant courts with the necessary information regarding ongoing market abuse cases in South Africa by assigning certain persons with the relevant expertise to assist the DPP and/or relevant courts in their prosecution of such cases in South Africa.

In conclusion, it is hoped that the suggestions and/or proposals stated in this chapter will be carefully employed in the future to enhance the enforcement of the market abuse ban in South Africa.

[136] See related analysis in paragraph 7 2 3 above.

References

Books

Avgouleas E *The Mechanics and Regulation of Market Abuse: A Legal and Economic Analysis* (Oxford University Press Oxford 2005)

Barnes P *Stock Market Efficiency, Insider Dealing and Market Abuse* (Gower Publishing Limited Surrey England 2009)

Beuthin RC and Luiz SM *Beuthin's Basic Company Law* 3rd ed (Butterworths Durban 2000)

Blair MQC & Walker GA (eds) *Financial Services Law* 1st ed (Oxford University Press Oxford United Kingdom 2006)

Lyon GJ & Du Plessis JJ *The Law of Insider Trading in Australia* (The Federation Press Sydney 2005)

Rider B, Alexander K, Linklater L & Bazley S *Market Abuse and Insider Dealing* 2nd ed (Tottel Publishing Haywards Heath 2009)

Russen J *Financial Services Authorisation, Supervision, and Enforcement: A Litigator's Guide* (Oxford University Press New York 2006)

Swan EJ *Market Abuse Regulation* 1st ed (Oxford University Press United States of America 2006)

Journal articles

Anonymous "The Financial Conduct Authority: An Overview" 2013 *Allen & Overy Investigations Insight* 3-42

Bhattacharya U & Daouk H "The World Price of Insider Trading" 2002 *Journal of Finance* 75-108

Black J & Nobles R "Personal Pensions Misselling: The Causes and Lessons of Regulatory Failure" 1998 *MLR* 789-820

Botha D "Control of Insider Trading in South Africa: A Comparative Analysis" 1991 *SA Merc LJ* 1-18

Botha D "Increased Maximum Fine for Insider Trading: A Realistic and Effective Deterrent?" 1990 *SALJ* 504-508

Cassim R "An Analysis of Market Manipulation under the Securities Services Act 36 of 2004 (Part 1)" 2008 *SA Merc LJ* 33-60

Cassim R "An Analysis of Market Manipulation under the Securities Services Act 36 of 2004 (Part 2)" 2008 *SA Merc LJ* 177-199

Cassim R "Some Aspects of Insider Trading – Has the Securities Services Act, 36 of 2004 Gone too Far?" 2007 *SA Merc LJ* 44-70

Chitimira H & Lawack VA "Overview of the Role-Players in the Investigation, Prevention and Enforcement of Market Abuse Provisions in South Africa" 2013 *Obiter* 200-217

Chitimira H "Overview of Selected Role-Players in the Detection and Enforcement of Market Abuse Cases and Appeals in South Africa" 2014 *Speculum Juris* 108-124

Henning JJ & Du Toit S "The Regulation of False Trading, Market Manipulation and Insider Trading" 2000 *Journal for Juridical Science* 155-165

Jooste R "A Critique of the Insider Trading Provisions of the 2004 Securities Services Act" 2006 *SALJ* 437-460

Kiernan P "The Regulatory Bodies Fraud: Its Enforcement in the Twenty-First Century" 2003 *The Company Lawyer* 293-299

Luiz SM "Market Abuse and the Enforcement Committee" 2011 *SA Merc LJ* 151-172

Luiz SM "Insider Trading Regulation – If at First You Don't Succeed…" 1999 *SA Merc LJ* 136-151

Osode PC "The New South African Insider Trading Act: Sound Law Reform or Legislative Overkill?" 2000 *Journal of African Law* 239-263

Rider BAK "Policing the City-Combating Fraud and Other Abuses in the Corporate Securities Industry" 1988 *Current Legal Problems* 47-68

Steinberg MI "Insider Trading Regulation–A Comparative Perspective" 2003 *The International Lawyer* 153-171

Van Deventer G "New Watchdog for Insider Trading" 1999 *FSB Bulletin* 2-3

Van Deventer G "Harnassing Administrative Law in Encouraging Compliance" 2009 *FSB Bulletin* 3-4

Case law

South Africa

Pretorius and Another v Natal South Sea Investment Trust 1965 3 SA 410 (W)

United Kingdom

Bell v Lever Brothers Ltd [1932] AC 161

Chase Manhattan Equities v Goodman [1991] BCLC 897

Chaston v SWP Group Ltd [2003] 4 Current Law 78

El Ajovu v Dollar Holdings [1993] 1 BCLC 760

FCA v David John Hobbs [2013] EWCA Civ 918

FCA v Da Vinci Invest Limited [2015] EWHC 2401 (Ch)

FCA v Hannam [2014] UKUT 0233

Financial Services Authority v Fitt [2004] EWHC 1669 Ch

Financial Services Authority v Martin and Anor [2005] 1 BCLC 495

Financial Services Authority v (1) Sean Fradley (t/a Top Bet Placement Services) (2) Gary Woodward [2004] EWHC 3008 (Ch)

Philip Jabre v Financial Services Authority (2006) 36 fin 06/2006

R v Caldwell [1982] AC 341

R v Ghosh [1982] QB 1053

R v Kylsant [1932] 1 KB 442

R v Rigby, Bailey & Rowley (2005) FSA/PN/106/2005 2005-10-07

R v Rollins [2010] UKSC 39

Scott v Brown [1892] QB 724

Seager v Copydex (No 2) [1969] 1 WLR 809

SIB v Pantell SA (No 2) [1993] BCLC 146 (CA)

7722656 Canada Inc. (t/a Swift Trade Inc) v FSA [2013] All ER (D) 266

Legislation

South Africa

Companies Act 61 of 1973
Companies Act 71 of 2008
Consumer Protection Act 68 of 2008
Financial Institutions (Protection of Funds) Act 28 of 2001 as amended
Financial Markets Act 19 of 2012
Financial Markets Control Act 55 of 1989
Securities Services Act 36 of 2004
Stock Exchanges Control Act 1 of 1985

United Kingdom

Companies Act 1980 (c 22)
Companies Act 1985 (c 6)
Companies Act 2006 (c 46)
Company Securities (Insider Dealing) Act 1985 (c 8)
Criminal Justice Act 1993 (c 36)
Criminal Justice Act 1987 (c 38)
Financial Services and Markets Act 2000 (c 8)
Financial Services Act 1986 (c 60)
Fraud Act 2006 (c 35)
Larceny Act 1861 (24 and 25 Vict c 96)
Powers of Criminal Courts (Sentencing) Act 2000 (c 6)
Prevention of Fraud (Investments) Act 1939 (c 16)
Prevention of Fraud (Investments) Act 1958 (c 45)
Supreme Court Act 1981 (c 54)

European Union

Commission Directive 2003/124/EC of 22 December 2003 implementing Directive 2003/6/EC of 28 January 2003 on the definition and public disclosure of inside information and the definition of market manipulation [2003] OJ L339/70

Commission Directive 2003/125/EC of 22 December 2003 on the fair presentation of investment recommendations and the disclosure of conflicts of interest [2003] OJ L339/073

European Union Directive on Insider Dealing and Market Manipulation, the Directive of the European Parliament and Council of 28 January 2003 on insider dealing and market manipulation (market abuse) 2003/6/EC [2003] OJ L96/16

European Union Insider Dealing Directive, Council Directive 89/592/EEC of 13 November 1989 [1989] OJ 1989 L334/30

Commissions, committees, statutory instruments and reports

South Africa

Financial Services Board *Annual Report* 2011

Financial Services Board *Annual Report* 2013

The King Task Group into Insider Trading Legislation *Minority Report on Insider Trading* 1997

The King Task Group into the Insider Trading Legislation *First Report* 15 May 1997

The King Task Group into the Insider Trading Legislation *Final Report* 21 October 1997

Van Wyk de Vries Commission of Inquiry into the *Companies Act* of 1973

United Kingdom

Enforcement (Settlement and Other Procedures) Instrument's *Decision Making Manual* October 2005

Financial Conduct Authority (Code of Market Conduct) *MAR Release 18* July 2017

Financial Conduct Authority Enforcement Guide 01 April 2014

Financial Services and Markets Act 2000 (Market Abuse) Regulations 2005 SI 2005/381

Financial Services and Markets Act 2000 (Prescribed Markets and Qualifying Investments) Order 2001, SI 2001/1996 as amended by Regulation 10 of the Market Abuse Regulations 2005

Financial Services Authority Handbook (Code of Market Conduct) *FSA Release* 19 July 2001

Financial Services Authority's *Market Abuse Directive Disclosure Rules Instrument* 2005, 17 March 2005

Financial Services Authority's *Market Abuse Directive Instrument* 2005, 17 March 2005

Insider Dealing (Securities and Regulated Markets) Order 1994

Traded Securities (Disclosure) Regulation 1994

United States of America

Commodity Futures Trading Commission and the United States Securities and Exchange Commission "A Joint Report of the SEC and the CFTC on Harmonization of Regulation" *Report* 16 October 2009

International Organisation of Securities Commissions Technical Committee Working Party 4 on *Principles for Memorandum of Understanding, XVI Annual Conference* 5 September 1991

Thesis and dissertations

Chitimira H *A Comparative Analysis of the Enforcement of Market Abuse Provisions* (LLD-thesis Nelson Mandela Metropolitan University 2012)

Chitimira H *The Regulation of Insider Trading in South Africa: A Roadmap for an Effective, Competitive and Adequate Regulatory Statutory Framework* (LLM-dissertation University of Fort Hare 2008)

Media releases and other relevant material

Herbert Smith "UK Market Abuse Update" 2009 *Financial Regulation Briefing* 1

Newspaper reports

Chanetsa B "Insider Trading is Notoriously Hard to Prosecute" *Business Report* (2004-04-26)

Internet sources

Barron C "Greg Draws a Blank in Belfort Parallel" (2014) <http://www.timeslive.co.za/Feeds/2014/02/02/greg-draws-a-blank-in-belfort-parallel> (accessed 03-03-2014)

Blincoe R "Datatec Directors Pay Up on Insider Trading Charges" (2001) <http://www.theregister.co.uk/2001/05/23/datatec_directors_pay_up/> (accessed 03-03-2014)

Commodity Futures Trading Commission & the Financial Services Authority FSA's *Memorandum of Understanding on Consultation, Cooperation and the Exchange of Information Related to Market Oversight* (2006) <http://www.fsa.gov.uk/pubs/mou/cftc.pd> (accessed 27-01-2014)

Financial Services Authority "FSA Signs Regulatory Cooperation Agreement with the CFTC" (20-11-2006) http://www.fsa.gov.uk/pages/Library/Communication/PR/2006/118.shtml > (accessed 27-01-2014)

FCA "Michael Coscia Final Notice" *FCA Final Notice* (03-07-2013) <http://www.fca.org.uk/your-fca/documents/finalnotices/2013/michael-coscia> (accessed 15-07-2017)

Financial Services Board "Enforcement Committee Actions" *Media Release* (28-06-2011) <http://www.fsb.co.za/ftp://ftp.fsb.co.za/public/documents/AReport2011.pdf> (accessed 22-11-2013)

Financial Services Board "List of Current Investigations of the Directorate of Market Abuse" *Media Release* (28-06-2011) <http://www.fsb.co.za/ftp://ftp.fsb.co.za/public/documents/AReport2011.pdf> (accessed 22-11-2013)

Hitchins "Focusing on the Latest Trends, Risks and Developments in Financial Services Investigations" *Allen & Overy Investigations Insight* (17-10-2016) <http://www.aoinvestigationsinsight.com/further-drop-in-number-of-market-abuse-cases-concluded-by-the-fca/> (accessed 13-07-2017).

Johannesburg Stock Exchange Limited "Insider Trading and other Market Abuses (Including the Effective Management of Price–Sensitive Information)" in the *Insider Trading Booklet*, (2013) <http://www.jse.co.za/Libraries/JSE_Regulatory_Environment_Insider_Trading/InsiderTrading_Booklet.sflb.ashx> (accessed 03-03-2014)

Loubser R "Insider Trading and other Market Abuses (Including the Effective Management of Price–sensitive Information)" in the *Insider Trading Booklet* final draft, (2006) <http://www.jse.co.za/public/insider/JSEbooklet.pdf> (accessed 03-03-2014)

Myburgh A & Davis B "The Impact of South Africa's Insider Trading Regime: A Report for the Financial Services Board" (25-03-2004) <http://www.genesis-analytics.com/public/FSBReport.pdf> (accessed 09-02-2013)

SIA Partners (Banking and Insurance) "Brexit and the Impact on the UK's Regulatory Framework" (2016) 1-4 <http://en.finance.sia-partners.com/brexit-and-impact-uks-regulatory-framework> (accessed 12-07-2017)

Van Deventer G "Anti-Market Abuse Legislation in South Africa" (10-06-2008) <http://www.fsb.co.za/public/marketabuse/FSBReport.pdf> (accessed 05-05-2013)

Chapter 8

Selected Anti-Market Abuse Preventative Measures in the United Kingdom and South Africa

8 1 Introduction

Various anti-market abuse enforcement approaches and preventative measures are employed in the United Kingdom (UK). Accordingly, the UK has to date successfully developed and/or adopted various measures aimed at discouraging insider trading and market manipulation (market abuse) practices in its financial markets.[1] Consequently, the market abuse preventative measures employed in the UK[2] will be investigated and, where necessary, contrasted with similar anti-market abuse measures in South Africa.[3] In this regard, only relevant UK market abuse provisions and cases will be discussed and contrasted with similar provisions and cases in South Africa for the purposes of identifying market abuse preventative methods that could be possibly incorporated in the South African anti-market abuse enforcement framework.[4] Therefore, the co-operation between the Financial

---

* This chapter is influenced in part, by an article that was initially published in the *Mediterranean Journal of Social Sciences* and this was done with legal permission from the editors of this *Journal*, see Chitimira "Overview of the Enforcement of the Market Abuse Prohibition in the United Kingdom" 2014(5)(20) *Mediterranean Journal of Social Sciences* 529-541.

[1] See the Criminal Justice Act 1993 (c 36) (Criminal Justice Act) & the Financial Services and Markets Act 2000 (c 8) (Financial Services and Markets Act). See further Steinberg "Insider Trading Regulation–A Comparative Perspective" 2003 *The International Lawyer* 153 154-171; Avgouleas *The Mechanics and Regulation of Market Abuse: A Legal and Economic Analysis* (2005) 307; 75-502; Bhattacharya & Daouk "The World Price of Insider Trading" 2002 *Journal of Finance* 75 75-108; Lyon & Du Plessis *The Law of Insider Trading in Australia* (2005) 159-168, for further related comparative analysis in other jurisdictions.

[2] Generally see Barnes *Stock Market Efficiency, Insider Dealing and Market Abuse* (2009) 125.

[3] Ss 78; 80; 81 & 82 of the Financial Markets Act 19 of 2012 (Financial Markets Act); also see related discussion by Chitimira *A Comparative Analysis of the Enforcement of Market Abuse Provisions* (Unpublished LLD thesis, Nelson Mandela Metropolitan University) 2012, 332-353.

[4] In relation to this, see the historical and comparative analysis of the enforcement of the market abuse ban in South Africa by Loubser "Insider Trading and other Market Abuses (Including the Effective Management of Price–sensitive Information)" in the *Insider Trading Booklet* final draft, (2006) 18-20; 24-27 <http://www.jse.co.za/ public/insider/JSEbooklet.pdf> (accessed 03-03-2014); the Johannesburg Stock Exchange Limited (the JSE) "Insider Trading and other Market Abuses (Including the Effective Management of Price–sensitive Information)" in the *Insider Trading Booklet*, (2013) 1-26

Services Authority (FSA) before its replacement by the Financial Conduct Authority (FCA), the Treasury, the Department of Trade and Industry (DTI) and the courts will be examined first. Secondly, the co-operation between the FSA, subsequently, the FCA and the local self-regulatory organisations (SROs) will be discussed. Thirdly, the co-operation between the FSA, subsequently, the FCA and similar international regulatory bodies will be scrutinised. Fourthly, other preventative measures that were adopted in the UK will be analysed. Thereafter, possible recommendations and conclusions will be given.

8 2 Co-operation between Enforcement Authorities

8 2 1 Co-operation between the FCA, the Treasury, the DTI and the Courts

Several notable achievements obtained by the market abuse regime in the UK have been largely influenced by a good co-operative relationship that existed between the FSA and other enforcement authorities like the Treasury, the courts and the DTI. The same *status quo* is currently maintained by the FCA,

---

<http://www.jse.co.za/Libraries/JSE_Regulatory_Environment_Insider_Trading/InsiderTrading_Booklet.sflb.ashx> (accessed 03-03-2014); Van Deventer "Anti-Market Abuse Legislation in South Africa" (10-06-2008) 1-5 <http://www.fsb.co.za/public/marketabuse/FSBReport.pdf> (accessed 05-05-2013); Myburgh & Davis "The Impact of South Africa's Insider Trading Regime: A Report for the Financial Services Board" (25-03-2004) 8-33 <http://www.genesis-analytics.com/public/FSBReport.pdf> (accessed 09-02-2013); Chanetsa "Insider Trading is Notoriously Hard to Prosecute" (2004-04-26) *Business Report* page number unknown; *Pather and Another v Financial Services Board and Others (57617/10)* [2014] 3 All SA 208 (GP); *Zietsman v Director of Market Abuse* 2016 1 SA 218 (GP); *Pretorius and Another v Natal South Sea Investment Trust* 1965 3 SA 410 (W), were the courts failed to convict the suspected insider trading offenders; Blincoe "Datatec Directors Pay Up on Insider Trading Charges" (2001) <http://www.theregister.co.uk/2001/05/23/datatec_directors_pay_up/> (accessed 03-03-2014), where two Datatec directors, Jens Montanana and Robin Rindel were reportedly fined about R1 million each for insider trading by the Financial Services Board (the FSB); Barron "Greg Draws a Blank in Belfort Parallel" (2014) <http:// www.timeslive.co.za/ Feeds/2014/02/02/greg-draws-a-blank-in-belfort-parallel> (accessed 03-03-2014), where Greg Blank was reportedly sentenced to eight years imprisonment for stock market-related fraud and front running in 1992; Osode "The New South African Insider Trading Act: Sound Law Reform or Legislative Overkill?" 2000 *Journal of African Law* 239 239-263; Jooste "A Critique of the Insider Trading Provisions of the 2004 Securities Services Act" 2006 *SALJ* 437 441–460; Van Deventer "New Watchdog for Insider Trading" 1999 *FSB Bulletin* 2 3; Beuthin & Luiz *Beuthin's Basic Company Law* (2000) 235–238; Luiz "Market Abuse and the Enforcement Committee" 2011 *SA Merc LJ* 151-172; Luiz "Insider Trading Regulation – If at First You Don't Succeed..." 1999 *SA Merc LJ* 136 136-151; Henning & Du Toit "The Regulation of False Trading, Market Manipulation and Insider Trading" 2000 *Journal for Juridical Science* 155 155-165; Botha "Control of Insider Trading in South Africa: A Comparative Analysis" 1991 *SA Merc LJ* 1 1-18; Botha "Increased Maximum Fine for Insider Trading: A Realistic and Effective Deterrent?" 1990 *SALJ* 504 504-508 & Chitimira *The Regulation of Insider Trading in South Africa: A Roadmap for an Effective, Competitive and Adequate Regulatory Statutory Framework* (Unpublished LLM dissertation, University of Fort Hare) 2008, 1–175.

the Treasury, the courts and the DTI, in relation to the enforcement of the anti-market abuse laws and preventative measures in the UK.

Firstly, the Treasury entered into an agreement with the FSA in October 1997 which outlines, among other aspects, the terms of their relationship and guiding principles on accountability, transparency and regular information exchange.[5] This agreement was introduced to enhance the efficiency and effectiveness of the securities and financial services industry regulation in the UK. In addition, the same agreement improved the FSA's monitoring and supervision of the clearing and settlements systems, relevant financial markets, and companies in order to detect and discourage market abuse violations. The aforementioned agreement also enabled the FSA to formulate adequate policy and principles regarding its general regulatory functions. The FCA has commendably continued to work hand in glove with both the Treasury and the Parliament to ensure that all anti-market abuse investigations and related regulatory aspects are executed in accordance with the relevant laws in the UK.[6]

Secondly, the FSA and the DTI had concurrent jurisdiction to investigate and prosecute certain matters involving serious corporate frauds and market abuse offences.[7] For example, it is reported that the DTI could appoint its own investigators and inspectors to deal with any specific or suspected securities violations.[8] The DTI could further disclose certain information to the FSA and other relevant enforcement authorities for them to take any appropriate action.[9] This could imply, notwithstanding the fact that some of the DTI's market abuse prosecutorial powers are now vested in the Department for Business Enterprise and Regulatory Reform (DBERR), that there was a better co-operation relationship between the DTI and the FSA in relation to the enforcement of securities and market abuse laws in the UK. It is hoped that such co-operation relationship will also be carried out between the DBERR, other relevant agencies and the FCA.

Lastly, the relevant courts[10] are mostly responsible for the criminal enforcement of the market abuse prohibition in the UK. In practice, the courts may, nevertheless, prosecute any market abuse cases referred to them by the FCA. As a result, the courts and the FCA have to date achieved some substantial progress in their quest to eradicate market abuse practices in the relevant

[5] Blair & Walker *Financial Services Law* (2006) 35.
[6] FCA "Reporting to Treasury and Parliament" (05-07-2017) https://www.fca.org.uk/about/reporting-treasury-parlia ment (accessed 17-07-2017).
[7] Blair & Walker *Financial Services Law* 299-300.
[8] Blair & Walker *Financial Services Law* 299-300.
[9] Blair & Walker *Financial Services Law* 299.
[10] These include the High Courts, Supreme Courts and the Courts of Appeal.

financial markets in the UK. Furthermore, the courts have on many occasions relied on the help of the Crown Prosecution Services (CPS), FSA and subsequently, the FCA to obtain a number of settlements and convictions in market abuse cases.[11] For example, in *Chase Manhattan Equities v Goodman*[12] Knox J held that the accused persons were guilty of misusing material non-public inside information. The court further held that the illicit trading of these accused persons was tantamount to an offence against public policy. Moreover, in *Seager v Copydex (No 2),*[13] damages were awarded against the person who misused confidential non-public inside information (insider trading) for personal gain. The FCA has relatively managed to successfully obtain some settlements and convictions in market abuse-related cases, including those Internet and/or social media-related cases in the UK to date.[14]

The effectiveness of the co-operation between the FSA and the courts was further revealed in *Financial Services Authority v Rourke,*[15] where Neuberger J imposed a declaratory injunctive relief against the accused persons who violated the Financial Services and Markets Act's provisions on the disclosure of confidential information.[16] Moreover, the courts of Appeal have to date been able to assist the FCA to make appropriate decisions in relation to any appeal raised by the aggrieved persons. Significant efforts have also been successfully made by both the courts and the FCA to curb cross-border market abuse activities. For example, the FCA may appoint specific competent persons and assign them to assist the courts to investigate and/or prosecute market abuse violations perpetrated in the UK by persons

---

[11] Blair & Walker *Financial Services Law* 300.

[12] [1991] BCLC 897.

[13] [1969] 1 WLR 809.

[14] See further the FCA "FCA Fines Former Investment Banker for Sharing Confidential Information over WhatsApp" (30-03-2017) *Press Release* <https://www.fca.org.uk/news/press-releases/fine-former-investment-banker-sharing-confidential-information-whatsapp> (accessed 18-07-2017); FCA "Two Charged with Insider Dealing" (16-06-2017) *Press Release* <https://www.fca.org.uk/news/press-releases/two-charged-insider-dealing> (accessed 18-07-2017); FCA "FCA Bans and Fines Two Individuals for Market Abuse" (07-04-2017) *Press Release* <https://www.fca.org.uk/news/press-releases/fca-bans-and-fines-two-individuals-market-abuse> (accessed 18-07-2017); FCA "Tesco to Pay Redress for Market Abuse" (28-03-2017) *Press Release* <https://www.fca.org.uk/news/press-releases/tesco-pay-redress-market-abuse> (accessed 18-07-2017); FCA "FCA Fines Deutsche Bank £163 Million for Serious Anti-money Laundering Controls Failings" (31-01-2017) *Press Release* <https://www.fca.org.uk/news/press-releases/fca-fines-deutsche-bank-163-million-anti-money-laundering-controls-failure> (accessed 18-07-2017); FCA "Mark Lyttleton Sentenced to 12 Months Imprisonment for Insider Dealing" (21-12-2016) *Press Release* <https://www.fca.org.uk/news/press-releases/mark-lyttleton-sentenced-12-months-imprisonment-insider-dealing> (accessed 18-07-2017).

[15] (HC, 2001-10-19).

[16] S 348. Also see Russen *Financial Services Authorisation, Supervision* (2006)148-149.

domiciled elsewhere.[17] Additionally, the FCA has to date proposed and introduced some measures aimed at enhancing the UK's debt listing regime and related anti-market abuse regulatory aspects.[18]

On the other hand, as is the position with the FCA,[19] the FSB has to date received considerable help, especially, in respect of the criminal prosecution of market abuse cases, from the courts and the Director of Public Prosecutions (DPP) in South Africa.[20] As stated above,[21] the DPP in South Africa, like the CPS of the UK,[22] usually prosecutes matters relating to market abuse after a referral from the FSB or other relevant authorities. This could, in a way, suggest that the DPP in South Africa may only commence its own investigations or prosecution of market abuse offences after consultation with the FSB.[23] As indicated above, although it may be *prima facie* presumed that the FSB supports the DPP and the relevant courts with the necessary information regarding ongoing market abuse cases in South Africa, it is not clear whether the FSB is statutorily mandated to assign certain persons with the relevant expertise to assist the courts in their prosecution of such cases.[24] Moreover, notwithstanding the outstanding effort that is being made by the courts and the FSB to prosecute market abuse cases timeously and effectively, the paucity of successful settlements or prosecutions that have been obtained in such cases remains a major challenge in South Africa to date.[25] Relatively few settlements have been obtained in cases involving market abuse activities like market manipulation in South Africa.[26] Thus, it remains to be seen whether the co-operation relationship between the FSB, the courts and the DPP will give rise to more convictions and settlements in matters involving market abuse in

---

[17] Also see related remarks by Blair & Walker *Financial Services Law* 34-38 & 302-303 & Rider, Alexander, Linklater & Bazley *Market Abuse and Insider Dealing* (2009) 190-195.

[18] FCA "FCA Proposes Measures to Improve the Effectiveness of UK Primary Listed Debt Markets" (27-04-2016) *Press Release* <https://www.fca.org.uk/news/press-releases/fca-proposes-measures-improve-effectiveness-uk-primary-listed-debt-markets> (accessed 18-07-2017).

[19] See related remarks above.

[20] Chitimira & Lawack "Overview of the Role-Players in the Investigation, Prevention and Enforcement of Market Abuse Provisions in South Africa" 2013 *Obiter* 200 200-217; Chitimira "Overview of Selected Role-Players in the Detection and Enforcement of Market Abuse Cases and Appeals in South Africa" 2014 *Speculum Juris* 108 108-124, for related analysis.

[21] Chitimira & Lawack 2013 *Obiter* 200-217; Chitimira 2014 *Speculum Juris* 108-124.

[22] See related remarks above.

[23] S 84(10) of the Financial Markets Act.

[24] Generally see Chitimira & Lawack 2013 *Obiter* 200-217; Chitimira 2014 *Speculum Juris* 108-124.

[25] Chitimira & Lawack 2013 *Obiter* 200-217; Chitimira 2014 *Speculum Juris* 108-124, for similar analysis.

[26] See *Pretorius v Natal South Sea Investment Trust Limited* 410, where the court held that the accused persons were guilty for prejudicing other investors by selling overpriced securities (market manipulation).

South Africa in the future.[27] It is further uncertain whether the courts and the FSB have been successful with regard to the combating of cross-border market abuse practices in South Africa.[28] For example, relatively few cases involving cross-border market abuse activities has been reported or successfully prosecuted and/or settled in South Africa to date.[29] Accordingly, this raises some doubt as to whether the co-operative efforts of the courts and the FSB have to date sufficiently and effectively dealt with the market abuse violations in South Africa and elsewhere.

8 2 2 Co-operation between the FCA and the Local SROs

As indicated earlier,[30] the FCA does not work in isolation. It involves SROs such as the London Stock Exchange (LSE), the London International Financial Futures and Options Exchange Administration and Management (LIFFOEAM), the Serious Fraud Office (SFO), the Financial Services and Markets Tribunal (FSMT), the Financial Ombudsman Service (FOS) and the Regulatory Decisions Committee (RDC) in order to enhance its anti-market abuse enforcement efforts. Consequently, this sub-heading scrutinises whether this co-operative enforcement approach has managed to reduce market abuse practices in the UK. A brief analysis of the functions of the FCA and selected SROs in relation to this co-operative approach will be therefore carried out under this sub-heading.

The FCA has entered into several operating arrangements (co-operation agreements) with certain SROs which are directly or indirectly involved in the enforcement of market abuse laws in the UK. For instance, the FCA and the LSE have stipulated relevant guidelines which help them to determine the appropriate action that will be taken by either the LSE or the FCA with regard to suspected market abuse cases in order to avoid unnecessary duplication of their functions. Moreover, both the FCA and the LSE employ the same computerised surveillance systems to detect and prevent market abuse practices in the UK's financial markets. This has enabled the FCA to investigate and prosecute market abuse violations that are committed over the Internet in respect of any prescribed financial markets in many instances.[31] Furthermore, the FCA obliges all companies, operators of trading venues, individuals

[27] In contrast to the UK, there is no person who has been convicted for insider trading in South Africa. See related analysis by Chitimira & Lawack 2013 *Obiter* 200-217; Chitimira 2014 *Speculum Juris* 108-124.

[28] Chitimira & Lawack 2013 *Obiter* 200-217; Chitimira 2014 *Speculum Juris* 108-124, for further discussion.

[29] Chitimira & Lawack 2013 *Obiter* 200-217; Chitimira 2014 *Speculum Juris* 108-124, for related analysis.

[30] See similar discussion in paragraph 8 2 1 above.

[31] Blair & Walker *Financial Services Law* 301-303, for generally related remarks.

and/or other professional market participants that are involved in arranging or executing transactions in certain securities or financial instruments to promptly report "suspicious transactions and orders" (STORs) to it for further investigation.[32] Notably, STORs are determined where there objective grounds to suspect that such transactions could constitute market abuse practices in the UK's financial markets.

Moreover, the FCA has forged some good co-operation agreements with the LIFFOEAM to detect, investigate and prosecute all market abuse cases relating to any qualifying investments that are dealt with on the LIFFOEAM or other prescribed financial markets.[33] Thus, the FCA, with the help of the LIFFOEAM, may detect and track any suspected market abuse activity in the prescribed financial markets situated in the UK or which are accessible electronically in the UK or in any member state of the European Union (EU).[34] However, it is unclear whether the UK will continue enforcing and abiding by the EU market abuse laws in light of the Brexit referendum outcome.

Furthermore, the SFO and the FCA are both responsible for investigating and curbing serious fraud and other illicit trading practices that amount to market abuse in the UK. This has nonetheless resulted in the duplication of some of the regulatory functions by either the FCA or the SFO, especially with regard to market abuse violations.[35] Therefore, one can assume that this overlap of functions that usually occurs between the SFO and the FCA could be an indication of an inconsistent co-operative enforcement relationship between these two regulatory bodies. Be that as it may, the FCA is mainly responsible for policing the market abuse prohibition in the UK. In view of this, the SFO may only prosecute certain market abuse cases if it reasonably believes that such cases also constitute serious fraud.[36] Where such market abuse violations are detected and investigated by the SFO, they may be referred to the CPS or the FCA for further prosecution.[37]

The FOS and the FCA have been co-operatively involved to curb market abuse activities in the UK. For instance, the FOS hears individual disputes

---

[32] FCA "Suspicious Transaction and Order Reports" (28-02-2017) <https://www.fca.org.uk/markets/market-abuse/suspicious-transaction-order-reports> (accessed 18-07-2017).

[33] S 118(5) of the Financial Services and Markets Act; also see Rider, Alexander, Linklater & Bazley *Market Abuse and Insider Dealing* 73-74.

[34] This has enabled the FCA to discourage and combat cross-border market abuse practices. Also see Rider, Alexander, Linklater & Bazley *Market Abuse and Insider Dealing* 74.

[35] Blair & Walker *Financial Services Law* 300.

[36] Blair & Walker *Financial Services Law* 300.

[37] Notably, before its replacement by the FCA, the FSA signed co-operation agreements with the Association of Chief Police Officers of England and Wales to enhance its investigation and prosecution of market abuse practices in the UK. See further Russen *Financial Services Authorisation, Supervision* 96.

involving cases of market abuse that do not necessarily fall under the ambit of the FCA.[38] In so doing, the FOS enables the FCA to resolve any outstanding matters involving market abuse cases in order to promote the efficiency and integrity of the UK's financial markets. Put differently, the FCA has put in place some guidelines that govern and allow the FOS to take independent and appropriate action regarding complaints against any decision of the FCA or other relevant enforcement authorities.[39] The FCA has permitted the FOS to administer independent claims under the Financial Services Compensation Scheme (FSCS) in order to afford all the aggrieved persons an opportunity to obtain adequate redress.[40]

Additionally, the FSMT offers a platform for prejudiced persons to appeal against the decisions of the FCA. In other words, the FSMT and the FCA have some co-operation guidelines in place to enable them to perform their functions more effectively. These guidelines further allow the FSMT to advise the FCA regarding its disputed decisions or any other relevant matter.[41] The FCA has further exploited its mutual co-operation with the RDC to investigate and prosecute market abuse violations in the UK.

The RDC is responsible and accountable to the FCA for its decisions in relation to market abuse cases. This could *prima facie* imply that there is a good co-operation relationship between the FCA and the RDC, especially, with regard to the enforcement of market abuse laws in the UK.[42] The FCA also entered into a co-operation agreement with the Bank of England and the Prudential Regulation Authority (PRA) in relation to the supervision of regulated financial markets and market infrastructure for the purposes of sharing

---

[38] See further related analysis above.

[39] See generally ss 226 & 227 read with ss 155 & 225 of the Financial Services and Markets Act; also see Avgouleas *The Mechanics and Regulation of Market Abuse* 409-411.

[40] See *R (on the application of Davies and others) v Financial Services Authority* [2003] 4 All ER 1196, where the applicants sought a judicial review to challenge the decision of the FSA to issue a warning notice pursuant to s 56 of the Financial Services and Markets Act without initially referring the matter to the FSMT.

[41] For example, in *Legal and General Assurance Society Limited v Financial Services Authority* (2005) FSMT 016 the FSMT upheld a decision made by the FSA to award a public censure and a financial penalty against the applicants and warned the FSA to be flexible in order to give appropriate penalties in such matters in the future; also see *Piggott v FSA* (2003) FSMT 004 the FSMT reduced the financial penalty imposed by the FSA from £40 000 to £10 000 citing that the applicants were having some difficulties in paying the initial penalty and see further *Mohammed v FSA* (2005) 013 the FSMT held that the applicant's other share dealings were not in themselves unlawful and were therefore not in contravention of s 118 of the Financial Services and Markets Act. Also see generally Russen *Financial Services Authorisation, Supervision* 194-195; Avgouleas *The Mechanics and Regulation of Market Abuse* 382-383.

[42] Swan *Market Abuse Regulation* (2006) 106-107.

relevant information and combating illicit trading activities such as market abuse.[43]

In addition, as is the position in the UK,[44] the FSB works hand in hand with other local SROs to complement its anti-market abuse enforcement efforts in South Africa.[45] Like the LSE,[46] the JSE has to date been assisting the FSB with the surveillance, detection and investigation of suspicious illicit activities which in most instances would be indicative of market abuse violations.[47] This shows that there is some co-operation and relevant information sharing between the FSB and the JSE.[48] Moreover, the JSE has now consolidated the functions of the Bond Exchange of South Africa in order to investigate and curb commodities-based market abuse practices in South Africa. This suggests that the FSB now relies on the JSE to detect and combat commodities-based market abuse practices in the South African financial markets.[49] Nevertheless, the fact still remains that a relatively few market abuse cases reported to the FSB by either the JSE or other enforcement authorities have been successfully settled and prosecuted in South Africa under the Financial Markets Act to date.[50] This status quo is likely to continue because the Financial Markets Act does not expressly and statutorily impose a mandatory co-operation obligation on both the FSB and the JSE to improve the enforcement of the market abuse prohibition in South Africa.[51]

Notably, the Directorate of Market Abuse (DMA) has similar roles as those of the RDC and it investigates and exercises some functions on behalf of the FSB.[52] Currently, the FSB and the DMA work closely and consult each other in relation to the making of market abuse rules, penalties and any other decisions.[53] It is hoped that this co-operation between the FSB and the DMA will in future produce more settlements and convictions, especially, in criminal

[43] FCA, PRA & Bank of England "Memorandum of Understanding between the Financial Conduct Authority and the Bank of England, including the Prudential Regulation Authority" (Date unknown) 1 2-11 <https://www.fca.org.uk/publication/mou/mou-bank-pra.pdf> (accessed 19-07-2017).

[44] See related remarks above.

[45] See related remarks above.

[46] See earlier comments above.

[47] Chitimira & Lawack 2013 *Obiter* 200-217; Chitimira 2014 *Speculum Juris* 108-124, for related discussion.

[48] Chitimira & Lawack 2013 *Obiter* 200-217; Chitimira 2014 *Speculum Juris* 108-124, for related discussion.

[49] Chitimira & Lawack 2013 *Obiter* 200-217; Chitimira 2014 *Speculum Juris* 108-124, for related analysis.

[50] See relevant provisions under Chapter X of the Financial Markets Act; also see related analysis by Chitimira & Lawack 2013 *Obiter* 200-217; Chitimira 2014 *Speculum Juris* 108-124.

[51] See relevant provisions under Chapter X of the Financial Markets Act; Chitimira & Lawack 2013 *Obiter* 200-217; Chitimira 2014 *Speculum Juris* 108-124, for related analysis.

[52] S 85 of the Financial Markets Act.

[53] S 84(2)(f) read with s 85 of the Financial Markets Act.

cases of market abuse.[54] Notwithstanding the fact that the FSB and the DMA convene regular meetings to discuss and share any relevant confidential information, especially, in respect of ongoing market abuse investigations, more may still need to be done to increase the number of market abuse cases that are successfully prosecuted and/or settled in South Africa.[55]

The Takeover Regulation Panel (TRP) offers additional support to the FSB in relation to the regulation and enforcement of securities laws in South Africa.[56] For example, the TRP has some requirements in place pertaining to the disclosure of price-sensitive information.[57] This is aimed at preventing insider trading and market manipulation by insiders in relation to the offeror or offeree company by dealing unlawfully in securities of the affected companies at an early stage of the negotiations. All parties to an offer relating to an affected transaction are required to take reasonable steps to prevent the making or publication of misleading statements, creation of false markets and other market abuse activities.[58] However, the extent of co-operation between the FSB and the TRP remains unclear. It appears as if the TRP does not involve itself much in the day-to-day enforcement of matters relating to market abuse as such matters usually concern the FSB. Consequently, the actual degree of co-operation between the FSB and the TRP is very difficult to ascertain since the TRP does not primarily deal with the enforcement of the market abuse prohibition in South Africa on a more regular basis.

Furthermore, like the FSMT of the UK,[59] the Enforcement Committee (EC)[60] provides all aggrieved persons with an opportunity to appeal against any decisions of the FSB, especially, with regard to the penalties for market abuse.[61] While this is important in that it helps the FSB to review its own decisions and to make appropriate decisions in relation to its market abuse

---

[54] See relevant provisions under Chapter X of the Financial Markets Act & Chitimira & Lawack 2013 *Obiter* 200-217; Chitimira 2014 *Speculum Juris* 108-124, for related analysis.

[55] For instance, relatively few market abuse cases were successfully investigated and/or settled by the DMA and the FSB, during the period between 1999 and 2015, see the DMA "Past Investigations" (23-06-2015) <https://www.fsb.co.za/Departments/marketAbuse/Documents/DMA_Past%20investigations%20until%202015-06-23.pdf>(accessed 19-07-2017).

[56] See related analysis by Chitimira 2014 *Speculum Juris* 108-124.

[57] See related analysis by Chitimira 2014 *Speculum Juris* 108-124.

[58] See the TRP Rules General Principles and/or Guidelines, see the TRP *Guideline on Approaching Shareholders Prior to Making a Firm Intention Annoucement* Guideline 1/2013; the TRP *Guideline on Annoucement* Guideline 3/2012; notably, the TRP was formerly called the Securities Regulation Panel (SRP), see especially, the SRP General Principles 6 & 9.

[59] See earlier remarks above.

[60] See ss 85 & 99 of the Financial Markets Act; ss 6A to 6I of the Financial Institutions (Protection of Funds) Act 28 of 2001 as amended (Protection of Funds Act).

[61] Chitimira & Lawack 2013 *Obiter* 200-217; Chitimira 2014 *Speculum Juris* 108-124, for related remarks.

enforcement and regulatory functions, only a minimum number of market abuse cases have been settled with the EC to date.[62] Accordingly, this could be an indication that there is inconsistent, little or no co-operation between the FSB and the EC. Likewise, the Appeal Board (AB) is empowered to independently hear and afford all the aggrieved persons an opportunity to appeal or lodge their complaints against any decisions of the Registrar of Securities Services[63] or the FSB executive officer regarding market abuse for them to be addressed. For instance, a person aggrieved by any decision of the Registrar of Securities Services may appeal to the AB for further adjudication under the Financial Markets Act.[64] Likewise, any person aggrieved by the decision of the claims officer as contemplated in the Financial Markets Act[65] may apply to the AB for a redress.[66] Despite these positive developments, relatively minimal market abuse cases have been successfully settled by the FSB to date.[67]

8 2 3 Co-operation between the FCA and Similar International RegulatoryBodies

Notably, before the introduction of the FCA, the FSA entered into some co-operation agreements (Memoranda of Understanding) with several regulatory bodies in other jurisdictions. For example, the FSA signed a separate Memorandum of Understanding (MOU) with the United States Securities and Exchange Commission (SEC) and the Commodity Futures Trading Commission (CFTC) in October 1997.[68] The main objective of this MOU is *inter alia* to improve the ability of the bodies concerned to exchange relevant information in respect of the activities, internal controls and management systems of the UK and the United States of America (USA)'s companies that operate interna-

---

[62] Generally see similar remarks by Chitimira & Lawack 2013 *Obiter* 200-217; Chitimira 2014 *Speculum Juris* 108-124; for related comments, see the EC "Enforcement Actions" (19-07-2017) <https://www.fsb.co.za/enforcementCommittee/Pages/enforcementActions.aspx> (accessed 19-07-2017).

[63] S 26A of the Financial Services Board Act 97 of 1990 (Financial Services Board Act); s 105(1)(a) of the Financial Markets Act. Notably, those aggrieved by the EC's determinations may now appeal to the High Court, (not to the AB), as indicated in s 6F of the Protection of Funds Act.

[64] S 105(1)(a).

[65] S 105(1)(j) read with s 82.

[66] FSB "Appeal Board Hearing Schedule: 20 June – 20 July 2017" *Appeal Board Publications* 20 July 2017; Chitimira 2014 *Speculum Juris* 114; for related comments.

[67] FSB "FSB fines Michiel Jakobus Bronn R350 000 plus Costs for FMA Contravention" *FSB Press Release* 15 March 2017; FSB "Report by the Directorate of Market Abuse" *FSB Press Release* 31 March 2017; FSB "FSB fines Robert Fourie R2 million for FMA Contravention" *FSB Press Release* 08 March 2017; FSB "FSB Fines Johan Franck R1 000 000 for FMA Contraventions" *FSB Press Release* 26 October 2016; FSB "Report by the Directorate of Market Abuse" *FSB Press Release* 28 September 2016; FSB "Administrative Penalties Imposed for Market Manipulation" *FSB Press Release* 1 December 2015; FSB "High Court Upholds Zietzman Conviction" *FSB Press Release* 28 August 2015.

[68] Blair & Walker *Financial Services Law* 37.

tionally.[69] In addition, this MOU developed procedures to increase co-operation, especially, in connection with important market events occurring in the UK and the USA's banking companies, securities and financial markets.[70] The FCA also entered into similar MOUs with the CFTC and the SEC in 2016 and 2013 respectively. For instance, the FCA entered into a co-operation MOU with SEC in relation to; *inter alia*, the supervision of the asset management industry and regulated financial markets in both the UK and the USA.[71] Likewise, the FCA and the CFTC concluded an MOU to improve the sharing of relevant information and the supervision of companies and regulated markets in order to curb market abuse activities in their respective jurisdictions.[72]

Furthermore, prior to its replacement by the FCA, the FSA forged bilateral and multilateral MOU with leading international regulatory bodies such as the Basel Committee on Banking Supervision (BCBS), the Financial Action Task Force (FATF), the Joint Forum on Financial Conglomerates,[73] the International Organisation of Securities Commissions (IOSCO), the Financial Stability Forum, and the Committee on the Global Financial System.[74] The FSA also entered into other short-term co-operation arrangements known as the Financial Information Sharing Agreements with SROs and regulators in other jurisdictions in order to share information that will be relevant to any ongoing investigations of securities and/or market abuse violations.[75] The FCA is a member of the IOSCO. This membership enables the FCA to exchange relevant information with other regulatory bodies that are also members of the IOSCO.[76] It further empowers the FCA to co-operate with similar regulatory bodies elsewhere in order to establish good corporate standards and better surveillance systems to combat cross-border market abuse practices.[77] In addition, the FCA specifically signed the IOSCO Multilateral Memorandum

---

[69] Generally see Blair & Walker *Financial Services Law* 37.

[70] Additionally, this MOU has generally improved the relations between the FSA, the CFTC & the SEC as well as the effectiveness of the financial supervision in discouraging cross-border market abuse activities in both the UK and the USA's financial markets.

[71] Orrick, Herrington & Sutcliffe LLP "FCA and SEC Publish a MOU on Investment Fund Supervision" (29-07-2013) http://www.lexology.com/library/detail.aspx?g=3b66b38a-535a-4c9a-afa1-da447bab9d95 (accessed 19-07-2017).

[72] The CFTC and the FCA "Memorandum of Understanding Concerning Cooperation and the Exchange of Information in the Context of Supervising Covered Firms" (06-10-2016) 1 2-10 <http://www.cftc.gov/idc/groups/public/@internationalaffairs/documents/file/cftc-fca-supervisorymou100616.pdf> (accessed 19-07-2017).

[73] This body is now known as the Joint Forum.

[74] Blair & Walker *Financial Services Law* 34-38.

[75] See generally Blair & Walker *Financial Services Law* 37.

[76] See generally Blair & Walker *Financial Services Law* 37-38.

[77] See generally Blair & Walker *Financial Services Law* 37-38.

Concerning Consultation, Cooperation and the Exchange of Information.[78] This MOU allows the FCA to obtain mutual assistance from other international regulatory bodies and to adopt better corporate standards that will enhance the enforcement and prosecution of cross-border market abuse offences.[79] For instance, during the period between 2015 and 2016, the FCA received about 971 requests to assist other likeminded regulatory bodies from 60 countries with their anti-market abuse and related investigations.[80] The UK co-chaired the IOSCO taskforce on unregulated financial entities with Italy. This enabled the FCA to focus closely on unregulated entities and hedge funds in order to devise alternative regulatory approaches that curb the negative effects associated with their trading and global opacity.[81]

The FCA co-operates with similar regulatory bodies in the EU member countries. As envisaged in the EU Market Abuse Regulation,[82] the FCA may investigate, track and prosecute market abuse activities conducted in the UK in relation to qualifying investments listed on a regulated financial market in any other EU member state.[83] Nevertheless, it remains unclear whether the FCA will continue to abide by the EU anti-market abuse laws after the UK's withdrawal from the EU (Brexit).

Likewise, the FCA has reportedly received assistance from other affiliated bodies such as the BCBS, the Joint Forum, the FATF and the Organisation for Economic Co-operation and Development (OECD) to develop principles and/or identify practices that will reduce illicit trading activities like market abuse as much as possible.[84] This has also enabled the FCA to improve its supervisory methods and market abuse enforcement approaches.[85]

---

[78] FCA "International Cooperation" (2015) <https://www.fca.org.uk/enforcement-annual-performance-account-2015-16/11-international-cooperation> (accessed 19-07-2017); Blair & Walker *Financial Services Law* 37-38 & 826-830.

[79] See further Blair & Walker *Financial Services Law* 826-830; Rider, Alexander, Linklater & Bazley *Market Abuse and Insider Dealing* 271-275.

[80] FCA (2015) <https://www.fca.org.uk/enforcement-annual-performance-account-2015-16/11-international-cooperation> (accessed 19-07-2017); Blair & Walker *Financial Services Law* 37-38 & 826-830.

[81] Blair & Walker *Financial Services Law* 826-830; Rider, Alexander, Linklater & Bazley *Market Abuse and Insider Dealing* 271-275, for a similar discussion.

[82] Regulation (EU) No 596/2014 of the European Parliament and of the Council of 16 April 2014 on market abuse (market abuse regulation) and repealing Directive 2003/6 of the European Parliament and of the Council and Commission Directives 200/124/EC, 2003/125/EC and 2004/72/EC, [2014] OJL 173/1 (EU Market Abuse Regulation).

[83] Also see articles 24 to 26 read with articles 32 to 33 of the EU Market Abuse Regulation, which provides some guiding principles which allow regulatory bodies in the EU member countries to co-operate whenever necessary for the purpose of effectively executing their duties, especially, with regard to the regulation of market abuse practices. Also see Blair & Walker *Financial Services Law* 302-303.

[84] See generally Blair & Walker *Financial Services Law* 34-35 & 830-836.

[85] See generally Blair & Walker *Financial Services Law* 34-35 & 830-836.

Additionally, the FCA has also concluded several regulatory and anti-market abuse-related co-operation agreements with regulatory bodies from several countries such as the Ontario Securities Commission (OSC),[86] Albanian Financial Supervisory Authority, Alberta Securities Commission, Australian Securities and Investments Commission, Autorité des marchés financiers, Québec, Bermuda Monetary Authority, Board of Governors of the Federal Reserve System, British Columbia Securities Commission, British Virgin Islands Financial Services Commission, Capital Markets and Securities Authority of Tanzania, Capital Markets Authority of Kenya, Capital Market Development Authority of Maldives, Capital Markets Board of Turkey, Cayman Islands Monetary Authority, Comissão de Valores Mobiliários do Brasil, Conseil Déontologique des Valeurs Mobilières of Morocco, Dubai Financial Services Authority, Egyptian Financial Supervisory Authority, Financial Markets Authority of New Zealand, Financial Services Agency of Japan, FSB, Financial Services Commission of Mauritius, Financial Supervision Commission of the Isle of Man, Guernsey Financial Services Commission, Hong Kong Securities and Futures Commission, Israel Securities Authority, New Zealand Financial Markets Authority and many others.[87]

In contrast to the FCA,[88] it is not certain whether the FSB has also entered into some co-operation arrangements with international regulatory bodies that deal with commodities-based market abuse practices such as the CFTC, the LIFFOEAM and the Trade Point Stock Exchange (TPSE).[89] Likewise, it is not clear whether South Africa has also ratified any agreement with the OECD[90] in order to enable the FSB to improve its policies regarding the monitoring, investigation, information gathering and the adoption of other appropriate market abuse enforcement approaches. Nevertheless, the FSB should be commended for its great efforts to respond to the mounting global concern over the negative effects of market abuse activities.[91] It has, for instance, joined the IOSCO in order to learn from the experiences of similar regulatory

---

[86] OSC & FCA "International Memoranda of Understanding: Notice of Co-operation Agreement Concerning Innovative Fintech Businesses with UK Financial Conduct Authority" (02-03-2017) <http://www.osc.gov.on.ca/en/mou_international_index.htm> (accessed 19-07-2017).

[87] FCA "National Private Placement Regime Supervisory Co-operation Arrangements (MOUs)" (07-07-2016) <https://www.fca.org.uk/firms/nppr/supervisory-co-operation-arrangements-mous> (accessed 19-07-2017).

[88] See related analysis above.

[89] This might further suggest that commodities-based cross-border market abuse practices are not being sufficiently detected and prosecuted in South Africa.

[90] Blair & Walker *Financial Services Law* (2006) 832-833.

[91] Chitimira & Lawack 2013 *Obiter* 200-217; Chitimira 2014 *Speculum Juris* 108-124, for further discussion.

bodies that are members of the IOSCO.[92] For example, in light of this, the FSB can rely on its IOSCO membership to co-operate with other regulators such as the Securities and Exchange Board of India (SEBI) to track and investigate market abuse activities that relate to the affected securities in South Africa by the perpetrators who anonymously dealt in such securities while in India.[93] However, it is unclear whether the FSB has concluded any binding co-operation MOU with the SEBI in relation to the enforcement of the cross-border market abuse prohibitions. Despite this, it is encouraging that the FSB has concluded binding co-operation MOUs with the FCA and the SEC for the purposes of mutual sharing of relevant information and combating cross-border market abuse practices.[94]

8 3 The Adoption of Adequate Preventative Measures

The UK, like many other countries, has developed and adopted several methods to prevent market abuse practices in all its prescribed financial markets. These methods include providing a definition of, and enumerating the conduct that amounts to market abuse, reliance on criminal, civil and administrative penalties, public censure and the use of surveillance systems.

For example, a wide but comprehensive definition of practices that constitute market manipulation and other related market abuse offences is statutorily provided for in the UK. Specifically, about seven types of conduct that amount to or that could give rise to market abuse are clearly stipulated in the Financial Services and Markets Act.[95] The UK's market abuse regime further discourages and prohibits Internet-based market manipulation practices.[96] Moreover, the Financial Services Act 2012[97] recently amended the Financial Services and Markets Act and introduced new market abuse offences and a new anti-market abuse regulatory system in the UK.[98] This has led to a substantial increase in compliance and enforcement of the market abuse laws in the UK to date.

---

[92] Generally see related comments by Chitimira & Lawack 2013 *Obiter* 200-217; Chitimira 2014 *Speculum Juris* 108-124.

[93] Chitimira & Lawack 2013 *Obiter* 200-217; Chitimira 2014 *Speculum Juris* 108-124, for further discussion.

[94] Chitimira & Lawack 2013 *Obiter* 200-217; Chitimira 2014 *Speculum Juris* 108-124, for further discussion; FCA (07-07-2016) <https://www.fca.org.uk/firms/nppr/supervisory-co-operation-arrangements-mous> (accessed 19-07-2017).

[95] S 118(1) to (8).

[96] The making or publishing of false, deceptive or misleading statements to manipulate the financial markets over the Internet is prohibited in the UK. See generally Cassim "An Analysis of Market Manipulation under the Securities Services Act 36 of 2004 (part 2)" 2008 *SA Merc LJ* 177 182-183.

[97] (c 21) (Financial Services Act 2012).

[98] Part 7 of the Financial Services Act 2012; also see related discussion in paragraph 6 3 in Chapter Six of this book.

Additionally, the UK's market abuse regime o employs appropriate penalties to discourage all persons from committing market abuse offences. For example, criminal penalties may be levied against the offenders under both the Financial Services and Markets Act and the Criminal Justice Act.[99] Notably, criminal penalties under the Criminal Justice Act are only limited to individuals who commit insider trading and very few convictions have been obtained in such cases so far. The Financial Services and Markets Act has, however, now extended this criminal liability to both individuals and companies.[100] Moreover, offenders may incur administrative and civil penalties for market abuse under the Financial Services and Markets Act and/or the Financial Services Act 2012. Therefore, the FCA may impose unlimited financial penalties on companies or individuals who indulge in market abuse practices.[101] The UK's market abuse regime also provides separate and different penalties for individuals and companies. This has arguably increased deterrence on the part of the offenders and improved the overall enforcement of the market abuse prohibition in the UK.[102]

Apart from relying on penalties, the FCA may further issue public statements to the effect that the accused person was involved in market abuse in some instances where it reasonably believes that issuing such statements is the more appropriate sanction.[103] These public statements are also employed in instances where the accused persons have taken responsibility for their market abuse conduct as well as reasonable steps to co-operate with the FCA and where such persons are unable to pay the imposed financial penalty.[104] This name and shame approach is usually employed to deter and prevent unscrupulous persons from wilfully indulging in market abuse activities in the UK's prescribed financial markets.[105]

---

[99] See related remarks in paragraph 8 1 above.

[100] See generally s 118(1) to (8).

[101] S 123(1) of the Financial Services and Markets Act.

[102] See generally Cassim 2008 *SA Merc LJ* 191-195.

[103] S 123(3) of the Financial Services and Markets Act; see further the FCA Handbook (MAR) "Market Conduct" (2017) *Release 18* MAR 1 & 2 https://www.handbook. fca.org.uk/handbook/MAR.pdf (accessed 20-07-2017); the FCA "Enforcement Information Guide" (2017) 1 1-9 <https://www.fca.org.uk/publication/corporate/enforcement-information-guide.pdf> (accessed 20-07-2017); the FCA Handbook "Disclosure Guidance and Transparency Rules (DTRs) Sourcebook" (2017) *Media Release 18* DTRs 1A to 1C; 2; 5; 6 & 8 <https://www.handbook.fca.org.uk/handbook/ DTR.pdf> (accessed 20-07-2017). See further FSA's Enforcement (Manual) Handbook *Release 064* April 2007 ("ENF"), see ENF 14.4.1G.

[104] FCA Handbook (2017) *Release 18* MAR 1 & 2 <https://www.handbook.fca.org.uk/handbook/MAR.pdf> (accessed 20-07-2017); also see ENF 14.6.2G(6).

[105] Generally see Cassim 2008 *SA Merc LJ* 195-196.

Furthermore, the FCA relies on the LSE's surveillance systems to detect possible market abuse activities in the UK's prescribed financial markets.[106] Specifically, the LSE reports any cases of suspected market abuse through the Suspicious Transaction Reports (STRs) to the FCA for further adjudication. Thus the FCA is responsible for the investigation and prosecution of market abuse practices which occur on the LSE and any other prescribed financial markets in the UK.[107]

The FCA further relies on various committees such the Executive Regulatory Issues Committee (ERIC), the Executive Diversity Committee (EDC), the Executive Operations Committee (EOC) & the Policy Steering Committee (PSC) to execute its anti-market abuse and other relevant regulatory roles in the UK.[108]

Investigation and information gathering is another tool used by the FCA's Enforcement Division to combat market activities in the UK's prescribed financial markets.[109] The Enforcement Division co-operates with other FCA Divisions, namely, the Authorisation Division, Supervision Division and Strategy and Competition Division to, *inter alia*, enforce market abuse laws in the UK divisions. Moreover, the FCA's Enforcement Division co-operates with other local regulatory authorities to detect and investigate market abuse activities in the UK. The FCA has powers to appoint specific skilled persons to investigate and submit reports pertaining to ongoing market abuse cases.[110] In addition, the FCA may summon and interrogate any persons suspected to have contravened the relevant market abuse provisions in the UK.[111] The FCA also has the power to impose Anton pillar orders and to search and seize any documents or material from any person or premises if it reasonably believes that such material or documents will be essential to its market abuse investigations. In most instances, the FCA searches any person or premises after having obtained permission from the competent courts in the UK. Consequently, a number of market abuse cases have so far been successfully investigated by both the RDC[112] and the FCA.[113]

---

[106] See related comments in paragraph 8 2 2 above.

[107] This could further imply that the FCA is empowered to combat market abuse practices in relation to both listed and unlisted qualifying investments. A central computerised system known as the Stock Exchange Electronic Trading Service (SEETS) is usually used to detect the occurrence of such practices in the relevant financial markets in the UK.

[108] FCA "Executive Committees" (09-11-2016) <https://www.fca.org.uk/about/executive-commit tees> (accessed 20-07-2017).

[109] See related discussion in paragraphs 8 2 1; 8 2 2 & 8 2 3 above.

[110] See related analysis in paragraphs 8 2 1; 8 2 2 & 8 2 3 above.

[111] See related discussion in paragraphs 8 2 1; 8 2 2 & 8 2 3 above.

[112] See related comments in paragraph 8 2 2 above.

[113] Wood *Regulation of International Finance (The Law and Practice of International Finance Series Volume 7)* (2007) 591.

The FCA further employs whistle-blowing immunity provisions to promote prompt disclosure (tip-offs) by all persons who are aware of any market abuse activities without fear of reprisals.[114] Whistle-blowers in the UK are therefore protected against the risk of being victimised, losing their jobs or sidelined in their careers. This has since improved the timeous disclosure of relevant information to the prescribed financial markets through the Internet or the STRs by all the market participants in the UK. The FCA also imposes a duty on directors, employees and other relevant persons to report or speedily publish non-public price-sensitive information relating to qualifying investments or their dealing in any qualifying investments in order to discourage illicit trading practices like insider trading.[115]

Additionally, the FCA uses awareness programmes to combat and discourage market abuse practices in the prescribed UK's financial markets. The FCA has also provided the Code of Market Conduct to guide and educate all relevant persons regarding market abuse. The FCA has, in some instances, relied on public lectures and publishing important information through the Internet to inform all the relevant stakeholders regarding any illicit trading activities. This has assisted the FCA to develop and establish a good anti-market abuse corporate ethics culture among all the market participants and issuers of qualifying investments. The FCA has formulated extensive Listing Principles which must be followed by all issuers of qualifying investments.[116] These Listing Principles allow all the listed companies to take reasonable steps to train their directors about their duties, maintain adequate procedures, systems and controls which enable them to execute their functions well, and to promote market integrity.[117]

The UK's market abuse regime has established the FCA as the main competent regulatory body to police the enforcement of the market abuse prohibition.[118] This is the so-called single regulator model and it is used in the UK as

---

[114] FCA "FCA Introduces New Rules on Whistleblowing" (19-04-2016) <https://www.fca.org.uk/news/press-releases/fca-introduces-new-rules-whistleblowing> (accessed 21-07-2017).

[115] FCA Handbook" (2017) *Media Release 18* DTRs 1A to 1C; 2; 5; 6 & 8 <https://www.handbook.fca.org.uk/handbook/DTR.pdf> (accessed 20-07-2017); also see the FSA's Disclosure and Transparency Rules 2.6.1; 2.6.2; 2.2.8; 2.2.9; 2.8.1; 2.8.1; 2.8.3 to 2.8.10; Wood *Regulation of International Finance* 591; Barnes *Stock Market Efficiency, Insider Dealing* 119-121.

[116] FCA Handbook" (2017) *Media Release 18* DTRs 1A to 1C; 2; 5; 6 & 8 <https://www.handbook.fca.org.uk/handbook/DTR.pdf> (accessed 20-07-2017); see further the FSA's Disclosure and Transparency Rules 2.6.1; 2.6.2; 2.2.8; 2.2.9; 2.8.1; 2.8.1; 2.8.3 to 2.8.10; Wood *Regulation of International Finance* 591; Barnes *Stock Market Efficiency, Insider Dealing* 119-121.

[117] FCA Handbook" (2017) *Media Release 18* DTRs 1A to 1C; 2; 5; 6 & 8 <https://www.handbook.fca.org.uk/handbook/DTR.pdf> (accessed 20-07-2017); see further the FSA's Disclosure and Transparency Rules 2.6.1; 2.6.2; 2.2.8; 2.2.9; 2.8.1; 2.8.1; 2.8.3 to 2.8.10; Wood *Regulation of International Finance* 591; Barnes *Stock Market Efficiency, Insider Dealing* 119-121.

[118] See related discussion in paragraphs 8 2 1; 8 2 2 & 8 2 3 above.

a measure to discourage and combat market abuse practices in its financial markets. Thus, although the FCA co-operates with and delegates some of its functions to other local SROs like the RDC;[119] it remains mainly responsible for the enforcement of the market abuse prohibition in the UK.

Moreover, the FCA uses transaction recording, telephonic tapping, exit interviews, staff vetting checks, review of unusual trades and regular internal audit review of policies, systems and controls of issuers to prevent market abuse activities.[120] For purposes of preventing cross-border market abuse activity, the FCA usually invokes its fellow regulators in other jurisdictions to prosecute market abuse offences committed in the UK by persons in other countries.[121]

A private right of action in relation to certain market abuse offences is further used to discourage market abuse activities in the UK.[122] Therefore, all the prejudiced persons are given an opportunity to claim their damages or compensation directly from the market abuse offenders.[123] This has, in a way, afforded the affected persons an alternative arbitration method to obtain their damages speedily from the market abuse offenders. On the other hand, this private right of action method has increased deterrence on the part of the market abuse offenders to disengage from their illegal trading activities.[124] Over and above, it is generally accepted that some of the persons have so far successfully relied on this private right of action to claim their damages from either the companies or the individuals who involved themselves in market abuse practices.[125]

In contrast to the UK position,[126] there was no attempt on the part of the South African legislature to define the concept of market abuse comprehensively.[127] In addition, unlike the position in the UK,[128] the FSB is not statutorily authorised to impose unlimited financial penalties on the market abuse

---

[119] See the discussion in paragraph 8 2 2 above.
[120] Barnes Stock Market Efficiency, Insider Dealing 122-123.
[121] See the discussion in paragraph 8 2 3 above.
[122] Ss 150; 380 & 382 of the Financial Services and Markets Act. Notably, the court orders for a private right of action were not applicable to market abuse violations regarding the repealed s 397 of the Financial Services and Markets Act; see further Part 7 of the Financial Services Act 2012.
[123] Ss 150; 380 & 382 of the Financial Services and Markets Act.
[124] Rider, Alexander, Linklater & Bazley *Market Abuse and Insider Dealing* 94.
[125] Barnes *Stock Market Efficiency, Insider Dealing* 164-175; also see *In Re A-G's Reference (No 1 of 1998)* [1998] BCLC 193, where Lord Lane CJ ruled in favour of a plaintiff who was prejudiced by any insider (offender) who had dealt dishonestly in respect of the affected securities concerned & *In Re A-G's Reference (No 1 of 1988)* [1989] AC 971 973-977 & 986, the court held that the defendant was guilty for misusing non-public price-sensitive information. See further Rider, Alexander, Linklater & Bazley *Market Abuse and Insider Dealing* 60.
[126] See similar remarks above.
[127] See Chapter X of the Financial Markets Act.
[128] See related analysis above & in paragraphs 8 2 1; 8 2 2 & 8 2 3 above.

offenders in South Africa.[129] Moreover, no separate and distinct penalties for violating market abuse provisions are given to individuals and companies in South Africa.[130] Nonetheless, like the situation in the UK,[131] the FSB is now statutorily empowered to issue public statements to expose the perpetrators of market abuse under the Financial Markets Act.[132] However, it is not very clear whether this name and shame approach may be used by the FSB in conjunction with another penalty for market abuse deterrence purposes under the Financial Markets Act.[133]

Detection and surveillance is another method employed by the enforcement authorities to prevent market abuse practices in South Africa. Thus, like the position in the UK where market abuse surveillance is extended to all the prescribed financial markets,[134] such surveillance is also usually restricted to the regulated financial markets in South Africa. Moreover, as is the position with the FCA,[135] the FSB uses the investigation and information gathering method to identify and prevent all possible contravention of market abuse provisions by both individuals and companies in South Africa.[136] In line with this, as has already been said,[137] in most instances the DMA may, on behalf of the FSB, summon, interrogate or search and seize documents or material from any person or premises when it objectively believes that such material or documents are relevant to the market abuse matter under investigation.[138] Nevertheless, the Financial Markets Act[139] do not expressly empower the FSB to appoint other additional competent persons apart from the members of the DMA to investigate the occurrence of market abuse activities in the South African financial markets.[140]

Furthermore, awareness and educational programmes are employed by the FSB in an attempt to prevent market abuse practices in the South African financial markets. The FSB, for example, issues some quarterly informative

---

[129] S 109(a) of the Financial Markets Act & also see analysis by Chitimira & Lawack 2013 *Obiter* 200-217; Chitimira 2014 *Speculum Juris* 108-124.

[130] This could probably fail to deter and prevent all persons especially companies or other entities from wilfully indulging in market abuse activities. S 109(a) of the Financial Markets Act.

[131] See related remarks above.

[132] S 84(2)(e).

[133] S 84(2)(e). It is generally believed that potential offenders might desist from committing market abuse offences if they are aware that their identity and illicit trading practices, if caught, will be made public.

[134] See generally related remarks in paragraph 8 2 2 above.

[135] See earlier related remarks above.

[136] S 84(2)(a) & (b); (3) read with subsecs (4) & (5) of the Financial Markets Act; see further Chitimira & Lawack 2013 *Obiter* 200-217.

[137] See further related remarks in paragraph 8 2 2 above; also see s 85 of the Financial Markets Act.

[138] S 85 read with s 84 of the Financial Markets Act.

[139] S 84 of the Financial Markets Act.

[140] See related analysis in paragraphs 8 2 1 & 8 2 2 above.

market abuse booklets on its website to increase the general awareness among the market participants and all the relevant stakeholders.[141] However, unlike the FCA which is statutorily obliged to publish a detailed Code of Market Conduct,[142] the FSB is not expressly and statutorily empowered to provide a similar code of market conduct to increase market abuse awareness and promote a good anti-market abuse corporate ethics culture in South Africa.[143]

8 4 Concluding Remarks

Numerous anti-market abuse preventative measures are employed in the UK and South Africa. For instance, as highlighted above,[144] the FCA has relatively managed to formulate high-level methods and preventative measures, especially, in relation to the enforcement of market abuse laws in order to obtain more settlements and prosecutions in market abuse cases in the UK. For instance, the UK's market abuse regime has a number of measures in place such as market abuse awareness programmes; appointing additional skilled investigators; technological surveillance mechanisms and about 2500 to 3000 competent persons who work for the FCA in order to enhance the enforcement of the market abuse provisions in the UK.[145] On the other hand, relatively few anti-market abuse preventative measures have been adopted in South Africa.[146] Consequently, South Africa has so far not been able to successfully and consistently enforce its market abuse prohibition, particularly in cross-border market abuse cases and over the counter markets.[147] Accordingly, it is suggested that the Financial Markets Act should be amended to enact provisions that expressly empower other SROs in South Africa, apart from the FSB, to impose their own penalties or take any other appropriate action against any persons who indulge in market abuse activities in South Africa.[148]

A significant number of flaws and challenges such as the adoption of few market abuse preventative measures and the failure to provide separate and distinct penalties for companies and individuals could also have marred the successful enforcement of the market abuse ban in South Africa to date.[149] It is further submitted that the FSB should be expressly and statutorily authorised to impose separate and different penalties on individuals and juristic

[141] See similar comments above & Chitimira & Lawack 2013 *Obiter* 200-217.
[142] See similar remarks above.
[143] See Chapter X of the Financial Markets Act, which outlines market abuse offences in South Africa; also see related analysis by Chitimira & Lawack 2013 *Obiter* 200-217.
[144] See related analysis in paragraphs 8 2 1; 8 2 2; 8 2 3 & 8 3 above.
[145] See related analysis in paragraphs 8 2 1; 8 2 2; 8 2 3 & 8 3 above.
[146] See related analysis in paragraphs 8 2 1; 8 2 2; 8 2 3 & 8 3 above.
[147] See related analysis in paragraphs 8 2 1; 8 2 2; 8 2 3 & 8 3 above.
[148] This should, however, be carefully utilised and enforced to avoid other possible constitutional-related conflicts and/or double jeopardy.
[149] See related remarks in paragraphs 8 1; 8 2 1; 8 2 2; 8 2 3 & 8 3 above.

persons or companies that engage in market abuse activities in South Africa. It is also recommended that the Financial Markets Act should be reviewed to enact provisions that give private rights of action to the affected persons for them to claim their damages directly from the market abuse offenders. Moreover, the Financial Markets Act should be reviewed to introduce whistle-blower immunity provisions for the purposes of encouraging all the persons to voluntarily disclose any information regarding market abuse activities to the FSB or other enforcement authorities in South Africa.

It is also suggested that the FSB should seriously consider establishing its own surveillance systems to improve and increase the timeous detection of market abuse activity in both the regulated and unregulated financial markets in South Africa. It is further submitted that the relevant provisions of the Financial Markets Act which now empower the FSB to assist foreign regulators with investigations pertaining to any cross-border market abuse cases should be effectively and consistently utilised to enhance the combating of such cases in South Africa and elsewhere. Furthermore, the FSB should enter into more co-operation arrangements with international regulatory bodies that enforce commodities-based market abuse laws such as the CFTC, the LIFFOEAM and the TPSE to increase the combating of commodities-based market abuse practices in South Africa.

The Financial Markets Act should be reviewed to enact provisions that expressly impose a mandatory co-operation obligation on both the FSB and the JSE to improve the enforcement of the market abuse prohibition in South Africa. It is also recommended that the FSB and the JSE should consider embarking more on awareness and educative programmes such as developing an adequate anti-market abuse curriculum to be taught to students from high school level up to tertiary level; publishing some quarterly informative market abuse booklets on their respective websites; conducting market abuse workshops and public lectures to prevent market abuse practices and increase the general awareness among the market participants and/or other relevant stakeholders in the South African financial markets.

In a nutshell, it is hoped that the recommendations as enumerated above will be utilised in the future to consistently discourage market abuse activity in both the UK and South African financial markets.

References

Books

Avgouleas E *The Mechanics and Regulation of Market Abuse: A Legal and Economic Analysis* (Oxford University Press Oxford 2005)

Barnes P *Stock Market Efficiency, Insider Dealing and Market Abuse* (Gower Publishing Limited Surrey England 2009)

Beuthin RC and Luiz SM *Beuthin's Basic Company Law* 3rd ed (Butterworths Durban 2000)

Blair MQC & Walker GA (eds) *Financial Services Law* 1st ed (Oxford University Press Oxford United Kingdom 2006)

Lyon GJ & Du Plessis JJ *The Law of Insider Trading in Australia* (The Federation Press Sydney 2005)

Rider B, Alexander K, Linklater L & Bazley S *Market Abuse and Insider Dealing* 2nd ed (Tottel Publishing Haywards Heath 2009)

Russen J *Financial Services Authorisation, Supervision, and Enforcement: A Litigator's Guide* (Oxford University Press New York 2006)

Swan EJ *Market Abuse Regulation* 1st ed (Oxford University Press United States of America 2006)

Wood PR *Regulation of International Finance (The Law and Practice of International Finance Series Volume 7)* 1st ed (Sweet & Maxwell Limited London 2007)

Journal articles

Bhattacharya U & Daouk H "The World Price of Insider Trading" 2002 *Journal of Finance* 75-108

Black J & Nobles R "Personal Pensions Misselling: The Causes and Lessons of Regulatory Failure" 1998 *MLR* 789-820

Botha D "Control of Insider Trading in South Africa: A Comparative Analysis" 1991 *SA Merc LJ* 1-18

Botha D "Increased Maximum Fine for Insider Trading: A Realistic and Effective Deterrent?" 1990 *SALJ* 504-508

Cassim R "An Analysis of Market Manipulation under the Securities Services Act 36 of 2004 (Part 1)" 2008 *SA Merc LJ* 33-60

Cassim R "An Analysis of Market Manipulation under the Securities Services Act 36 of 2004 (Part 2)" 2008 *SA Merc LJ* 177-199

Cassim R "Some Aspects of Insider Trading – Has the Securities Services Act, 36 of 2004 Gone too Far?" 2007 *SA Merc LJ* 44-70

Chitimira H & Lawack VA "Overview of the Role-Players in the Investigation, Prevention and Enforcement of Market Abuse Provisions in South Africa" 2013 *Obiter* 200-217

Chitimira H "Overview of Selected Role-Players in the Detection and Enforcement of Market Abuse Cases and Appeals in South Africa" 2014 *Speculum Juris* 108-124

Henning JJ & Du Toit S "The Regulation of False Trading, Market Manipulation and Insider Trading" 2000 *Journal for Juridical Science* 155-165

Jooste R "A Critique of the Insider Trading Provisions of the 2004 Securities Services Act" 2006 *SALJ* 437-460

Kiernan P "The Regulatory Bodies Fraud: Its Enforcement in the Twenty-First Century" 2003 *The Company Lawyer* 293-299

Luiz SM "Market Abuse and the Enforcement Committee" 2011 *SA Merc LJ* 151-172

Luiz SM "Insider Trading Regulation – If at First You Don't Succeed…" 1999 *SA Merc LJ* 136-151

Osode PC "The New South African Insider Trading Act: Sound Law Reform or Legislative Overkill?" 2000 *Journal of African Law* 239-263

Rider BAK "Policing the City-Combating Fraud and Other Abuses in the Corporate Securities Industry" 1988 *Current Legal Problems* 47-68

Steinberg MI "Insider Trading Regulation–A Comparative Perspective" 2003 *The International Lawyer* 153-171

Van Deventer G "New Watchdog for Insider Trading" 1999 *FSB Bulletin* 2-3

Van Deventer G "Harnassing Administrative Law in Encouraging Compliance" 2009 *FSB Bulletin* 3-4

Case law

South Africa

Pather and Another v Financial Services Board and Others (57617/10) [2014] 3 All SA 208 (GP)

Zietsman v Director of Market Abuse 2016 1 SA 218 (GP)

Pretorius and Another v Natal South Sea Investment Trust 1965 3 SA 410 (W)

United Kingdom

Bell v Lever Brothers Ltd [1932] AC 161

Chase Manhattan Equities v Goodman [1991] BCLC 897

Chaston v SWP Group Ltd [2003] 4 Current Law 78

El Ajovu v Dollar Holdings [1993] 1 BCLC 760

Financial Services Authority v Fitt [2004] EWHC 1669 ch

Financial Services Authority v Martin and Anor [2005] 1 BCLC 495

Financial Services Authority v (1) Sean Fradley (t/a Top Bet Placement Services) (2) Gary Woodward [2004] EWHC 3008 (Ch)

In Re A-G's Reference (No 1 of 1998) [1998] BCLC 193

In Re A-G's Reference (No 1 of 1988) [1989] AC 971

Legal and General Assurance Society Limited v Financial Services Authority (2005) FSMT 016

Mohammed v FSA (2005) 013

Philip Jabre v Financial Services Authority (2006) 36 fin 06/2006

Piggott v FSA (2003) FSMT 004

R v Caldwell [1982] AC 341
R v Ghosh [1982] QB 1053
R v Kylsant [1932] 1 KB 442
R (on the application of Davies and others) v Financial Services Authority [2003] 4 All ER 1196
R v Rigby, Bailey & Rowley (2005) FSA/PN/106/2005 2005-10-07
Scott v Brown [1892] QB 724
Seager v Copydex (No 2) [1969] 1 WLR 809
SIB v Pantell SA (No 2) [1993] BCLC 146 (CA)

Legislation

South Africa

Companies Act 61 of 1973
Companies Act 71 of 2008
Consumer Protection Act 68 of 2008
Financial Institutions (Protection of Funds) Act 28 of 2001 as amended
Financial Markets Act 19 of 2012
Financial Markets Control Act 55 of 1989
Financial Services Board Act 97 of 1990
Securities Services Act 36 of 2004
Stock Exchanges Control Act 1 of 1985

United Kingdom

Companies Act 1980 (c 22)
Companies Act 1985 (c 6)
Companies Act 2006 (c 46)
Company Securities (Insider Dealing) Act 1985 (c 8)
Criminal Justice Act 1993 (c 36)
Criminal Justice Act 1987 (c 38)
Financial Services and Markets Act 2000 (c 8)
Financial Services Act 1986 (c 60)
Financial Services Act 2012 (c 21)
Fraud Act 2006 (c 35)
Larceny Act 1861 (24 and 25 Vict c 96)
Powers of Criminal Courts (Sentencing) Act 2000 (c 6)
Prevention of Fraud (Investments) Act 1939 (c 16)
Prevention of Fraud (Investments) Act 1958 (c 45)
Supreme Court Act 1981 (c 54)

European Union

Commission Directive 2003/124/EC of 22 December 2003 implementing Directive 2003/6/EC of 28 January 2003 on the definition and public disclosure of inside information and the definition of market manipulation [2003] OJ L339/70

Commission Directive 2003/125/EC of 22 December 2003 on the fair presentation of investment recommendations and the disclosure of conflicts of interest [2003] OJ L339/073

European Union Directive on Insider Dealing and Market Manipulation, the Directive of the European Parliament and Council of 28 January 2003 on insider dealing and market manipulation (market abuse) 2003/6/EC [2003] OJ L96/16

European Union Insider Dealing Directive, Council Directive 89/592/EEC of 13 November 1989 [1989] OJ 1989 L334/30

Market Abuse Regulation (EU) No. 596/2014 of the European Parliament and of the Council of 16 April 2014 on market abuse (market abuse regulation) and repealing Directive 2003/6 of the European Parliament and of the Council and Commission Directives 200/124/EC, 2003/125/EC and 2004/72/EC, [2014] OJ L 173/1

Commissions, committees, statutory instruments, media releases and reports

South Africa

Financial Services Board "FSB fines Michiel Jakobus Bronn R350 000 plus Costs for FMA Contravention" *FSB Press Release* 15 March 2017

Financial Services Board "Report by the Directorate of Market Abuse" *FSB Press Release* 31 March 2017

Financial Services Board "FSB fines Robert Fourie R2 million for FMA Contravention" *FSB Press Release* 08 March 2017

Financial Services Board "FSB Fines Johan Franck R1 000 000 for FMA Contraventions" *FSB Press Release* 26 October 2016

Financial Services Board "Report by the Directorate of Market Abuse" *FSB Press Release* 28 September 2016

Financial Services Board "Administrative Penalties Imposed for Market Manipulation" *FSB Press Release* 1 December 2015

Financial Services Board "High Court Upholds Zietzman Conviction" *FSB Press Release* 28 August 2015

Financial Services Board "Appeal Board Hearing Schedule: 20 June – 20 July 2017" *Appeal Board Publications* 20 July 2017

Financial Services Board *Annual Report* 2011

Financial Services Board *Annual Report* 2013

The King Task Group into Insider Trading Legislation *Minority Report on Insider Trading* 1997

The King Task Group into the Insider Trading Legislation *First Report* 15 May 1997

The King Task Group into the Insider Trading Legislation *Final Report* 21 October 1997

Van Wyk de Vries Commission of Inquiry into the *Companies Act* of 1973

United Kingdom

Enforcement (Settlement and Other Procedures) Instrument's *Decision Making Manual* October 2005

Financial Services and Markets Act 2000 (Market Abuse) Regulations 2005 SI 2005/381

Financial Services and Markets Act 2000 (Prescribed Markets and Qualifying Investments) Order 2001, SI 2001/1996 as amended by Regulation 10 of the Market Abuse Regulations 2005

Financial Services Authority Handbook (Code of Market Conduct) *FSA Release* 19 July 2001

Financial Services Authority's *Market Abuse Directive Disclosure Rules Instrument* 2005, 17 March 2005

Financial Services Authority's *Market Abuse Directive Instrument* 2005, 17 March 2005

Insider Dealing (Securities and Regulated Markets) Order 1994

Traded Securities (Disclosure) Regulation 1994

Thesis and dissertations

Chitimira H *A Comparative Analysis of the Enforcement of Market Abuse Provisions* (LLD-thesis Nelson Mandela Metropolitan University 2012)

Chitimira H *The Regulation of Insider Trading in South Africa: A Roadmap for an Effective, Competitive and Adequate Regulatory Statutory Framework* (LLM-dissertation University of Fort Hare 2008)

Newspaper reports

Chanetsa B "Insider Trading is Notoriously Hard to Prosecute" *Business Report* (2004-04-26)

Internet sources

Barron C "Greg Draws a Blank in Belfort Parallel" (2014) <http://www.timeslive.co.za/Feeds/2014/02/02/greg-draws-a-blank-in-belfort-parallel> (accessed 03-03-2014)

Blincoe R "Datatec Directors Pay Up on Insider Trading Charges" (2001) <http://www.theregister.co.uk/2001/05/23/datatec_directors_pay_up/> (accessed 03-03-2014)

Commodity Futures Trading Commission & the Financial Conduct Authority "Memorandum of Understanding Concerning Cooperation and the Exchange of Information in the Context of Supervising Covered Firms" (06-10-

2016) 1 2-10 <http://www.cftc.gov/idc/groups/public/@internationalaffairs/documents/file/cftc-fca-supervisorymou100616.pdf> (accessed 19-07-2017).

Commodity Futures Trading Commission & Financial Services Authority's *Memorandum of Understanding on Consultation, Cooperation and the Exchange of Information Related to Market Oversight* (2006) <http://www.fsa.gov.uk/pubs/mou/cftc.pd> (accessed 27-01-2014)

Directorate of Market Abuse "Past Investigations" (23-06-2015) <https://www.fsb.co.za/Departments/marketAbuse/Documents/DMA_Past%20investigations%20until%202015-06-23.pdf>(accessed 19-07-2017)

Enforcement Committee "Enforcement Actions" (19-07-2017) <https://www.fsb.co.za/enforcementCommittee/Pages/enforcementActions.aspx> (accessed 19-07-2017)

Financial Conduct Authority "Suspicious Transaction and Order Reports" (28-02-2017) <https://www.fca.org.uk/markets/market-abuse/suspicious-transaction-order-reports> (accessed 18-07-2017)

Financial Conduct Authority "FCA Introduces New Rules on Whistleblowing" (19-04-2016) <https://www.fca.org.uk/news/press-releases/fca-introduces-new-rules-whistleblowing> (accessed 21-07-2017)

Financial Conduct Authority "Executive Committees" (09-11-2016) <https://www.fca.org.uk/about/executive-committees> (accessed 20-07-2017)

Financial Conduct Authority "International Cooperation" (2015) <https://www.fca.org.uk/enforcement-annual-performance-account-2015-16/11-international-cooperation> (accessed 19-07-2017)

Financial Conduct Authority Handbook "Market Conduct" (2017) *Release 18* <https://www.handbook.fca.org.uk/handbook/MAR.pdf> (accessed 20-07-2017)

Financial Conduct Authority "Enforcement Information Guide" (2017) <https://www.fca.org.uk/publication/corporate/enforcement-information-guide.pdf> (accessed 20-07-2017)

Financial Conduct Authority Handbook "Disclosure Guidance and Transparency Rules (DTRs) Sourcebook" (2017) *Media Release 18* <https://www.handbook.fca.org.uk/handbook/DTR.pdf> (accessed 20-07-2017)

Financial Conduct Authority, Prudential Regulation Authority & Bank of England "Memorandum of Understanding between the Financial Conduct Authority and the Bank of England, including the Prudential Regulation Authority" (Date unknown) <https://www.fca.org.uk/publication/mou/mou-bank-pra.pdf> (accessed 19-07-2017)

Financial Conduct Authority "FCA Proposes Measures to Improve the Effectiveness of UK Primary Listed Debt Markets" (27-04-2016) *Press Release* <https://www.fca.org.uk/news/press-releases/fca-proposes-measures-improve-effectiveness-uk-primary-listed-debt-markets> (accessed 18-07-2017)

Financial Conduct Authority "FCA Fines Former Investment Banker for Sharing Confidential Information over WhatsApp" (30-03-2017) *Press Release*

<https://www.fca.org.uk/news/press-releases/fine-former-investment-banker-sharing-confidential-information-whatsapp> (accessed 18-07-2017)

Financial Conduct Authority & Ontario Securities Commission "International Memoranda of Understanding: Notice of Co-operation Agreement Concerning Innovative Fintech Businesses with UK Financial Conduct Authority" (02-03-2017) <http://www.osc.gov.on.ca/en/mou_international_index.htm> (accessed 19-07-2017)

Financial Conduct Authority "National Private Placement Regime Supervisory Co-operation Arrangements (MOUs)" (07-07-2016) <https://www.fca.org.uk/firms/nppr/supervisory-co-operation-arrangements-mous> (accessed 19-07-2017)

Financial Conduct Authority "Two Charged with Insider Dealing" (16-06-2017) *Press Release* <https://www.fca.org.uk/news/press-releases/two-charged-insider-dealing> (accessed 18-07-2017)

Financial Conduct Authority "FCA Bans and Fines Two Individuals for Market Abuse" (07-04-2017) *Press Release* <https://www.fca.org.uk/news/press-releases/fca-bans-and-fines-two-individuals-market-abuse> (accessed 18-07-2017)

Financial Conduct Authority "Tesco to Pay Redress for Market Abuse" (28-03-2017) *Press Release* <https://www.fca.org.uk/news/press-releases/tesco-pay-redress-market-abuse> (accessed 18-07-2017)

Financial Conduct Authority "FCA Fines Deutsche Bank £163 Million for Serious Anti-money Laundering Controls Failings" (31-01-2017) *Press Release* <https://www.fca.org.uk/news/press-releases/fca-fines-deutsche-bank-163-million-anti-money-laundering-controls-failure> (accessed 18-07-2017)

Financial Conduct Authority "Mark Lyttleton Sentenced to 12 Months Imprisonment for Insider Dealing" (21-12-2016) *Press Release* <https://www.fca.org.uk/news/press-releases/mark-lyttleton-sentenced-12-months-imprisonment-insider-dealing> (accessed 18-07-2017).

Financial Conduct Authority "Reporting to Treasury and Parliament" (05-07-2017) <https://www.fca.org.uk/about/reporting-treasury-parliament> (accessed 17-07-2017)

Financial Services Authority "FSA Signs Regulatory Cooperation Agreement with the CFTC" (20-11-2006) http://www.fsa.gov.uk/pages/Library/Communication/PR/2006/118.shtml > (accessed 27-01-2014)

Financial Services Board "Enforcement Committee Actions" *Media Release* (28-06-2011) <http://www.fsb.co.za/ftp://ftp.fsb.co.za/public/documents/AReport2011.pdf> (accessed 22-11-2013)

Financial Services Board "List of Current Investigations of the Directorate of Market Abuse" *Media Release* (28-06-2011) <http://www.fsb.co.za/ftp://ftp.fsb.co.za/public/documents/AReport2011.pdf> (accessed 22-11-2013)

Johannesburg Stock Exchange Limited "Insider Trading and other Market Abuses (Including the Effective Management of Price–Sensitive

Information)" in the *Insider Trading Booklet,* (2013) <http://www.jse.co.za/Libraries/JSE_Regulatory_Environment_Insider_Trading/InsiderTrading_Booklet.sflb.ashx> (accessed 03-03-2014)

Loubser R "Insider Trading and other Market Abuses (Including the Effective Management of Price–sensitive Information)" in the *Insider Trading Booklet* final draft, (2006) <http://www.jse.co.za/public/insider/JSEbooklet.pdf> (accessed 03-03-2014)

Myburgh A & Davis B "The Impact of South Africa's Insider Trading Regime: A Report for the Financial Services Board" (25-03-2004) <http://www.genesis-analytics.com/public/FSBReport.pdf> (accessed 09-02-2013)

Orrick, Herrington & Sutcliffe LLP "FCA and SEC Publish a MOU on Investment Fund Supervision" (29-07-2013) <http://www.lexology.com/library/detail.aspx?g=3b66b38a-535a-4c9a-afa1-da447bab9d95> (accessed 19-07-2017)

Van Deventer G "Anti-Market Abuse Legislation in South Africa" (10-06-2008) <http://www.fsb.co.za/public/marketabuse/FSBReport.pdf> (accessed 05-05-2013)

Chapter 9

Conclusion and Recommendations

9 1 Introduction

Market abuse practices are still prevalent in some securities and financial markets of both developed and developing countries. For instance, as highlighted in this book, insider trading, market manipulation and other related illicit trading activities have been occurring and affecting regulated financial markets in the United States of America (USA), the United Kingdom (UK) and South Africa as early as the 1920s to date.[1] Consequently, various anti-market abuse regulatory and enforcement approaches that are employed in the UK, the USA and South Africa are outlined in this book. Nonetheless, as discussed in this book, such anti-market abuse enforcement approaches are sometimes either inadequate or inconsistently enforced by the enforcement authorities in the UK, the USA and South Africa. This has, at times, given rise to rampant illicit trading practices in the UK, the USA and South African financial markets. In this regard, the recent surge of market abuse practices such as spoofing and layering in both the USA and the UK financial markets is a good example.[2] Moreover, the recent collusion and market manipulation involving the price-fixing, market allocation and rigging in the trading of foreign currency pairs of the South African rand as early as year 2007 by lenders and several local and international banks is another case in point.[3] Market abuse-related activities also culminated into numerous regulatory and enforcement challenges on the part of enforcement authorities during the 2007 to 2009 global financial crisis in the USA, the UK, South Africa and several countries in other jurisdictions.[4] In light of this, possible recommendations that could improve the enforcement of the market abuse prohibition in the USA, the UK and South Africa are provided.

---

[1] See the regulatory and historical aspects of the anti-market abuse laws in Chapters Two to Eight of this book.

[2] Aitken "Market Abuse: Spoofing, Layering & the Complexity of Proving Intent" (12-04-2016) https://www.b-next.com/general/market-abuse-spoofing-layering-the-complexity-of-proving-intent/ (accessed 13-07-2017); *7722656 Canada Inc. (t/a Swift Trade Inc) v FSA* [2013] All ER (D) 266, where both "layering" and "spoofing" activities were discussed and the offenders were accordingly found guilty.

[3] Anonymous "How Banks Allegedly Colluded on Currency Trades" (15-02-2017) <http://www.fin24.com/Companies/Financial-Services/why-the-competition-commission-wants-17-banks-prosecuted-20170215> (accessed 21-03-2017).

[4] See Chapters One to Eight of this book, for related discussion.

9 2 General Observations

It was noted that market abuse practices are still occurring in developed countries such as the USA and the UK as well as the developing countries such as South Africa. Furthermore, it was noted that, unlike the position in other jurisdictions like the USA,[5] and the UK,[6] South Africa does not seem to have an express statutory prohibition on Internet-based market abuse practices.[7] Nevertheless, the book has pointed out that both the USA and the UK do not expressly prohibit social media-related market abuse practices.

The book also revealed that both the USA[8] and the South African[9] market abuse regimes have similar regulatory and enforcement goals and missions. Despite this, they adopt and implement very different approaches to achieve their enforcement goals or targets.[10] For instance, it was observed that the USA, unlike South Africa, employs a multi-functional regulatory approach which allows more positive competition among the regulatory bodies in order to give rise to a much better and consistent enforcement of the market abuse prohibition in its financial markets.[11] It was also noted that although the South African market abuse legislation[12] was relatively influenced by the corresponding legislation in the USA,[13] it appears to lack a more practical enforcement approach to combat market manipulation activities in South Africa.[14]

Moreover, the book revealed that, in contrast to South Africa, the UK employs the so-called single regulator model to combat market abuse activities in all its relevant financial markets.[15] It was additionally noted that although South Africa has adopted some of the enforcement methods that are employed in the UK,[16] more may still need to be done to prevent and curb market abuse practices in the South African financial markets.[17]

---

[5] See related analysis in Chapters Two to Five of this book.

[6] See related analysis in Chapters Six to Eight of this book.

[7] Chitimira *A Comparative Analysis of the Enforcement of Market Abuse Provisions* (Unpublished LLD thesis, Nelson Mandela Metropolitan University) 2012, 27-566.

[8] See Chapters Two to Five of this book.

[9] See discussions in Chapters One to Nine of this book.

[10] See discussions in in Chapters One to Nine of this book; Chitimira *Enforcement of Market Abuse Provisions* 27-187; 421-496.

[11] See related analysis in Chapter Four of this book.

[12] This is mainly true especially in relation to the insider trading prohibition.

[13] See related analysis in Chapters Two to Five of this book.

[14] See the relevant discussions in Chapters One to Eight of this book.

[15] See related remarks in Chapters Six to Eight of this book; Chitimira *Enforcement of Market Abuse Provisions* 305-353; 497-566.

[16] See related remarks in Chapters Six to Eight of this book; Chitimira *Enforcement of Market Abuse Provisions* 305-353; 497-566; also see Armour "Enforcement Strategies in UK Corporate Governance:

This book has exposed that although the USA, the UK and South Africa have enacted anti-market abuse laws in a bid to combat market abuse practices in their respective financial markets; such laws are sometimes inadequate and/or poorly enforced. Thus, the book has usefully pointed out that the enforcement authorities in the USA, the UK and South Africa have, from time to time, struggled to consistently and effectively enforce their anti-market abuse laws. Accordingly, the book has muckraked illicit trading activities such as market abuse practices which are still occurring in the USA, the UK and South African many financial markets. In light of these observations, the book has underscored the need for the policy makers in the USA, the UK and South Africa to amend and/or enact adequate anti-market abuse laws and ensure that such laws are robustly and consistently enforced to effectively combat market abuse practices in their respective financial markets.

9 3 Recommendations

Various recommendations that could improve the enforcement of the market abuse prohibition in South Africa are outlined in this chapter. Moreover and where appropriate, recommendations that could enhance the enforcement of the anti-market abuse laws in the USA and the UK are outlined below. These recommendations are broadly divided into four categories, namely, those that deal with (a) the adoption of adequate and/or appropriate penalties for market abuse, (b) the adoption of adequate market abuse preventative measures, (c) mutual co-operation between the relevant stakeholders and, (d) the adoption of adequate market abuse awareness measures as enumerated below.[18]

9 3 1 Adoption of Adequate and/or Appropriate Penalties for Market Abuse

It is recommended that:

The Financial Markets Act[19] should be amended in line with the position in the UK and the USA to enact specific provisions for separate and distinct maximum penalties (civil, criminal or administrative) that can be imposed upon any individual or juristic person that commits or attempts to commit or that incites, aids and abets or attempts to incite, aid and/or abet another person to commit insider trading or market manipulation offences in South

---

A Roadmap and Empirical Assessment" in Armour and Payne (eds) *Rationality in Company Law Essays in Honour of DD Prentice* (2009) 71-119.

[17] See discussions in Chitimira *Enforcement of Market Abuse Provisions* 27-187; 421-496.

[18] It is submitted, depending on the merits of each case, that the regulatory authorities should co-operatively select or flexibility consider employing the most suitable enforcement measures that are listed in any of the aforesaid categories, to effectively combat market abuse, especially, in South Africa.

[19] 19 of 2012 (Financial Markets Act), see ss 78; 80; 81 & 82.

Africa, with much higher maximum criminal penalties being imposed on such juristic person. It is also submitted that the anti-market abuse penalties that are employed by the different enforcement authorities such as the Prudential Regulation Authority (PRA) and the Financial Conduct Authority (FCA) in the UK as well as the State and federal authorities in the USA, must be carefully enforced to avoid double jeopardy on the part of the offenders. In this regard, it is hoped that the Prudential Authority (PA) and the Financial Sector Conduct Authority (FSCA) which were recently established by the Financial Sector Regulation Act[20] will enhance the regulation and enforcement of anti-market abuse penalties in South Africa when this Act comes into force;[21]

Additionally, the FSB should be expressly and statutorily authorised in line with the position in the UK and the USA to impose its own additional separate and distinct unlimited monetary and other appropriate (civil, criminal or administrative) penalties on individuals and juristic persons that engage in market abuse activities in South Africa; and/or to use the seizure and forfeiture method to recover or confiscate assets and other illegal benefits from the market abuse offenders. Likewise, the PRA and the FCA of the UK and the United States Securities and Exchange Commission (SEC) and the Commodity Futures Trading Commission (CFTC) of the USA should carefully enforce their unlimited anti-market abuse penalties to avoid the possible effects of over-criminalization;

Furthermore, apart from the anti-market abuse penalties that are currently contained in the Financial Institutions (Protection of Funds) Act,[22] the Financial Markets Act should be reviewed to expressly provide civil penalties for market manipulation just like it does for insider trading offences for consistency and desist from rigidly relying on the policy goal of deterrence alone. Moreover, the provisions of the Financial Markets Act which now empowers the FSB to claim from the insider trading offenders, legal costs and civil compensatory penalties of up to three times the profit gained or loss avoided plus interest should be carefully amended for them to be equally and consistently applicable to market manipulation offences in South Africa. The policymakers in the USA, the UK and South Africa should also consider enacting new provisions for social media-related anti-market abuse penalties in their respective jurisdictions. Moreover, the relevant authorities in the UK and the USA should carefully adopt adequate anti-market abuse enforcement approaches to combat the current regulatory challenges caused by disruptive

[20] 9 of 2017 (Financial Sector Regulation Act).

[21] See Chapters 3 and 4 of the the Financial Sector Regulation Act. The FSCA is set to replace the Financial Services Board (FSB) once the Financial Sector Regulation Act comes into force.

[22] 28 of 2001 as amended (Protection of Funds Act), see ss 6A to 6I.

technology such as automated financial services, computerised trading, algorithms and artificial intelligence, especially, in the USA financial markets;

The relevant courts in South Africa should be expressly and statutorily empowered to impose other additional penalties (apart from those stipulated in the Financial Markets Act) upon the market offenders without the fear of violating the *autrefois* acquit or *autrefois* convict doctrine. In relation to this, the enforcement authorities in the UK and the USA should carefully utilise their additional anti-market abuse penalties to avoid violating the *autrefois* acquit or *autrefois* convict doctrine;

Lastly, the relevant provisions of the Financial Markets Act which now empowers the FSB to publish by notice on its official website or by means of other appropriate public media, any outcome, status or details of market abuse investigations (public censure or name and shame approach) if such publication is in the public interest should consistently enforced to discourage market abuse practices in the South African financial markets.

9 3 2 Adoption of Adequate Market Abuse Preventative Measures

It is recommended that:

The Financial Markets Act should be amended in line with the USA and UK position to provide for specific market abuse whistle-blower immunity provisions and bounty rewards for the purposes of encouraging all the persons to report market abuse activities to the FSB or other relevant enforcement authorities in South Africa. Accordingly, the anti-market abuse enforcement authorities in the UK and the USA should guide against the abuse of the whistle-blower immunity provisions by some unscrupulous persons who report frivolous instances of market abuse to gain monetary rewards from both the FCA and the SEC respectively;

The relevant courts and/or the FSB should be statutorily empowered to make a declaration of contravention of the market abuse provisions in South Africa and/or to seek a court order for such declaration in South Africa whenever a contravention occurs, for deterrence purposes;

Moreover, the Financial Markets Act should be reviewed to establish a specific regulatory body that prohibits and investigates Internet and social media-related market abuse practices in South Africa, and to specifically discourage the dissemination or publication of rumours, false, deceptive or misleading information through the Internet and/or through the electronic media (disclosure-based manipulation with regard Internet related to publications) by insiders or any person who knows or ought to have known that such information is false, deceptive or misleading. It is also submitted that the policymakers in the USA and the UK should expressly extend their anti-market abuse laws to social media-related market abuse activities;

The Financial Markets Act should be reviewed to explicitly provide a statutory private right of action for the issuers of listed securities and/or other aggrieved or prejudiced persons to claim their market abuse damages directly from the offenders. Moreover, the anti-market abuse laws in South Africa, the USA and the UK should be reviewed to enact provisions that statutorily define the concept of market abuse. This definition should provide adequate and comprehensive statutory definitions of the concepts of insider trading and market manipulation, involving all the elements of these offences (how they are committed) as well as the various types of market manipulation practices to enhance the combating of such practices in South Africa, the USA and the UK;

Furthermore, the Financial Markets Act should be reviewed to enact provisions that expressly prohibit a person who inadvertently aided or abetted another person to make or publish a false, misleading or deceptive statement, promise or forecast that relates to any security in South Africa. The Financial Markets Act should be further amended to enact provisions that expressly prohibit commodity-based market manipulation, and to introduce a specific anti-commodities-based market abuse enforcement commission or a regulatory body like the CFTC, to effectively and exclusively deal with the commodities-based market manipulation violations in South Africa;

The Protection of Funds Act and the Financial Markets Act should be reviewed to enact provisions that expressly empower the Enforcement Committee (EC) to enact or make its own independent market abuse rules, decisions, regulations and other appropriate disciplinary or administrative actions on matters involving market abuse practices to enhance the combating of such practices in South Africa;

Notwithstanding the potential negative effects of bureaucracy, balkanisation, conflict of interests and confusion that may be associated with many regulatory bodies, it is submitted that more self-regulatory organisations, apart from the FSB, should be statutorily empowered to enforce the market abuse prohibition and/or to impose their own penalties or take any other appropriate action against any persons who indulge in market abuse activities in South Africa;

It is also submitted, as is the position in Delaware (where there is a system in place for the periodic revision of the Delaware Codes), that the South African policymakers should seriously consider appointing a National Market Abuse Commission to examine and review, from time to time, all the matters and laws pertaining to market abuse in South Africa; or the Directorate of Market

Abuse (DMA) and/or a new self-regulatory organisation should be statutorily established and authorised to independently engage in public consultation from time to time, to review or make proposals to the legislature and/or other relevant authorities in relation to any matter dealing with the securities law reform and the general regulation or enforcement of the market abuse prohibition in South Africa;

In light of the position in the USA, the South African policymakers should consider introducing provincial market abuse statutes to: (a) create regulatory competition among the provinces to attract investors by effectively combating market abuse activities, and (b) promote dual or concurrent regulation and enforcement of the market abuse ban both at a provincial and national level. However, this should be managed well to avoid creating potential problems such as balkanisation and/or violating the *autrefois* acquit or *autrefois* convict doctrine;

Over and above, the Financial Markets Act should be reviewed in line with the position in the UK to enact provisions that mandate companies and all the relevant persons to have market abuse codes of conduct and to appoint market abuse compliance officers;

In light of the 2007 to 2009 global and economic crisis, the Financial Markets Act should be amended to enact provisions which broadly extend the scope of the market abuse ban to cover securities or financial instruments traded on regulated markets, over the counter markets, organised trading facilities (OTFs) or multilateral trading facilities (MTFs) in South Africa or elsewhere, to enable the FSB and other relevant regulatory authorities to curb the market abuse challenges posed by high frequency trading and other related illicit activities associated with the new trading platforms. In the same vein, the UK should carefully decide whether or not to continue abiding by the European Union (EU) anti-market abuse laws. It will also be more beneficial for the UK to promote legal certainty by continuing to abide by the new EU anti-market abuse laws that are now applicable to a wide range of OTFs and MTFs;

The relevant anti-market abuse laws in South Africa, the UK and the USA should be amended in line with the EU Market Abuse Regulation and the Wholesale Energy Market Integrity and Transparency Regulation to enact a specific definition of inside information for commodity derivatives, spot commodity derivatives and related spot commodity contracts to curb insider trading and cross-market manipulation in the UK, the USA and the South African physical (non-financial markets) commodities markets;

It is submitted that the Financial Markets Act should be reviewed to enact adequate provisions on emission allowances in order to discourage cross-border market abuse activities in the spot secondary markets or related emission allowances markets in South Africa and elsewhere;

The Financial Markets Act should be amended to enact specific, adequate and separate provisions that distinguish and prohibit both actual and attempted insider trading and market manipulation practices to enable the prosecuting authorities and/or the FSB to increase the number of successful prosecutions and settlements of cases involving such practices in South Africa;

Moreover, the Financial Markets Act should be amended to enact provisions that oblige issuers and other relevant persons to draw and update their insiders' lists to enhance the detection and prevention of market abuse practices in South Africa. In addition, the South African legislature should consider introducing mandatory, structured (periodic) and continuous statutory disclosure requirements coupled with civil penalties for non-compliance to enable the Johannesburg Stock Exchange Limited (JSE) and/or the FSB to oblige all the issuers or listed entities and directors (insiders) of such entities to promptly, consistently and publicly disclose the relevant non-public price-sensitive inside information (including their lending or pledging of securities or financial instruments), transactions executed on behalf of the issuers and/or their interests in the securities of those entities to prevent market abuse practices in the regulated markets, over the counter markets, small and medium-sized growth markets and/or other related trading platforms in South Africa;

The Financial Markets Act should be reviewed to enact provisions that expressly discourage any market abuse activity or illicit dealing in securities on unregulated over the counter markets through agents or professional intermediaries and face-to-face transactions between non-professional intermediaries in South Africa; and/or provisions that expressly prohibit natural persons (agents or corporate insiders) who participate in the execution of transactions on behalf of a primary insider who is a legal or juristic person from committing market abuse practices and other related organised crime activities in the South African financial markets;

Additionally, the FSB should have its own surveillance systems or other mechanisms in place to detect and prevent market abuse activity in the South African securities and financial markets. Moreover, that the FSB should be statutorily empowered to intercept telephonic data from the suspected market abuse offenders, to take over the real-time surveillance of the South African securities and financial markets from the JSE and to develop its own adequate technological mechanisms for market abuse cross-market surveillance in order to effectively and timeously detect, investigate and prevent market abuse practices in South Africa by eradicating the delays that might be associated with the FSB's investigations into the JSE's market abuse referrals;

The Financial Markets Act should be amended to enact provisions that clearly enumerate sufficient guidelines or conditions under which the extra-territorial application of the market abuse ban will be employed and/or to introduce a more adequate, feasible and practically enforceable extra-territorial approach which enforces the market abuse prohibition only where a violation of the South African securities listed on a foreign market has a territorial (nexus) link to South Africa, in order to prevent cross-border market abuse activities consistently in South Africa and elsewhere;

Likewise, the JSE should consider establishing its own Markets Disciplinary Tribunal which specifically deals with any illicit violations of its Listing Requirements and/or market abuse cases in South Africa;

The Financial Markets Act should be amended to expressly provide some rebuttable presumptions or reduce the evidentiary burden of proof in criminal cases in order to assist the Director of Public Prosecutions (DPP) and/or the relevant courts in the prosecution of market abuse cases in South Africa. In relation to this, insider trading and market manipulation should be statutorily treated as indictable offences in South Africa;

In addition, the Financial Markets Act should be amended to enact specific and adequate statutory provisions that deal with Chinese walls to reduce and discourage market abuse practices in South Africa; and/or other adequate and additional defences for market manipulation so as not to discourage legitimate securities trading by issuers or other potential investors;

The Financial Markets Act should be reviewed to provide adequate special or complementary definitions of inside information in relation to derivatives on commodities and/or to the persons (professional intermediaries) involved in the execution of orders relating to listed securities or other related derivative financial instruments. It is submitted that this could prevent the commission of front-running or other market abuse activities pertaining to commodities derivatives by some unscrupulous financial brokers and/or other related market participants in South Africa. Likewise, the anti-market abuse laws in the USA and the UK should continue to be consistently enforced to combat illicit market abuse practices such as layering and spoofing;

The definition of an insider which is provided in the Financial Markets Act should be amended in order to expressly acknowledge that a company (legal person) which repurchases its own shares would be an insider to itself. It is submitted that this will protect shareholders of a company against such company taking advantage of the non-public price-sensitive information to repurchase their shares at a lower price than what the company would have paid if the information had been made public;

Lastly, the FSB should consider employing infringement notices and enforceable undertakings to discourage market abuse activities in South Africa.

9 3 3 Mutual Co-operation between the Relevant Stakeholders

It is recommended that:

The FSB should consider concluding a binding co-operation and information-sharing Memorandum of Understanding (MOU) or other specific binding co-operation agreements with more local self-regulatory organisations such as the JSE and the Takeover Regulation Panel (TRP) to increase co-operation in relation to the detection and combating of market abuse practices in the South African financial markets. Moreover; the Financial Markets Act should be reviewed to enact provisions that expressly impose a mandatory co-operation obligation on both the FSB and the JSE to improve the enforcement of the market abuse prohibition in South Africa. The FCA and the SEC should also continue co-operating with other enforcement authorities in their respective jurisdictions and elsewhere to combat cross-border market abuse practices. In relation to this, it is submitted that the FCA and other relevant authorities in the UK should continue to co-operate and abide by the EU market abuse laws despite its decision to withdraw from the EU after the 2016 British EU (Brexit) referendum;

It is further submitted that the Financial Markets Act should be reviewed to enact a specific provision that obliges the JSE to give reasonable assistance to the FSB regarding the combating of market abuse whenever it is necessary by, *inter alia*, searching the premises of the accused persons who are suspected of engaging in market abuse practices and by summoning any such persons to furnish it with other relevant information relating to ongoing market abuse investigations;

The provisions of the Financial Markets which empowers the FSB to assist foreign regulators with investigations pertaining to any cross-border market abuse cases should be carefully enforced to enhance the combating of such cases in South Africa and elsewhere;

Additionally, the FSB should be statutorily mandated to support the DPP and/or the relevant courts with the necessary information regarding ongoing market abuse cases in South Africa by assigning from time to time certain persons with the relevant expertise to assist the DPP and relevant courts in their prosecution of such cases in South Africa. Moreover, the FSB and the DPP should consider concluding a binding co-operation and information-sharing MOU to enhance their co-operation and enforcement of the market abuse prohibition in South Africa;

The FSB should be statutorily authorised in line with the UK position to appoint other relevant stakeholders and/or additional skilled persons, apart from its own employees, to provide it with reports or relevant information relating to any suspected market abuse violations;

In accordance with the USA position, the South African legislature should consider enacting specific provisions which empower the FSB and the JSE to jointly form, fund, and operate a Joint Market Abuse Advisory Committee that would be tasked with considering and developing solutions to emerging and ongoing market abuse issues of common interest involving commodity and commodity derivatives as well as futures and/or securities traded in both the regulated and over the counter markets in South Africa. In other words, the aforesaid Joint Market Abuse Advisory Committee should identify emerging regulatory risks, assess and quantify their implications for investors and other market participants, and recommend possible solutions to the FSB and the JSE;

The South African legislature should consider enacting specific provisions which empower the FSB, the TRP, the JSE and other relevant stakeholders to create a Joint Anti-Market Abuse Enforcement Task Force to harness synergies from shared market surveillance data; improve market oversight; enhance enforcement; and to reduce duplicative regulatory burdens and/or balkanisation. The Joint Anti-Market Abuse Enforcement Task Force should prepare and offer market abuse training programmes for the employees of all the relevant enforcement authorities, develop practical market abuse investigation and enforcement measures and timeously coordinate the sharing of relevant market abuse information. Moreover, the Joint Anti-Market Abuse Enforcement Task Force should oversee the general execution of the day-to-day duties by the employees of all the relevant enforcement agencies to enhance the enforcement of the market abuse ban in South Africa;

Regulatory agencies such as the FSB and the JSE should establish a Joint Market Abuse Cross-Agency Training Programme for their employees to increase the enforcement of the market abuse provisions in South Africa. This could be achieved by developing a training programme to increase the consistent and/or regular sharing of relevant information and rotating of employees between the FSB and the JSE. This programme could, each year, give the employees of both the FSB and the JSE the opportunity to work at the other agency for a temporary specified period of time to enhance greater collaboration and coordination between these two agencies;

Likewise, the FSB and the JSE should consider developing a Joint Market Abuse Information Technology Task Force to link their relevant information pertaining to on-going market abuse investigations if they consider such information to be jointly useful and/or in the public interest in South Africa. This could promote transparency and facilitate the use and understanding of such information by providing a comprehensive, consolidated database on persons and entities investigated by both the FSB and the JSE to combat market abuse activities in the South African regulated financial markets;

The South African Police Services and/or the Financial Services Board should be statutorily empowered to co-operatively work together and jointly have measures in place to intercept or access telephone and existing data traffic records from companies, issuers of securities and any other suspected offenders in matters involving market abuse investigations in South Africa. Moreover, the FSB and the South African Police Services should also consider concluding a binding MOU relating to market abuse investigations in order to track down and meritoriously discourage the commission of market abuse offences in South Africa and elsewhere (cross-border market abuse activities);

Lastly, like the FCA and the SEC position, the FSB should enter into more co-operation arrangements with other renowned international regulators such as the Ontario Securities Commission and the Australian Securities and Investments Commission and similar bodies that enforce commodities-based market abuse laws such as the CFTC, the London International Financial Futures and Options Exchange Administration and Management and the Trade Point Stock Exchange to increase the combating of commodities-based market abuse practices and cross-border market abuse activities in South Africa and elsewhere.

9 3 4 Adoption of Adequate Market Abuse Awareness Measures

It is recommended that:

The South African legislature should consider statutorily establishing more specialised courts and mediation, arbitration and settlement tribunals that are manned with judges and other persons with the relevant expertise in all the provinces of South Africa to increase awareness, improve the negotiation, settlement and prosecution of market abuse cases and/or the general combating of market abuse practices in the South African financial markets. Moreover, the FCA and the SEC should continue to employ additional people with the relevant expertise to improve the investigation and prosecution of market abuse cases in the UK and the USA respectively;

Furthermore, the FSB should be statutorily required to provide its own adequate market abuse policy guidelines or Code of Market Abuse Conduct containing sufficient and adequate guidelines on factors that should be considered from time to time in determining whether a trading practice and/or behaviour will give rise to or amount to market abuse practices to increase awareness and the combating of such practices in South Africa;

Lastly, the legislature, the JSE, the FSB and/or other enforcement agencies should co-operatively engage more on preventative, educative and awareness programmes such as developing an adequate anti-market abuse curriculum to be taught to students from high school level up to tertiary level; publishing some quarterly informative market abuse booklets on their respective websites; and conducting anti-market abuse workshops and public lectures to increase the general awareness among the market participants and/or other relevant stakeholders in the South African financial markets. Likewise, the FCA, the CFTC, the SEC and other enforcement agencies in the UK and the USA should provide more anti-market abuse preventative, educative and awareness programmes to curb market abuse in their respective financial markets.

9 4 Concluding Remarks

The book has underscored that market abuse is still an enigma in several countries, including the USA, the UK and South Africa. Thus, notwithstanding the fact that various anti-market abuse laws and enforcement approaches are employed in the USA, the UK and South Africa, such laws and approaches have been sometimes inadequately and inconsistently enforced by the relevant authorities to curb market abuse practices in the aforesaid countries to date. The book has also usefully exposed that the Financial Markets Act is still flawed in some respects, especially, regarding the provision of adequate market abuse penalties and the employment of sufficient anti-market abuse enforcement approaches to combat market abuse practices in South Africa. Likewise, the book has successfully uncovered the uncertainties surrounding the future regulation and enforcement of the anti-market abuse laws in the UK after the Brexit and/or its withdrawal from the EU. Moreover, it was noted that the relevant enforcement authorities in the UK and the USA have sometimes grappled with the combating spoofing, layering and other related illicit practices in their respective financial markets. Given this background, it is hoped that these and other flaws as pointed out in this book will be carefully addressed by the relevant authorities in the USA, the UK and South Africa. Accordingly, it is submitted that various recommendations that were enumerated in this book will be carefully utilised by the enforcement authorities to curb market abuse practices in the USA, the UK and South Africa. Lastly, this book has buttressed the need for the relevant enforcement authorities in the USA, the UK and South Africa to flexibly rely on a variety of enforcement measures for the purposes of effectively combating market abuse practices on a case-to-case basis in their respective jurisdictions.

References

Books

Avgouleas E *The Mechanics and Regulation of Market Abuse: A Legal and Economic Analysis* (Oxford University Press Oxford 2005)

Barnes P *Stock Market Efficiency, Insider Dealing and Market Abuse* (Gower Publishing Limited Surrey England 2009)

Beuthin RC and Luiz SM *Beuthin's Basic Company Law* 3rd ed (Butterworths Durban 2000)

Blair MQC & Walker GA (eds) *Financial Services Law* 1st ed (Oxford University Press Oxford United Kingdom 2006)

Lyon GJ & Du Plessis JJ *The Law of Insider Trading in Australia* (The Federation Press Sydney 2005)

Rider B, Alexander K, Linklater L & Bazley S *Market Abuse and Insider Dealing* 2nd ed (Tottel Publishing Haywards Heath 2009)

Russen J *Financial Services Authorisation, Supervision, and Enforcement: A Litigator's Guide* (Oxford University Press New York 2006)

Swan EJ *Market Abuse Regulation* 1st ed (Oxford University Press United States of America 2006)

Wood PR *Regulation of International Finance (The Law and Practice of International Finance Series Volume 7)* 1st ed (Sweet & Maxwell Limited London 2007)

Journal articles

Bhattacharya U & Daouk H "The World Price of Insider Trading" 2002 *Journal of Finance* 75-108

Black J & Nobles R "Personal Pensions Misselling: The Causes and Lessons of Regulatory Failure" 1998 *MLR* 789-820

Botha D "Control of Insider Trading in South Africa: A Comparative Analysis" 1991 *SA Merc LJ* 1-18

Botha D "Increased Maximum Fine for Insider Trading: A Realistic and Effective Deterrent?" 1990 *SALJ* 504-508

Cassim R "An Analysis of Market Manipulation under the Securities Services Act 36 of 2004 (Part 1)" 2008 *SA Merc LJ* 33-60

Cassim R "An Analysis of Market Manipulation under the Securities Services Act 36 of 2004 (Part 2)" 2008 *SA Merc LJ* 177-199

Cassim R "Some Aspects of Insider Trading – Has the Securities Services Act, 36 of 2004 Gone too Far?" 2007 *SA Merc LJ* 44-70

Chitimira H & Lawack VA "Overview of the Role-Players in the Investigation, Prevention and Enforcement of Market Abuse Provisions in South Africa" 2013 *Obiter* 200-217

Chitimira H "Overview of Selected Role-Players in the Detection and Enforcement of Market Abuse Cases and Appeals in South Africa" 2014 *Speculum Juris* 108-124

Henning JJ & Du Toit S "The Regulation of False Trading, Market Manipulation and Insider Trading" 2000 *Journal for Juridical Science* 155-165

Jooste R "A Critique of the Insider Trading Provisions of the 2004 Securities Services Act" 2006 *SALJ* 437-460

Kiernan P "The Regulatory Bodies Fraud: Its Enforcement in the Twenty-First Century" 2003 *The Company Lawyer* 293-299

Luiz SM "Market Abuse and the Enforcement Committee" 2011 *SA Merc LJ* 151-172

Luiz SM "Insider Trading Regulation – If at First You Don't Succeed…" 1999 *SA Merc LJ* 136-151

Osode PC "The New South African Insider Trading Act: Sound Law Reform or Legislative Overkill?" 2000 *Journal of African Law* 239-263

Rider BAK "Policing the City-Combating Fraud and Other Abuses in the Corporate Securities Industry" 1988 *Current Legal Problems* 47-68

Steinberg MI "Insider Trading Regulation–A Comparative Perspective" 2003 *The International Lawyer* 153-171

Van Deventer G "New Watchdog for Insider Trading" 1999 *FSB Bulletin* 2-3

Van Deventer G "Harnassing Administrative Law in Encouraging Compliance" 2009 *FSB Bulletin* 3-4

Case law

South Africa

Pretorius and Another v Natal South Sea Investment Trust 1965 3 SA 410 (W)

United Kingdom

Bell v Lever Brothers Ltd [1932] AC 161

Chase Manhattan Equities v Goodman [1991] BCLC 897

Chaston v SWP Group Ltd [2003] 4 Current Law 78

El Ajovu v Dollar Holdings [1993] 1 BCLC 760

Financial Services Authority v Fitt [2004] EWHC 1669 ch

Financial Services Authority v Martin and Anor [2005] 1 BCLC 495

Financial Services Authority v (1) Sean Fradley (t/a Top Bet Placement Services) (2) Gary Woodward [2004] EWHC 3008 (Ch)

In Re A-G's Reference (No 1 of 1998) [1998] BCLC 193

In Re A-G's Reference (No 1 of 1988) [1989] AC 971

Legal and General Assurance Society Limited v Financial Services Authority (2005) FSMT 016

Mohammed v FSA (2005) 013

Philip Jabre v Financial Services Authority (2006) 36 fin 06/2006

Piggott v FSA (2003) FSMT 004

R v Caldwell [1982] AC 341

R v Ghosh [1982] QB 1053

R v Kylsant [1932] 1 KB 442

R (on the application of Davies and others) v Financial Services Authority [2003] 4 All ER 1196
R v Rigby, Bailey & Rowley (2005) FSA/PN/106/2005 2005-10-07
Scott v Brown [1892] QB 724
Seager v Copydex (No 2) [1969] 1 WLR 809
SIB v Pantell SA (No 2) [1993] BCLC 146 (CA)

Legislation

South Africa

Companies Act 61 of 1973
Companies Act 71 of 2008
Consumer Protection Act 68 of 2008
Financial Institutions (Protection of Funds) Act 28 of 2001 as amended
Financial Markets Act 19 of 2012
Financial Markets Control Act 55 of 1989
Financial Sector Regulation Act 9 of 2017
Securities Services Act 36 of 2004
Stock Exchanges Control Act 1 of 1985

United Kingdom

Companies Act 1980 (c 22)
Companies Act 1985 (c 6)
Companies Act 2006 (c 46)
Company Securities (Insider Dealing) Act 1985 (c 8)
Criminal Justice Act 1993 (c 36)
Criminal Justice Act 1987 (c 38)
Financial Services and Markets Act 2000 (c 8)
Financial Services Act 1986 (c 60)
Fraud Act 2006 (c 35)
Larceny Act 1861 (24 and 25 Vict c 96)
Powers of Criminal Courts (Sentencing) Act 2000 (c 6)
Prevention of Fraud (Investments) Act 1939 (c 16)
Prevention of Fraud (Investments) Act 1958 (c 45)
Supreme Court Act 1981 (c 54)

European Union

Commission Directive 2003/124/EC of 22 December 2003 implementing Directive 2003/6/EC of 28 January 2003 on the definition and public disclosure of inside information and the definition of market manipulation [2003] OJ L339/70

Commission Directive 2003/125/EC of 22 December 2003 on the fair presentation of investment recommendations and the disclosure of conflicts of interest [2003] OJ L339/073

European Union Directive on Insider Dealing and Market Manipulation, the Directive of the European Parliament and Council of 28 January 2003 on insider dealing and market manipulation (market abuse) 2003/6/EC [2003] OJ L96/16

European Union Insider Dealing Directive, Council Directive 89/592/EEC of 13 November 1989 [1989] OJ 1989 L334/30

Commissions, committees, statutory instruments and reports

South Africa

Financial Services Board *Annual Report* 2011

Financial Services Board *Annual Report* 2013

The King Task Group into Insider Trading Legislation *Minority Report on Insider Trading* 1997

The King Task Group into the Insider Trading Legislation *First Report* 15 May 1997

The King Task Group into the Insider Trading Legislation *Final Report* 21 October 1997

Van Wyk de Vries Commission of Inquiry into the *Companies Act* of 1973

United Kingdom

Enforcement (Settlement and Other Procedures) Instrument's *Decision Making Manual* October 2005

Financial Services and Markets Act 2000 (Market Abuse) Regulations 2005 SI 2005/381

Financial Services and Markets Act 2000 (Prescribed Markets and Qualifying Investments) Order 2001, SI 2001/1996 as amended by Regulation 10 of the Market Abuse Regulations 2005

Financial Services Authority Handbook (Code of Market Conduct) *FSA Release* 19 July 2001

Financial Services Authority's *Market Abuse Directive Disclosure Rules Instrument* 2005, 17 March 2005

Financial Services Authority's *Market Abuse Directive Instrument* 2005, 17 March 2005

Insider Dealing (Securities and Regulated Markets) Order 1994

Traded Securities (Disclosure) Regulation 1994

Thesis and dissertations

Chitimira H *A Comparative Analysis of the Enforcement of Market Abuse Provisions* (LLD-thesis Nelson Mandela Metropolitan University 2012)

Chitimira H *The Regulation of Insider Trading in South Africa: A Roadmap for an Effective, Competitive and Adequate Regulatory Statutory Framework* (LLM-dissertation University of Fort Hare 2008)

Newspaper reports

Chanetsa B "Insider Trading is Notoriously Hard to Prosecute" *Business Report* (2004-04-26)

Internet sources

Aitken R "Market Abuse: Spoofing, Layering & the Complexity of Proving Intent" (12-04-2016) <https://www.b-next.com/general/market-abuse-spoofing-layering-the-complexity-of-proving-intent/> (accessed 13-07-2017)

Anonymous "How Banks Allegedly Colluded on Currency Trades" (15-02-2017) <http://www.fin24.com/Companies/Financial-Services/why-the-competition-commission-wants-17-banks-prosecuted-20170215> (accessed 21-03-2017)

Barron C "Greg Draws a Blank in Belfort Parallel" (2014) <http://www.timeslive.co.za/Feeds/2014/02/02/greg-draws-a-blank-in-belfort-parallel> (accessed 03-03-2014)

Blincoe R "Datatec Directors Pay Up on Insider Trading Charges" (2001) <http://www.theregister.co.uk/2001/05/23/datatec_directors_pay_up/> (accessed 03-03-2014)

Commodity Futures Trading Commission & the Financial Services Authority FSA's *Memorandum of Understanding on Consultation, Cooperation and the Exchange of Information Related to Market Oversight* (2006) <http://www.fsa.gov.uk/pubs/mou/cftc.pd> (accessed 27-01-2014)

Financial Services Authority "FSA Signs Regulatory Cooperation Agreement with the CFTC" (20-11-2006) http://www.fsa.gov.uk/pages/Library/Communication/PR/2006/118.shtml > (accessed 27-01-2014)

Financial Services Board "Enforcement Committee Actions" *Media Release* (28-06-2011) <http://www.fsb.co.za/ftp://ftp.fsb.co.za/public/documents/AReport2011.pdf> (accessed 22-11-2013)

Financial Services Board "List of Current Investigations of the Directorate of Market Abuse" *Media Release* (28-06-2011) <http://www.fsb.co.za/ftp://ftp.fsb.co.za/public/documents/AReport2011.pdf> (accessed 22-11-2013)

Johannesburg Stock Exchange Limited "Insider Trading and other Market Abuses (Including the Effective Management of Price–Sensitive Information)" in the *Insider Trading Booklet*, (2013) <http://www.jse.co.za/Libraries/JSE_Regulatory_Environment_Insider_Trading/InsiderTrading_Booklet.sflb.ashx> (accessed 03-03-2014)

Loubser R "Insider Trading and other Market Abuses (Including the Effective Management of Price–sensitive Information)" in the *Insider Trading Booklet* final draft, (2006) <http://www.jse.co.za/public/insider/JSEbooklet.pdf> (accessed 03-03-2014)

Myburgh A & Davis B "The Impact of South Africa's Insider Trading Regime: A Report for the Financial Services Board" (25-03-2004) <http://www.genesis-analytics.com/public/FSBReport.pdf> (accessed 09-02-2013)

Van Deventer G "Anti-Market Abuse Legislation in South Africa" (10-06-2008) <http://www.fsb.co.za/public/marketabuse/FSBReport.pdf> (accessed 05-05-2013)

Index

F

L

M

N

O

P

R

S

T

U

W

www.ingramcontent.com/pod-product-compliance
Lightning Source LLC
LaVergne TN
LVHW010721210926
848485LV00007B/1408/J
* 9 7 8 1 6 2 2 7 3 2 6 0 9 *